THE RIGHT BALANCE

HUGH SEGAL

The

RIGHT

CANADA'S CONSERVATIVE TRADITION

BALANCE

Douglas & McIntyre

D & M PUBLISHERS INC.

Vancouver/Toronto

Douglas & McIntyre
An imprint of D&M Publishers Inc.
2323 Quebec Street, Suite 201
Vancouver BC Canada V5T 4S7
www.douglas-mcintyre.com

Cataloguing data available from Library and Archives Canada
ISBN 978-1-55365-549-7 (cloth)
ISBN 978-1-55365-790-3 (ebook)

Editing by Susan Folkins
Copy editing by Pam Robertson
Jacket design by Peter Cocking
Text design by Jessica Sullivan
Printed and bound in Canada by Friesens
Text printed on acid-free, 100% post-consumer paper

We gratefully acknowledge the financial support of the Canada Council
for the Arts, the British Columbia Arts Council, the Province of British Columbia
through the Book Publishing Tax Credit and the Government of Canada
through the Canada Book Fund for our publishing activities.

*To the Honourable William Grenville Davis, cc,
who, as premier of Ontario from 1971 to 1985,
and as an MPP and minister for a quarter of a century,
reflected the essential balance, decency, compassion and courage
that anchored and still reflects what modern
Canadian conservatism is at its inclusive and humane best*

Contents

Foreword

This is a self-help book for the intellectually starved, the history deprived and for those who know that the media's take on today's politics is all too often a fact-free zone. Articulated by one of the brightest and authentically compassionate conservative thinkers of our time—my Senate colleague and long-time friend Hugh Segal—*The Right Balance* is a scholarly examination of the roots of Canadian conservatism and of the contemporary Canadian state.

His thesis, eloquently explored, is that each Tory leader since Confederation has, in turn, consciously constructed a vital piece of our national architecture. But history, too, has foreshadowed an interesting pattern, namely that "Tories propose, engage and face the brunt and political cost for national and necessary policy innovation, while Liberals sort out how to more expertly profit politically in terms of seat totals and electoral outcomes." And today, too many still confuse liberal "tactical flexibility" with competence and integrity.

Threaded throughout this book, you will find a reasoned critique of the Liberal/Conservative divide, which is seldom about left and right, but always about attitude, moral leadership and a sense of nation.

Not surprisingly, Hugh's most cogent commentary is on the contemporary, with a view to the road ahead. Hugh is long known and well loved in this country for his sharp political wit and analytical precision and he and I have spent many an early morning together on the set of *Canada AM* so I am witness to this fact. But as he casts his eye back over the pages of history, the same finely honed skills come into play.

It has long been held that conservatives, by nature and ideology, are just that—conservative, mistrustful of the future, suspicious of change or improving things. As the late patron saint of American conservatism, William F. Buckley Jr., famously put it: the task for conservatives was to "stand athwart history, yelling 'Stop.'" But nothing could be further from the reality of our incredible country and Hugh has tapped into the spirit of Conservative leaders who, through deed and not just word, have inspired our nation's story.

Conservatives are not opposed to modernity, only to some of its excesses. And rather than being resistant to change, conservatism throughout our history has been about embracing it and managing it!

Canadian conservatism is unique—not derivative, nor transplanted, but rather the child of geography and history. And those who, for partisan purposes, try to suggest that conservatives are *Republicans North* fundamentally fail to grasp both history and reality.

In the pages that follow you will find a story not often told because of the myths that persist—perpetuated by the conceit of partisans who continue to cast the country as a Liberal one and themselves as midwives to our heart and humanity.

Yet, the record tells another tale.

Hugh's grand theme of "nation and enterprise" captures the conservative belief that the Canadian approach to governing is found at the intersection of market freedom and public interest, and that this is the tie that binds this great nation. Sir John A. Macdonald's embrace of the twin forces of nation and enterprise fostered a national economy and forged a political consolidation, not to mention helped build the railway that gave life to a Dominion from sea to sea! Wartime leader Robert Borden introduced national instruments such as income tax and the NRC. And Arthur Meighen opened up universal suffrage (again—nation building!), and helped define a national stance, declaring that we need not be cowed by British condescension or American exceptionalism.

A later prime minister, R.B. Bennett, sought to help a young country meet the Depression head-on by supporting pensions, unemployment insurance, a minimum wage and health insurance. But he also levered Canada's independent World War I effort and contribution to make certain that, in the future, we would have a "Canadian voice proudly articulated." That would mean Canada had to be prepared to defend her values and that domestic political issues should not excuse us from carrying our weight or from engaging in the defence of those principles—a concept that even today often separates Liberals from Conservatives. It shaped our foreign and defence policy. Even the golden age of Pearsonian diplomacy was made possible, in part, because of the respect afforded our nation by the actions of its soldiers. And despite years of Liberal governments short-changing our military, our men and women in Afghanistan have reclaimed that lost ground for us because they have been such committed and brave warriors. And their extraordinary humanitarian effort, combined with war fighting, has again earned Canada a respected place at the international table of allies.

Hugh describes John G. Diefenbaker, a son of Saskatchewan, as a tireless promoter of an unhyphenated Canada, and as a leader who shaped the nation by giving the First Nations the vote, passing the first Canadian Bill of Rights and building the Trans-Canada Highway. Dief was dismissed as a populist outsider by many mainstream liberal historians—but then again, as Hugh points out, they tend to see any Tory victory as an aberration.

As an aside, Hugh notes that this view has become a self-fulfilling prophecy for partisans and those in the media and civil service who both wish it and compel it to become true! And I hope his take on the politicization of the civil service will be the subject of his next book.

Hugh embraces Robert Stanfield with a particular affection. The two cannot abide excesses in either government or ideology. At different points in history, Stanfield and Hugh have advocated for the fiscally sensible view that a GAI—a basic income for all now beneath the poverty line—would do away with many of the politically motivated and ill-conceived income supplement programmes that have fallen short.

Hugh reminds readers that Brian Mulroney, against all odds and his own political self-interest, decided that it was in the national interest to seek both free trade and constitutional renewal. Mulroney fought back when Liberals used language as a wedge issue and followed in the shoes of his Tory predecessors, who knew that the Canadian way was to accommodate and make common cause with the French, the English and the First Nations.

As a Red Tory, Hugh is accurately and generously kind to Prime Minister Harper for his role in nation building that began with the merging of the Reform and Progressive Conservative parties. Conservatism has become not only reflective of the times, but a larger and larger national tent—political real estate always claimed by the liberals as theirs.

Hugh has been a partisan since childhood. I come to my recent affiliation with party politics through public service, most particularly my experience working and living in the United States in the period post-9/11, where, as Hugh notes, terrorism has been a powerful game changer.

Watching a country and a people that have long resisted and constrained the role of government in their lives allowed me an amazing vantage and the opportunity to re-examine my views on how and when government can best serve its people. Whether it was rebuilding Ground Zero or filling a pothole in the local road, Americans look first—and instinctively—to themselves for answers.

I am not as troubled by politics stateside as Hugh is, and when he suggests that some American conservatives might actually encourage "dysfunctional government" to ensure that private interests can run amok, I think this is a little over the top. I have come to believe the sheer size and power and the radical roots of America mean its system can tolerate more rancour and range than we can.

And perhaps this belies my Western roots, but I am content that some of those American influences still resonate here, probably as a result of the huge American settlement—in western Canada—in the 1890s. Being less deferential to authority or even to government itself is not anti-state. It's about defining the limits of government's empowerment in defence of freedom and local choice.

It is, as Hugh says, a reflection of a conservative belief in self-reliance and a sense of obligation to each other.

I grew up in the Saskatchewan of the CCF and NDP, who were often very narrow in their thinking about collective good, and at a time when the Liberals were increasingly becoming not only cautious defenders of the status quo, but began pandering to all manner of special interests.

And today, when we look stateside, we see the intense debate about the dramatic expansion of the role and reach of federal government there. That is why the timing of this book is so important to informed debate.

Some have argued that the conservative idea factory may be moribund. But not so here. Hugh is a one-man assembly line proposing everything from a North American Assembly to better manage trade, security and financial issues with our neighbours in the Americas to a social policy shift that sees poverty and income security as defining issues.

On foreign policy he is clear that we must offer freedom from fear as well as freedom from want, and Hugh believes that the liberal promotion of ideas like "the responsibility to protect" is a fiction unless we have a larger, better equipped military.

The unfailingly generous and polite senator abandons political correctness and offers up a blunt assessment of what he calls our regular existential crisis over Quebec and our endless neuroses about the United States. These are symptoms, he says, of the Canadian disease . . . a paralyzing combination of self-doubt and insecurity. But we can't fix it if we can't name it and Hugh has done just that.

Statecraft, Hugh says, must be more heroic, if we are to manage risk and sovereignty in our own national self-interest. Conservatives believe in the need for structure. That is what "nation and enterprise" is really about!

It's a question of the Right Balance.

You will be wiser for having read this book. It will incite you to take your citizenship more seriously. And that is a very good thing for the country we love and serve.

PAMELA WALLIN
September 2010
Wadena, Saskatchewan

Introduction

THE CANADIAN
TORY IDEA

This book is not about the present Conservative Party of
Canada or its leadership. It is about the intellectual history
and deeply rooted ideas of nation, identity, order, economy, freedom and community that today's Conservative Party
has inherited, and how and why they matter. It is about more than
the obvious reality that all of today's leaders stand on the shoulders of those who have come before. It is about the uniqueness of
Canadian conservatism, and why it is important to distinguish it
from the American or European varieties.

Politics in any democracy is about choice—those roads taken
and those roads not taken. And while the choices faced by societies like Canada, with vast access to natural resources, have been
profoundly easier than those faced by geographically less fortunate places, choices still had and have to be made. In the end, to
live in a free society requires that we use our freedom to make
wise choices. In democratic and free societies, larger choices are
made via elections, political parties, leading political figures and
sets of ideas. How all these idea systems and personalities engage

with each other, with reality, with the public, and with the past and the future is at the core of what politics is all about. Today's choices about what tomorrow's policies should be are shaped by yesterday's realities and historical forces.

Political philosophies—organized perspectives on how societies and communities should work—are central to the options from which citizens get to choose. In an open democracy, citizens have an opportunity to join or support those parties with which they feel most comfortable, or whose leadership and ideas they most admire. But few, if any, large ideas about what matters in society, what constitutes freedom, how a democracy should operate, what fairness really means, what defines the role of government(s) at home and abroad, are recent. The key views and systems of ideas that have shaped the choices we now face, and the political parties and philosophies that are often at odds about what choices are best, go back many centuries.

In Canada, one of those systems of political beliefs is the Tory idea. Canadian Toryism is not the result of a transplanted foreign philosophy moulding Canada. It is, instead, the story of how Canadian geography, demographics, climate, communities and generations shaped a unique brand of conservatism, one not replicated anywhere else in the world.

Any political party, whatever its formal name—in Canada, conservative ideas have been branded as Tory, Conservative, Liberal-Conservative, Conservative-Unionist, Progressive Conservative, Social Credit, Union Nationale (Québec), Reform, and Alliance—, changes its public brand and official role over time to suit the circumstances. Today's Conservative Party—with the large "C"—is the present incarnation of Canadian conservative political thought. But small "c" conservative trends, biases and ideas reflect a continuous, multi-source evolution of events and decisions that pre-date today's Conservative or Progressive Conservative parties, leaders and organizations. To fully understand why, one must recognize that the Canadian conservative idea started long before Canada was formalized in 1867.

In a general way, that small "c" conservative stream was cautious about change, and protected the tradition of societies operating without undue new or excessively reformed institutions. It was wary of change for its own sake, or for the sake of abstract goals or purposes. It favoured the local over the centralized and the traditional over the untried. These approaches and biases had roots in institutions of great longevity, such as the monarchy and the established faiths—roots that would turn into beliefs and values around stability and the rule of law, and essentially the importance of law and order as the framework for stability and reliable freedom.

In this digital age, in which the fascination with how ideas are transmitted often overtakes interest in the ideas themselves, the notion of mapping how economic, foreign policy, cultural, linguistic, constitutional and sovereignty choices over the centuries may have important connections to today might strike some as quaint. Well, in our rapidly changing and increasingly smaller world, context matters. Contextual awareness is one of the primary obligations and exigencies of any military, humanitarian or corporate leader. And there is no way to understand context without knowing the history of events, people and ideas that helped shape the specifics of any time or place. The same is true of today's Canadian conservatism. History matters. Not all change is good; not all change is inevitable.

Every contemporary society, every approach to how we should organize today's world, stands on the foundations of how others have done so in the past, for better or for worse. The ideas that shape Canada today—those that define our society, our courts, our schools, our businesses, our families, our very way of life—did not emerge as a published operating manual on July 1, 1867. One chapter of our operating manual certainly did: the chapter that defined how the mechanics of government would operate, how different orders of government would determine their scope and would create, through the ensuing confederal structure of our union, the nature of our electoral process and the rules necessary to sustain both. But those specific confederal provisions relate only to governing, and even those guiding ideas reflected an earlier history of cultural, religious, linguistic and community values already deeply rooted in Canadian society. That history is what this book will explore. How did Canadian society—at the farm, in the church, in the fishery, in the factory, in the town and classroom, or around the family table—form and affect these core ideas and make them uniquely Canadian? How did our climate and geography contribute to this shaping and tailoring? Why is Canadian conservatism unique and, in moulding the Canada we now share, why does it matter?

Obsession with a new tax, a dispute over the census or a debate over which jet fighter to purchase may well occupy our time and media space. And, through miscalculations, histrionic or ideological excess on both sides of any debate, and media focus on the apparently urgent, these issues might also dominate the public narrative regarding politics at any particular time. But it does not mean that they are of fundamental importance to the way we live our lives or find the right balance between competing rights and responsibilities over the long term, for our children and for their children.

When leaders in government or opposition lose perspective, and, more importantly, are seen to lose perspective, this, more than other threats or challenges, erodes democracy and loosens the sinews of our social coherence and sense of freedom and opportunity. The loss of perspective on any issue is the most unpardonable sin for any conservative—large "C" or small "c."

In the same way, and for the same reason, Canadian conservatism is not a derivative form of American, British or European forms. It is, without diluting the value of pollination from else-where in the seventeenth, eighteenth and nineteenth centuries, deeply indigenous to our geography, history and culture. Cana-dian conservatism is not just one part of the debate across the aisle in Parliament. And it is far more than one part of a label on a ballot.

There are elements of our day-to-day life—in families, at work, at play, at worship, at study—that have been unchanged for centuries. There are also elements that are relatively new. Some of the ways we live as citizens and neighbours in our communi-ties are important and shape the framework for other practices of lesser importance. Understanding the difference between those seminal ideas that shape the framework for other practices and those that are a less important part of our larger life together is a helpful way to look at the role large philosophical ideas play in our lives. This understanding applies very much to Canadian conservatism as it evolved over the centuries, running from the First Nations confederacy, the French Ancien Régime, British North America and pre- and post-confederation Canada.

The dynamics of our Canadian politics—the dynamics of our Canadian political parties, investment philosophies, approaches to community and social justice—are formed in an open and free society by a clash of different world views, dissimilar approaches advanced by diverse people around critical priorities such as freedom, justice, order and the rule of law. One Canadian's free speech may very well be another's sedition or hate speech; one Canadian's stability may seem oppressive to someone else. A pri-ority for one Canadian community may seem like undue impo-sition on another. In Canadian democracy, the battle among political parties and other competing interests is often over the *agenda* for the debate itself. The journey to the decision is often deemed more important than the decision itself, which means that a consensual solution can become the source of a new problem down the road.

It is a conservative truism that society and its challenges recast themselves generation after generation and that core challenges to peace, freedom and a balanced, humane state of affairs also re-emerge to test the human condition. How Canadian society organizes itself—the room that it creates for family, identity, hard work, success and common and free enterprise—and where these all fit in along with education, culture, security and freedom is essential to the quality of life experienced by all Canadians. The very structure of Canadian society, what values and practices are at its centre, what values and practices are at its periphery, all matter very much to the people who seek to live and prosper within our society and the communities that form its reality.

Travelling over parts of Canada by air, flying low enough to see how towns and farms are arranged, affords one a tiny glimpse of how historic organizing principles can matter. Small towns in Québec, near the St. Lawrence, are usually clustered around a large Roman Catholic church steeple, with neighbouring farms laid out in long strips down to the water, reflecting the original seigneurial grants provided by New France to its most trusted settlers. Protestant villages in what was Upper Canada, however, look quite different from the air, with grids that embrace commercial town centres and more than one Christian house of worship. Neither of these two approaches to town planning is better than the other. But they are clearly different, and the two organizing principles have a huge role to play in our history together today and our future together tomorrow. A young refugee arriving in Canada to be welcomed and afforded an opportunity for personal freedom, growth and success may not know it but these two different aerial views will also impact her life in ways that will matter intensely. And both town plans are absolutely reflective of early conservative principles as to how society was to be organized.

The words "Conservative," "Liberal" and "Socialist" often lead Canadians to think only of a particular government or leader, or political party or candidate. In the United States, where the dominant parties have "Republican" and "Democratic" labels, words like "liberal" and "conservative" are adjectives as opposed to nouns. In Canada, for reasons I will explain, the nature of our political spectrum is remarkably different.

In the late 1970s, Frank Mankiewicz, Robert Kennedy's former press secretary, introduced the journalist, author, columnist and former president of the Progressive Conservative Party of Canada Dalton Camp to the National Press Club in Washington. (In 1966, Mr. Camp had led the democratization movement of the Progressive Conservative Party over the objections of Mr. Diefenbaker.) During his introduction, Mr. Mankiewicz revealed, by implication, why in America there are only two political adjectives—not three, as there are in Canada. "Mr. Camp," Mankiewicz said, "is Progressive Conservative; the other parties in Canada are the Liberals—whom we would call 'socialists'; and there are New Democrats, whom we would also call 'socialists'; Mr. Camp's Progressive Conservatives, we would call 'moderate socialists.'" Well, Canadian conservatism is not socialism at all, but it is to the left of the American brand for good and solid historical, philosophical and critical reasons.

The Canadian conservative tradition—a tradition that predates Confederation—is much larger and broader than any single partisan brand. As I mentioned earlier, it has gone through several incarnations. It has been "Conservative" or "Liberal-Conservative" under Macdonald; "Conservative-Unionist" under Meighen and Bennett; "Progressive Conservative" from Manion through to Drew, Diefenbaker, Stanfield, Clark, Mulroney, Campbell, Charest, Clark and MacKay; "Reform" and "Alliance" under Manning and Day; and "Conservative" again under Harper. In its formation, Canadian conservatism was certainly affected by the initial French and British colonial outreach that brought the cultures of Europe to our shores. But the land the Europeans found, replete with rich and pervasive First Nations societies, governments, traditions and confederacies, would have its distinct role in shaping the way European political philosophies took root in, and were profoundly changed by, Canadian reality. This helps explain why Canadian society is in many ways conservative in tone and demeanour—whatever the political trends du jour are elsewhere.

My partisan and non-partisan research, and my working and political biases over four decades, are on the public record, but this book is not about extolling one of today's political parties or leaders over another. The conservatism revealed, sorted and probed here is a conservatism that has developed over centuries and that has helped create a notion of Canadian civility and order, which most of the world also seeks and which Canadians too often take for granted.

Political traditions are larger than the temporary partisan custodians each generation may choose or tolerate. Our Canadian conservative tradition may not be exportable to other societies, but the institutions it has helped shape, such as federalism, our judicial system, the rule of law and our parliamentary democracy, most definitely are. Canadian experts on federalism, a very Canadian form of government, have advised governments and those developing constitutions in places like Pakistan, South Africa, Nigeria, Mexico, China, Russia, Australia and Spain on how federalism dilutes conflict and tolerates difference.

In essence, federalism says to different ethnic, regional, linguistic or geographic populations that there is a way to maintain important local authority and jurisdiction on things that really matter. And recognition of local authority on some issues does not detract from the larger economic and political relationship, with certain powers exercised at the central or countrywide level. A battle, war or prolonged debilitating political or violent conflict is avoidable if powers and authorities can be distributed between players in ways that respect local rights and requirements while still protecting the broader needs of the larger political entity.

Some things, such as defence or military policy, and especially in large, multi-ethnic countries, are best dealt with at the centre in the name of all. Other priorities, such as the management of education or the resolve of civil disputes, are best done locally by the level of government closest to the reality on the ground.

Political philosophies, as systems of belief, do not exist in an efficacy spectrum of one to ten: "one" being those that have failed miserably and been destructive and "ten" being those that have been overwhelmingly successful as a plan for society to use in all its endeavours. Understanding the failures and setbacks of the Conservative Party in appreciating its roots is as important as embracing the value of its successes.

When considering how the roots of conservatism took hold, grew and then nourished the Canadian conservative idea over the generations, it is helpful to reflect on where conservatives often find themselves in today's political culture. Today's Conservatives often worry about the way in which modern society seems to embrace "freedom" as a contrary value to "order." The media and some in the academic world often associate liberalism with the former and conservatism with the latter. Conservatives' very strong bias is that without order, freedom itself is quite illusory. Simplistic ideas about "freedom of speech" are of little worth if they do not also assess the value of "responsibility" in making that freedom real, defensible and sustainable. The balance between the two is always a matter of debate and calibration; but the notion that the balance no longer matters is the greatest threat to freedom we could possibly know. Order and stability—and the social and economic framework of opportunity that they nurture—generate the capacity for freedom to flourish, or even to exist at all. A social framework or political philosophy that fails to produce order simply fails, whatever else of value it may champion. The absence of order usually presages the erosion of freedom from fear, as vital as any other freedom. A society without order, through the rule of legitimate laws, democratically passed, is one where the strongest, the wealthiest and those most free to use violence and intimidation always win. The rule of law, one of the notions at the centre of the modern Commonwealth, for example, guarantees that all are equal before the law, and that those who make the laws are not above them. It is precisely when there are those who are above the law, for reasons of wealth or violent power, that arbitrary powers can be used to destroy a business, crush a religion, oppress a village or engage in genocide. Order is about the freedom we all have to invest, vote, worship, dissent, write and speak as we choose.

Today's conservatives also worry that a world view that negates or misunderstands the force of history leads to the kind of self-reverence that for any generation is truly paralytic. There can be no more tragic distortion than the political frame set by the media which implies, every minute, of every hour, of every day, that the challenges we face, the risks alive in our world, the threats to our well-being, outstrip what prior generations faced. On every conceivable plane, from fairness to work, to poverty, to conflict, to longevity, to geopolitical and catastrophic threats, we are living through comparatively easy times. There were single days and weeks during World Wars I and II when more people, more soldiers, more Americans and Canadians died than in the Afghanistan, Iraq and September 11, 2001 engagements combined. Every death, civilian or military, is tragic and deeply felt. But our present geopolitical context is far more peaceful and less destructive of innocent lives than that of previous eras. The thermonuclear risk, now deeply diminished, did, during most of the tense Cold War activity, constitute the most serious threat to the environment and the planet as of yet—and this includes even the recent alarmist, and Cassandra-style, climate change scenarios. Climate change, both as a cyclical reality and as a condition that the developed and developing worlds must face together and with the full benefit of available science, is most definitely serious. But compared to other challenges the world has faced around poverty, conflict, plagues and the reality of "man's inhumanity to man," it is a minor test. And it must not generate a lack of engagement in all the other serious challenges that destroy lives and people around the world today. For today's proponents of fear, this is the most "inconvenient" truth of all. In Canada, despite the endless navel-gazing of our media, and the tendency for media and politicians in all parties to exaggerate, the challenges we do face pale in comparison to those faced during the Great Depression, the 1812–14 war with the Americans or either of the World Wars.

A sound sense of context really matters, both historically and geopolitically. We have all, in every walk of life, known leaders who, if one put a good-sized mirror on their desk, would never go to lunch! That self-centred narrowness is distressing because it reveals a lack of perspective and a disconnection from the demands of genuine service and responsibility. Context—the actual state of affairs regarding threat, need, importance and impact—is crucial. Losing contextual balance is the first sign of a party or leader's detachment from the larger world they seek to serve. When any leader, party or even country begins to take itself too seriously, to overstate its relative importance, it is usually a serious sign of trouble. Real conservatism is the triumph of perspective over myopia, of balance over enthusiasm.

Canada is not the most important country in the world; few, if any, leaders of other countries wake each morning to ask their partner or deputy minister what the Canadian prime minister said in our Parliament or at a press scrum in Regina. It is the ultimate liberal conceit to overemphasize one's own impact, one's own ideas or one's own party or country. Genuine perspective, realistic context, not overestimating one's own importance (or that of one's party, government or time) is truly the beginning of wisdom—and also inherently conservative. (U.S. "exceptionalism" is a liberal and revolutionary legacy that has produced some benefits but also great geopolitical blunders over time. The country's "aren't we special" exceptionalism is hyperbolic, immature, self-preening and distinctly unhelpful.) If pessimism and bad manners are profoundly obstructive, excessive starry-eyed optimism about the human condition or one's own value is equally destructive.

The supposed perfectibility of the human condition, the much vaunted and assumed intrinsic trustworthiness and goodness of all people and every individual, is a pointlessly optimistic liberal excess and indulgence conservatives reject. Every family, every neighbourhood, every community, every organization, every church or religion, every country, every military and police force, every aid agency or university, every international body has within it inspired, talented, devoted, good, giving people who care deeply and behave ethically. These people would be incapable of malfeasance or selfishness of any kind. But sadly they are not alone. In every human association, there are selfish, venal, self-centred and small-minded people. This is as true of grand geopolitical frameworks and alliances as it is of any church auxiliary. The presumption that everyone is equally trustworthy is the height of folly and self-delusion and the ultimate liberal conceit. Understanding why laws, penalties, responsibilities and deterrents are essential does not demean the majesty of the human condition; it is simply an acknowledgement of the hard realities history still teaches.

The most powerful conceit of any ideology on the left or the right, most often expressed by the young firebrand or determined self-promoter, is also the greatest delusion of some intellectuals: namely, that ideas shape nations and that it is the battle of ideas that shapes history. Hence the great analyses of wars as battles between one concept of society versus another: national socialism versus democracy in World War II; Communism versus capitalism in the Cold War. These analyses are not without substantial merit but they are not the whole story. They often attribute too much power to the intellectual abstraction of an idea or set of ideas as an uber-force greater than the forces of geography,

demography and the simple history of events. For the intellectually arrogant on either side of the left-right spectrum, these analyses provide both motivation and justification for some of the worst
excesses throughout history. Religious extremism, along with the
intolerance it engenders, is often responsible for most of the rest.

There is a huge difference between the power of ideas and the
tyranny of ideology. Ideas about how to organize society, how
to promote individual freedom and social well-being, can be
and have been positive forces. Everything—from public education and health care to moderate and progressive taxation and
representative government—has benefitted from these sorts of
organizing principles. National and international stability, the
balanced rule of law and a tolerance for dissent and diversity have
developed as a result of progressive ideas and approaches to society and government. Canada is not alone among those countries
that have benefitted from ideas such as democracy, responsible
government, public education and universal health care. Nor have
we been laggards in terms of our own contribution to the development, implementation and improvement of these and related ideas
over the decades.

The evolution of our local and national politics (which have, by
comparison to most other post-colonial societies, been both civil
and humane), speaks most eloquently to the confluence of ideas
with local geography, demography and history. The nature of the
development of French and English settlements of the sixteenth,
seventeenth and eighteenth centuries, the nature of their interac-
tive impact on First Nations, the role of global conflicts like the
Seven Years' War, the Napoleonic struggles and the early stir-
rings of American colonial dissatisfaction all had resonance and an
impact on how the founding concepts of Canada came into being.

It would be wrong to look at the nineteenth century and conclude that Gladstone's liberalism or Disraeli's "one nation" Toryism ("one nation" refers to addressing the interests of both the
rich and the poor) had no impact on Canadian Toryism, because

they did. As did Mr. Roosevelt's New Deal and the post–World War II National Health Service introduced in the war-ravaged United Kingdom by the Labour Party with Tory (i.e., Mr. Churchill's) support. Intellectual traditions, political texts, news coverage of debates, elections, revolutions elsewhere all seeped into the Canadian narrative. But the Canadian conservative narrative has roots all its own.

Every new generation of conservatives and Conservatives in any province, society or country will put their own stamp and hue on the bridge their generation builds between the conservative tradition they inherited and the one they will leave for those who follow. Understanding the interaction between the conservative foundations of Canadian society and the changing demands of present and future local, national and geopolitical forces is no esoteric, theoretical exercise. It lies at the very heart of a conservative's ultimate duty: to protect the very best of our democratic, free and pluralist society today and then lay down the economic, social, industrial and strategic essentials to strengthen our society's future.

Democracy means different things to different people. But the evolution of democracy in Canada—the particular role of the Crown, the legislatures and parliaments, the courts and institutions and the way those roles come together—is unique. And while a Briton, American, Australian or Western European would see elements with which they were comfortable and, in their own country and culture, quite familiar, there would be many aspects of our democracy that would be foreign to them.

Some have seen the Charter of Rights and Freedoms from the early 1980s as unique and a truly Canadian watershed. Others have treated it very much as an Americanization by Trudeau of what had been, before 1982, a British "Parliament is sovereign" framework for rights and freedoms, in which citizens had all rights not removed by Parliament.

The Charter—which in 1982 was made part of our basic law, the Constitution—brings the courts in as arbitrators of how individual laws stack up against the Charter's contents. The fact that it was only made possible after the inclusion of the "notwithstanding clause," protecting parliamentary supremacy, means that, far from being a simple adoption of the American model, which has its roots in the Napoleonic view of a "basic law" beyond the reach of parliaments, our Charter of Rights and Freedoms anticipates and accepts the absolute right of parliaments to suspend the Charter when demonstrable circumstances make that cause essential, and to do so for up to five years. In this way, it reflects both the British view of the supremacy of Parliament and the French historical view of written and specified rights in a manner no other Charter of Rights or the American Constitution ever would or could. And in that very Canadian compromise, put in place because Conservatives forced it upon Mr. Trudeau, a unique Canadian conservative blend was born. It was Mr. Diefenbaker's Bill of Rights that passed Parliament on August 10, 1960, that, in so many ways, started the ball rolling on this balance between government and individual rights.

The compromise was deemed essential by the differentiated roles of Ottawa and the provinces and the place of Parliament in the historical evolution of Canadian democracy. It relates to how Canada was settled. It relates to the unique relationship between Canadian institutions and our two mother countries, France and Great Britain. Our democracy did not burst forth in an eighteenth-century revolt against each of our mother countries or the British Empire, of which we were then a loyal part. It was founded through an evolution from Crown-appointed governments to responsible legislatures and parliaments within the broad pre-Victorian outreach of the British Empire. American democracy revolted against the Crown; Canadian democracy evolved with the Crown.

"Responsible government democracy" and "Canadian Constitutional Monarchy," as they both evolved in pre-Confederation and post-Confederation Canada, are very much core Canadian conservative values. But their uniqueness comes from more than the British and French philosophical dowries at their roots. They come from a very Canadian sense of the balance between order and freedom, as reflected by the institution of the Crown. When our neighbours to the south set aside that institution, they began a journey down a very different road, a road that would turn away from inclusion as a basic and founding value.

"Inclusion" is not only a tenet for a society that seeks to involve all of its people in a prosperous and humane way of life, or that seeks to broaden the economic mainstream. Inclusion also means, in historical terms, that a society evolves and develops traditions from the past that served and will continue to serve a constructive purpose. These traditions are often important to large segments of the population. Some of these traditions are about symbols that evoke certain principles or stabilities. Some are about a British approach to presumption of innocence or parliamentary democracy. Some are about a French approach to the way a community is organized or structured. It is intrinsically conservative not to shunt these traditions aside, because to do so is to deny our history and to dilute our sense of identity. For Canada, history is a very good teacher! This is as true of our internal relationships today as it was of the relationships among the First Nations who lived here originally and the French and British who came ashore in the sixteenth and seventeenth centuries.

There is nothing wrong with the free-for-all structure of American democracy: it has a populist Congress with more than four hundred members who must face re-election every two years; a Senate that seats one hundred, where small states with just thousands of voters have the same clout as those with thirty-plus million; a Supreme Court that makes laws in competition with the legislative branch; elected judges at many levels who can "campaign" and raise money for their campaigns; and state attorneys who can politicize prosecutions on the way to political careers. The latter seems, in some remarkable way, to accurately reflect an American economic and social system that is very much about competition, the primacy of accumulating wealth and a very substantive commitment to outcomes—economic, social and political—that embrace "winners" and "losers." The tendency for some in Europe and Canada to turn up their noses at this is both unseemly and unbecoming. It is who Americans are. It reflects the attractiveness of the American dream that has for so many millions been a positive force over the span of history.

America was colonized and overtaxed during the eighteenth century and, through acts of insurgent courage and local resentment created by commercial intensity, it broke free. This act was not so much evolutionary but revolutionary and it became a celebrated keystroke of U.S. and world history. And that keystroke not only differentiated, once and for all, American society from the rest of British North America, but it also redefined American conservatism, which then went down an individualistic, Patriot-Republican, "life, liberty and the pursuit of happiness" road. And because Empire Loyalist conservatism took a "peace, order and good government" route, which was more about communitarian and responsible choices as lynchpins for society, it helped form the Canada that emerged in the late eighteenth and early nineteenth centuries.

The decision by Québec elites to resist revolutionary blandishments from Americans leading up to 1776 was, in no small way, shaped by the Québec Act of 1774, which guaranteed French language rights and the role of the Roman Catholic Church in Québec society. The passage of this act was the first time the British Parliament had granted such guarantees anywhere in the Empire. The Québec Act was about a formal inclusion of French language traditions, the Roman Catholic clergy and established civil law, by a British Empire maturing in its approach to ethnic and cultural diversity. The American Revolution was about many things that were positive, including an affirmation of the American desire for independence and self-determination. But it was also about the exclusion of those who did not wish to separate from the Crown.

According to the United Empire Loyalists' Association of Canada, the number of people who were residents of the American colonies prior to the Treaty of Paris of 1783, and who joined the Royal Standard and settled in territory that remained under the rule of the Crown, ranges from 30,000 to 100,000. These thousands of American Empire Loyalists, who emigrated from the colonies to New Brunswick, Nova Scotia, southern Québec and Ontario, did more than simply leave one idea of society behind to embrace another. Their preference for the British Crown and Empire over the new republicanism of the colonies was also an embrace of a specific social order, a specific construct of society itself. Their migration to the Canadian colonies not only shaped a core element of our national and historical identity, but also established (in the years 1776–1850) the very nature of English-Canadian conservatism.

If the basic relationship between the Crown and French Canadians (in Québec particularly) influenced the French Canadian concept of the conservative brand, then the Empire Loyalists' view of an ordered society fashioned by the Crown and centred on institutions and values—not only on money—was also fundamental to the Anglo-Tory brand. Together, these two streams moulded the foundations of the Tory brand in Canada.

This cascading dynamic of Canadian conservatism was built and sustained over five centuries through French, English and First Nations cooperation (with some conflict) and through the aid of the regular British regiments in the defence of Canada in the War of 1812. Relationships with the First Nations established in the fifteenth century, however conflicted and difficult, also formed the basis of First Nations loyalty in the defence of Canada in 1812–14, and were a part of the development of the conservative view of Canada. The dynamic referred to above continued in the formation of the "Château Clique," a small group of officials—mostly members of the Anglophone merchant community, including John Molson and James McGill—who dominated the executive and legislative councils, the judiciary and senior bureaucratic positions in Lower Canada until the 1830s; in Upper Canada, the "Family Compact" performed a similar role, and the members of its executive and legislative councils also helped to prevent an American form of democratization from developing in the early 1830s.

Tory nationalism, as reflected in the early days through loyalty to the Crown, was different in tone and substance in Québec from what it was in Ontario. But in the early pre-Confederation days of Canada's emergence, Tory nationalism became very clear and well-defined: in essence, it was about balance. And the Tory balance can be described simply and directly as a political system of beliefs in which fairness and compassion are not threatening to enterprise, profit, growth or freedom. Fairness and compassion are, in fact, the very foundations of a society within which the reality of a durable freedom can rest and prosper. That is a central ingredient of the right balance within the Tory mainstream, and not, as some would suggest, a quaint Red Tory indulgence.

There are many ways to encapsulate the story of Confederation: as an evolution towards statehood; as a merger of colonies into a country with continental reach; as the development in North America of a country with both French and British roots; as the liberation of Québec from a potentially suffocating dominance by Ontario within the Province of Canada—the list is endless. But in the essence of our founding, in our history and geography, there is a unique Canadian conservative philosophy and brand. And this brand is about the cementing of Canada to the Crown and the institutional protection of historical rights, for both groups and individuals. The fact that the First Nations negotiated with the Queen's representatives and that, to this day, they continue to view their treaties as solemn engagements with the "Crown" underlines this principle. So, too, does the notion of one "criminal law" for all—the equality of all subjects before the Crown—established by the federal parliament. This approach is opposite to that in the U.S., where individual states have their own criminal codes.

The concept of separate provincial orders of government, with precise jurisdictions all emanating from the Crown, is an extension of the respect for "particularity" that goes right back to the Québec Act of 1774. Monetary, military and foreign policy powers taken up by the new federal government did not mean very much in 1867 as, in those pre–Statute of Westminster (pre-1931) days, London ran foreign policy for the entire Empire and defence constituted simply local militias raised in the counties and provinces, sustained by regular British forces as appropriate. The central monetary power, weights and measures, banking, transport, borders and criminal laws, the legislative structure paralleling that the U.K., reflected the dynamics of the intercolonial negotiation. The mix of local requirements and trade-offs and the fundamental desire to have a greater British North American footprint to countervail the bellicose, robustly military industrial behemoth to the south was the other competing priority.

Confederation was and is a structural road map to the central compromise and vision of the Canadian conservative idea: unity under the Crown; common and similar institutions in each province and Ottawa; accommodation and respect for particularity; and no overpowering impositions of federal restrictions on provincial powers or overly centralized federal jurisdictions. Conservative federalism uses different orders of government and division of powers as a way of dissipating acute areas of potential conflict in the greater interest of one country, its survival and its prospects.

The Canadian conservative idea is the opposite of a narrow ideology. Ideologies assemble core philosophies, premises and societal visions into rigid and all-inclusive belief systems in ways that, while coherent, can also be disturbingly insensitive and, over history, inhumane and oppressive.

Ideas, such as the Canadian conservative idea, have deep roots, varied histories, many custodians and both strengths and weaknesses, but they are formed by realities on the ground, then informed and expanded by actual social, economic and geopolitical events and challenges. Canadian conservative and Tory ideas have been on just such a journey, from deep, pre-colonial riots in the late 1700s to Throne Speeches since 2000, and the journey has been remarkable.

Understanding how that "ideas journey" unfolded, with its successes and setbacks, is the best way to cast a bright light on the path ahead and on the turns in the road that conservatives and Canadians have the right to see as clearly as possible. It is towards that modest goal that this book on the history of Canadian conservatism is aimed.

ACCOMMODATION, RESPECT

The Tory View of Our National Soul

There is little ambiguity about the difference of opinion between the Liberals and Conservatives concerning Québec, and that division reflects their very different core beliefs on the role of duality and the key elements of a partnership of equals between English and French cultures as the basis of the Canadian idea itself. This division runs right to the essential conservative respect for the particularities of language, culture and "les instruments du société" fundamental to the Québec Act of 1774, in which Québec language, religion and civil law were protected by the U.K. Parliament.

The communities that shaped the "Old Regime" of New France had their unique form and structure, with faith and loyalty at the heart of their purpose. When, in 1759, after the Battle of the Plains of Abraham, the British regime began the embrace of accommodation, and when, in 1774, the British Parliament embraced "French facts on the ground," Canada's future was established. This was not about, as some historians like to suggest, who we were *not* (i.e., Americans); it was very much about who we were and who we wanted to become. And through the grafting process, the Ancien Régime in Québec and the subsequent protection through the Québec Act of 1774 of the language, religion and civil law of Québécers (two years before the events of 1776) and the resilience of loyalty to the Crown as an organizing principle of Canadian society, the structure of our way of life was very much defined.

There was, after all, an explicit decision by Québécers to stay under the British Crown despite an open invitation from the American colonies to join them in revolution. The leadership in Québec, including the clergy and some among the business elite, determined *inter alia* (and not without controversy) that they were, in terms of language, culture, religion and commerce, better protected in British North America under the Crown than they might be in a mercantile American democracy that espoused republican values and assertions that would undoubtedly swamp the French-speaking minority, its language and its cultural heritage.

In the *bleu* conservative Québec tradition, this central identity was based on an entrenched respect for faith, language and "nation" and has prevailed in important measure to this day. There is a direct causal line from the Québec Act of 1774 to the rejection of the American revolutionaries by the Québécois leadership, from the structure of the Province of Canada, and its subsequent replacement by the fundamental guarantees of Confederation for a Québec with its own constitutionally protected institutions, to Canadian conservative philosophy today.

In the 1950s, Maurice Duplessis, an established provincial conservative who started the Union Nationale, campaigned under *"coopération toujours, assimilation jamais"* (always cooperate, never assimilate); in the 1960s, Daniel Johnson and Jean-Jacques Bertrand's Union Nationale campaigned under a partnership affirming *"égalité ou indépendence"* (equality or independence); in the 1960s, Liberal Jean Lesage campaigned under *"maître chez nous"* (masters in our own home). Robert Stanfield embraced the "one country, two peoples," *"deux nations"* premise in the late

1960s, and Brian Mulroney forged the Meech Lake Accord (an agreement reached by all first ministers on constitutional reform, enhanced provincial policy discretion and consultation), whose primary purpose was to bring Québec in as a signatory of the 1982 Constitution Act by, in part, giving Québécers explicit status as an historical founding people. Robert Bourassa, after the failure of Meech Lake in 1990, campaigned under *"jamais au genoux"* (never on our knees) after two first ministers essentially went back on their word prior to ratification.

These are all aspects of the same particular conservative fidelity to the foundational understanding between Québec and the Crown reached by the British and the Ancien Régime in 1774. And this fidelity has defined the conservative brand in Canada, as Stephen Harper underlined when he spoke in the 2005–2006 election about *"un fédéralisme d'ouverture"* (open federalism), and subsequently "un nation des Québécois et Québécoise" (a nation of all Québécers) in a unified Canada. This conservative respect for identity stands in stark contrast to the centralizing liberal view dating back to Lord (Jack) Durham, who argued against regional French Canadian particularity. The liberal view can also be traced to George Brown's opposition to the French papists, to Mackenzie King's federal spending in specific areas of provincial jurisdiction, to Pierre Trudeau's intolerance of French Canadian nationalism, and to Jean Chrétien and Stéphane Dion's insensitivity to the critical issue of Québécers' identity and national aspiration within Canada. Prime Minister Pearson, on the other hand, was a more subtle and considerate supporter of Québec particularity on important issues like the Canada Pension Plan (making room for Québec's Caisse de dépôt) and social policy overall; he was also too decent and confederal to be an integral part of the liberal tradition of top-down *"fédéralisme dominateur."* Modern debates between Canadian conservatism and postwar centralist liberalism date back to the eighteenth century and are vital to understanding the Canadian conservative tradition of today.

This strong Tory bias regarding respect for Québec particularity within Canada also informs our conservative anxiety about a too-centralized state, where the divisions between federal and provincial powers are blurred by overly aggressive federal spending, taxation or legislation outside its federal duties as defined in Section 91 of the Constitution. The notion of separate orders of government, with separate and precise jurisdictions, all emanating from the Crown, is an extension of the respect for "particularity" that reflects the intent of the Québec Act.

In the French areas of North America, especially in the "St. Lawrence empire" region and elsewhere on the Atlantic coast, land was granted and settled under the seigneurial system of the Ancien Régime, imported from France. In fact, from the early seventeenth century on, that system, which was very much a Canadianized offshoot of French feudal social structure, was inherently conservative with power transferred to the Compagnie des Cent-Associés by the French king (Louis XIII) under the advice of his senior minister, Cardinal Richelieu—resembling very much an initial "Crown corporation" initiative. The governance of each seigneurie was established by a contract that was enforced by the king's intendant, the chief administrator for New France, of whom one of the first was Jean Talon, who was installed in 1665. This kind of settlement was a structure that focused on control, order and cooperation with *"les habitants,"* who were the tenants on the land and the working core of the community.

A classic seigneurial manor house was the source of local authority and justice in sorting out disputes. Tenants, or *colons*, were allowed, on good and productive behaviour, to be promoted to *habitants*, or "free farmers," with rights to marry. Here, citizenship was earned. The cooperation of the intendant's people, the local seigneur, the Church and the neighbouring seigneurs established a series of social roots and community structures that provided governance and stability. Once a year, the *habitants* paid the local seigneur the annual *cens* (dues) for the land they farmed, either in cash or in kind. Loyalty, faith, and fealty to the seigneur's rights and discretion were all rock-edged parts of the core premises of early Québec society. The land that passed from generation to generation was the central underlying currency at the base of the social capital that framed Québec society. That, much later, Duplessis would build a coalition called Union Nationale to nationalize private power companies, speaks to this tradition. The tradition, simply stated, was that a public interest/community purpose had to coexist with private and other local interests. The seigneurial manor house defined that interest as Québec was settled and expanded. The decision by Duplessis (himself a Conservative and a long-serving nationalist premier of Québec) to unite with left-wing Liberals in order to nationalize those private power companies that were thought to be exploiting all aspects of the Québec economy reflected a seventeenth century manor-house principle.

This tradition speaks to the deeply rooted practices of the Ancien Régime. The rights of *habitants* were earned but were structured around respect for, and collaboration with, authority. This system was different from, and more humane than, the pure feudalism alive and well in so many parts of Europe at the time, but it was still feudal by any definition. The traditional sources of order and opportunity, the communitarian role of Church as educator and the role of the seigneur as arbiter and representative of the intendant, who was the agent of the king, all spoke to a view of governance and stability that persisted in some measure for decades and even centuries. It was a hierarchy more egalitarian than those in feudal Europe, but a hierarchy nonetheless. Even today, the role of government is more central to life in Québec than elsewhere in Canada, for better or for worse.

There was, to be sure, some exploitation of the "peasant" by commercial, governing, religious and military parts of the structural hierarchy that were imported and took root on Canadian soil.

Powerful forces like the Comte de Frontenac, who established the first fortification at what is now Kingston, exercised immense military, commercial and political influence, with authority that came from the royal court in France. There was nothing that reversed the feudal structures of imperial France. But there was, in the community organization, in the interaction and conciliation with the First Nations, and in the seigneurial social and authoritarian structure, the moderating effect of local and decentralized mediation. The Empire would look very different as arranged from seigneury to seigneury, from local town to farm; local authority, tribal dynasties, intermarriage, and the economies of small scale agriculture and the fur trade would all help to form a French society that was unlike anything in France, which had dispatched Champlain in 1603.

But it was not a system or society that produced massive population growth or intense settlement. Indeed, as Québec City and Montréal grew, they were dwarfed by centres of growth like Boston, New York and Philadelphia. By the late 1760s, French-speaking North America contained about 80,000 souls compared to the 1,500,000 souls in the British colonies to the south. So, along with the order, the communitarian structure and the leadership of the Church also came the sense of being outnumbered and, with it, all the sensitivities that kind of imbalance cannot help but generate and promote. The distinguished historian Marcel Trudel, in his book *Introduction to New France* emphasizes that New France was "a virgin country where it was necessary to introduce clear lines of administration for the first time in order to enable a society to develop." Establishing "clear lines of administration" was the only way for the French state to ensure that New France's inhabitants would continue to be French-speaking then and in the future. The survival of their culture depended on it.

What had begun as an obstacle to the passage to Asia was now a full-fledged French colony with an all-powerful "royal administrator" and a social structure to perpetuate the old system within the French-controlled regions of the new continent. Global geography and trade routes and the search for colonial riches had brought the French to Canada's shores. The community they built now had a structure that would encourage the development of a self-sustaining, French-speaking society. The rivers, forests and clearings of New France required a certain kind of community organization. Small populations spread over large geography needed firm structural and hierarchical organization to survive. This was about order and the survival and configuration of community; it was not about personal liberty or individual choice. Nor was it about an imperial branch plant. It was about a deeply rooted and unique North American French civilization and culture, centred in Québec. (For those business scholars or practitioners who have tried from outside Québec to understand "Québec Inc." or the "Québec model" of a cooperative mix of economic, social and state instruments, this one basic fact of Québec's history is deeply helpful and important to note.)

Key parts of the French Canadian roots of Canadian conservatism come from the views of community, history and order brought to Canada by the Roman Catholics. These views were instrumental in the development of our country. Their impact on everything from community organization and commerce to the evolving political trend is very much part of the kind of conservatism that was shaped by the particularities of Canadian geography, demographics and history, and cannot be underestimated. Any country with multinational roots of the kind moulded by the two warring empires (joined with First Nations) must be competent at managing transition and adaptation.

The France that was reaching out to the world when Samuel de Champlain established Stadacona (Québec City) was a France very much dominant in the Europe of its time. It was made strong by industrious workers of the land and by determined and capable businessmen who ran thousands of stores in the many thriving cities across France. And with the coming of Cardinal Richelieu's service to Louis XIII, the monarchy would be strengthened, the French state consolidated, a powerful army and navy built, and the idea of a French nation clearly established as something greater than the individual loyalties or intrigues of the nobility du jour. This sense of "nation" under the Bourbon sovereign was something that did not exist at the end of the sixteenth century, but was built by Richelieu through to 1642. Richelieu's intendant system under Jean Talon in Québec focused on strong local government building a society for "the glory of God" in a way that reflected not the challenges of the Métropole, but the geographic realities of what became New France and would be the basis of Canada itself. The French fact had taken root in the demography and topography of the Atlantic and St. Lawrence regions of Canada, creating the former and, in part, defined by the latter. It had also become a defining reality of national identity for the foreseeable future.

It seems self-evident that competing First Nations would battle over territorial limits, or that competing European empires would contest around colonial reach and conflicting geographical aspirations. What is truly amazing and unique about Canada is the extent to which geography, and its role in defining or protecting interests, has been and remains deeply central, influencing almost every political debate, ideology and party that has come to have any role in the public life of Canada and Canadians. And the disputes mentioned above—to which we can add debates over conscription, French language rights, Métis rights or First Nations land claims—can really be sourced back to domestic geopolitics as we became part of the colonial outreach of the French and British.

While it may be extreme to suggest that "geography is destiny," it is surely fair, based on our history, to accept the fact that geography influences the way people, ideas and economic forces actually can and do affect destiny. Sparse, low-density settlement patterns, with communities formed near waterways and requiring large land- and sea-crossing efforts to establish and sustain, all conspired to produce a particular culture made ever-more unique by its climate. This culture would be very different from the ancient or historic cultures of Europe or Asia, where intense population density was a core reality.

The geography that met those who preceded Jacques Cartier—and Jacques Cartier himself—was one that was both compelling and difficult. For all the attraction of the plentiful fur and fish, both soon to be economic drivers of frontier colonial expansion and conflict, the network of rivers that led into the heart of the continent itself, and to different First Nations territories, initiated a fortress-based approach to expansion and exploration.

Europeans who came to Canada found organized First Nations societies in place with traditions, laws and governance, and economic systems that had served them for centuries. While there were geographic and land bases for many of the First Nations whom the French began to work with upon arrival, tribal interaction with each other and with the new colonists brought about change and mobility. Professor Richard White, in *The Middle Ground: Indians, Empires and Republics in the Great Lakes Region, 1650–1815*, argues that there was a sustained, not always stable, but coherent set of working relationships and alliances between the tribes of the Algonquian confederacy and the French, characterized by military cooperation, intermarriage, economic exchange and cultural tolerance. White's portrayal of a "middle ground of culture" speaks eloquently to the mode of accommodation that the French empire and its emissaries accepted here while other empires sought domination and destruction, if not conversion and cultural absorption of indigent occupants. There was, of course, no lack of missionaries and "savers of souls" for "the glory of God" in and among the waves of French settlers. But the reality on the ground of accommodation, alliance, intermarriage, and cultural and linguistic exchanges is irrefutable. One of the most conservative and imperial of world empires had landed in Canada to be taken in, largely helped, and, in part, accommodated in return for trade, cultural tolerance and respect for local survival skills. Dr. White further argues that this middle ground only works when means other than force are engaged. Dr. Graham Reynolds of Cape Breton University, in his essay "Teaching First Nations History as Canadian History," has more recently reflected that there is a consensus among serious historians that the interaction between the First Nations and the settlers was real, especially in Acadia and in the eastern part of New France. In 1668, the French Crown began encouraging intermarriage between First Nations and settlers. This, he suggests, foreshadows the notion of a coming Canadian history in which First Nations and settler narratives become one.

Despite wars, raids, massacres, and inhumanity on all sides, conservative settler societies were also about accommodation and a certain measure of joint enterprise. A core strand of Canadian conservatism can, in part, be found there.

Very quickly, in terms of the sweep of exploratory history, Canada, and the larger continent of which it was part, became a geography of competing zones of influence and interest, each with different economic and political antecedents and sponsors in Europe. Even with territories so vast and a robust First Nations template of regions of control already in place, the settlement possessed intense competition and substantive discord. The "where" of our local politics and early government and development began very much with the dawn of the seventeenth century. As the competing aspirations that geography evoked took hold during that century, the reality of British colonies and French colonies all overlaid on First Nations territorial communities began to intensify—and by the end of that century, the French and English were seriously disputing the Newfoundland fishery and the fur trade of Hudson Bay and the interior. The English holdings on the coast and the substantial French holdings in the interior and along the

St. Lawrence were not cooperative ventures, but highly competitive ventures. Attracted by rich agricultural land, fur-filled forests and teeming seas, both sides met the challenges of cold and ice. The mix of elements, large spaces and climatic variation would help define how communities were built, locations chosen and inhabitant cultures implanted.

The geographical grandeur of Canada, along with the often difficult relations with the First Nations, whose territory the Europeans were "taking up," became a new tableau against which the brush strokes of European conflict would be applied by the colonial, missionary and commercial interests of competing European-based empires.

In the conflicts that would come with the English colonies, in the extension of European wars to Canadian soil, the allies and enemies of the French and English would emerge among First Nations, whose development and economic settlement patterns were imposed upon, used and, in significant measure, exploited by European settlement. First Nations alliances were about survival. And survival meant finding ways to mediate the exploitation that Europeans, true to their time and ethos, confused with settlement and development.

The relationships the French and then the British built with the First Nations communities were defining in terms of trade, economic viability, social organization and military defence. The French found a northern tier of the continent that already had fifty-three indigenous languages grouped in eleven language families. The French faced seven different cultural zones, including the Algonquian (in the eastern and east central part of New France), and the southeastern Ontario region Iroquois, each with numerous tribes with specific regional and sub-regional reach. Coming to terms and cooperating with these First Nations societies was a vital requirement of survival. The Canadian geographic and demographic realities were already imposing a "Canadian" imperative on those who would seek to take root in our land: cooperate and accommodate, or perish. And while the dynamics of that accommodation and cooperation would vary and, in some cases, be more difficult or viable than in others, the Montagnais, Naskapi, Huron, Algonquian, Chippewa, Micmac, Maliseet, Cree, Penobscot and Iroquois would all be among those First Nations whose presence and regional force, whose social organization and structures, made cooperation and accommodation vital.

But, in the end, after the events of 1759, the British Crown held fast to its colonial offspring while the French Métropole lost interest, leaving "French" Canada to fend for itself in an Anglo continent. The British Crown hung in and remained central to Canadian colonial roots as laid down. It also embraced Québec particularity and its accommodation became central to the state-craft of Canada itself. It is important that we understand how important the Québec Act of 1774 actually was to the roots of French Canadian survival in North America.

> And, for the more perfect Security and Ease of the Minds of the Inhabitants of the said Province, it is hereby declared, That His Majesty's Subjects, professing the religion of the Church of Rome, of and in the said Province of Quebec, may have, hold, and enjoy, the free Exercise of the Religion of the church of Rome ... and that the Clergy of the said Church may hold, receive, and enjoy, their accustomed Dues and Rights, with respect to such Persons only as shall profess the said Religion.

Canada's founding nations had founding faiths. However some may embrace ecumenical and non-denominational beliefs today, our founding faiths were those of the Catholic Church and the Protestant derivations that followed. Not only did the act embrace the Roman Catholic faith and clergy and their land reserves, it went on to legitimize and protect the French civil law.

This paragraph from the Québec Act of 1774, which passed in the seventh session of the Thirteenth Parliament of Great Britain, was a critical bridge between the Ancien Régime of New France—its culture, history, language and inhabitants—and Canada's tomorrow. The new boundary definitions for Québec included in the act would upset American colonists and become one more *casus belli*. The protection of French language and culture infuriated some local Montréal Anglo-business interests over time and laid the basis for imperial protection of French rights in Québec for years to come. In a geopolitical sense, the Québec Act reflected a British government and Parliament that had learned from the earlier 1746 slaughter at Culloden, in which two thousand Scottish rebel combatants perished. This British government understood that the faith and language of Québec's francophone *habitants* were fundamental parts of how they lived, who they were and how they would survive. It was a government that understood that the clergy, who had come to heal the sick, teach and advance the faith, and who were at the centre of parish and community life, were pillars of the nationalism and identity of a people. There is precious little evidence of any other colonial power, at that point in history, having acted in a similar way. That is, truly respecting and enshrining the established social and cultural preferences of a people who had been "defeated" after military conflict. Mason Wade, in his seminal work *The French Canadians, 1760–1945*, calls the Québec Act "virtually the Magna Charta of the French Canadians." And, as it re-established the commercial empire of the St. Lawrence, at the expense of American colonial borders, it assured Québec's loyalty while fanning the anger and insurgent spirit in the American colonies.

The Church of Rome, as licensed by the French Métropole and the Jesuit, Oblate and other orders who were dispatched after

Champlain, was a conservative church professing a conservative faith of hierarchy and discipline. And the Church's involvement in education, language, health care, family and civic life, made it central to the sinews of French Canadian identity and national spirit. Its survival created a bedrock for all that would follow: a bedrock of resistance at elite levels to the blandishments of the American Revolution; a bedrock of resistance to the relations that would ensue with the Loyalists, who would soon be leaving the American colonies and who were largely Protestant, English, Scottish and Dutch, and more interested in commerce; a bedrock of resistance that would survive to define the nation that, with British regulars, First Nations allies and *habitant* militia would repel the American invasion of 1812–14.

To say that the British government, in its endorsement of the Québec Act, envisioned all of this would be to press the point too far. But it is quite reasonable to say that the British Parliament, in its protection of the *habitants* and their faith and in its definition of new borders for Québec, produced not only a Québec *securisé* in its own language, culture and faith, but a geographic definition of British North America that was secured by a working agreement with its occupants. The foundation of British North America now included a solid and massive pillar of French Canadian language, culture and identity. As a defining and central value it characterized one of the principle tenets of an emergent Canadian Tory and conservative world view: respect for the foundational duality of who Canadians were. And as the gradual move to responsible government evolved in the ensuing century, that century would be marked by some realities that this core conservatism would protect: respect for the origins and hierarchy of the founding European cultures and the conservative bias in favour of dealing respectfully with the ultramontane francophone Catholic Church and its supporting *bleu* and nationalist fellow travellers. The commonly shared English and French Canadian fear of the Republican forces to the south was a reaction to the disrespect for minority rights evoked by America's bustling mercantile ways. And the very origins of the Québec Act as the first territorial/cultural/religious recognition of, and official acceptance of, a distinct French language, culture and civilization also began a tradition of conservative nationalism in Canada that would distinguish it from American perspectives. It was a conservatism that respected the history and particularity of place. In Canada, every aspect of public society would evolve to accommodate who people were as a collective, where in the country they lived, and what special nature their geography, language and history created. In America, the route from the pre- and post-revolutionary days led inexorably to an individualist, arms-bearing, anti-government and self-centred "life, liberty and the pursuit of happiness" vision of governance. The Canadian conservatism of accommodation, of dealing respectfully with what people believed in and cared about and the institutions that protected those beliefs, led naturally to a constitutional process structured around the remarkably more conservative notion of "peace, order and good government."

The Québec Act, passed some twenty-six years before the eighteenth century's turning, was the *pierre angulaire*, the absolute cornerstone, of a unique Canadian identity and the conservatism it would help create. The mismanagement by the British under George III of their relationship, both fiscal and political, with the American colonies stands in stark contrast to their sensitivity towards French Québec.

British insensitivity to legitimate patriot and Loyalist angst in the American colonies would cost the U.K. dearly and create huge new influences to broaden and deepen Canadian conservative roots and reach. The "accommodationist" school, which served so well to cement the loyalty of the Catholic Church and French Canadian society during the American Revolution and during the skirmishes that constituted the successful military defence of Canada from 1812–14 against American attack, would not be officially contested until the arrival of Lord Durham, the prominent British Liberal dispatched by the Colonial Office to deal with the causes of rebellion in 1837. The mix of history, language rights, Crown loyalties, identities and compromises that shaped who we are is complex. But in that complexity is found the immense strength and durability that forms the foundation of Canadian identity.

[2]

CROWN, ORDER,
IDENTITY
AND FREEDOM

In Canada, freedom and identity are deeply tied to the Crown
and the concept of order. Freedom may well be one of the
most difficult qualities for any society to both define and
understand. Its absence, and the travails of a country or society
in which it is repressed or diluted, is more easily perceived and
explained. Not having the right to worship one's own way or not
at all, has always been a symbol of freedom denied. Since the
nineteenth century's midpoint, not having the right to elect or
defeat the government of one's choice has been an almost classic
definition of freedom denied. The absence of the presumption of
innocence would strike most residents of Anglosphere countries
as a sign that freedom was severely constrained. Yet, in France,
Italy or other countries with a Roman law legacy, where the mag-
istrate is a prosecuting officer within the administration of justice,
are citizens less free than in the U.K. or Canada? In a country
like Great Britain, steeped in the presumptions of innocence and
freedom that date all the way back to the Magna Carta of 1512,
but where closed-circuit television cameras record almost every

out-of-home (so far at least) activity, is freedom diminished? In a system such as that found in the United States, where the quality of the defence bar, the presumption of innocence, and the legal costs of a stout and competent defence tilt the outcomes of the judicial process towards the very wealthy, and where, like Canada, the prison populations are wildly over-represented with black, First Nations and poor citizens, can we be sure that freedom is evenly distributed and protected?

The shape, tone and nature of freedom in any society, notwithstanding laudable international norms, differ according to the nature of that society: its history, geography and founding values. A society whose basic political framework is founded on "peace, order and good government," as is the case with Canada, will be different than one founded on the basic premise of "life, liberty and the pursuit of happiness," as is the case with the U.S. This is not about being better or worse. It is simply about fundamental differences at the foundation of the national idea. National identity matters very much to how freedom is shaped.

The Canada that was structured by the Articles of Confederation (1865–67) is not the only source of our national identity. A range of local, cultural, religious, linguistic, community and geographic realities combined to form our identity and, in turn, spawned the politics of the confederal union. Canadian conservatism was shaped in a similar way and, from its very beginnings, became a critical force in forming Canadian identity itself.

The nature of our relationship with the Crown, made unavoidable upon the arrival of British warships on the St. Lawrence in the spring of 1760, to relieve the successful French blockade of Québec City after the Plains of Abraham skirmish, would become a critical part of how that identity would characterize our sense, our Canadian sense, of what freedom really means. Less than two decades later, in 1776, American "patriots" would expel the Loyalists who were no less "democratic" than they were but remained loyal to the Crown and the British connection. And the manner of this expulsion would further define the Crown-centred part of both our national order and the balance between order and freedom that became, without armies or bloodshed, the Canadian idea.

It has been said that if the Liberals view themselves as the party of the Charter of Rights and Freedoms, that most American of Canadian constitutional innovations, then the Conservatives see themselves as the party of the British North America Act. This act established a clear, institutional order for the architecture of our statehood around the centrality of the Crown.

I remember, as a youngster in Montréal, attending religious schools where the non-religious curriculum was governed by provincial regulation. The front wall over the classroom blackboard had a series of sketches representing the great figures of the Old Testament: Abraham, Moses, Joshua and various prophets. But at the centre, elevated over them, was the classic mid-1950s photograph of a young Queen Elizabeth and her husband, Prince Philip, in his naval uniform. When I asked one afternoon why the picture of the queen and Prince Philip occupied a more prominent place than the biblical figures, the answer was clear: "Because, Mr. Segal, in Canada we are all equal under the Crown and we are all free to practise our faith, live and worship in freedom and maintain our tradition and culture. That's why Canada is the most decent country in the world." Over the top, no doubt, but grade school teachers have to sometimes hit the ball out of the park for youngsters to get it. And to the extent that Canadians are not Americans, it is not just because of a border, the Treaty of Ghent of 1814 or the failure of successive American military incursions between 1812 and 1814. It is also due to the arrival of the Loyalists after 1783, who were a cornerstone to the lasting relationship between Crown and country.

Despite what some historians argue, there is almost no meaningful evidence of the Loyalists coming to Canada with uniform anti-democratic biases. Quite the contrary. Those who would leave the American colonies would do so to return to the closest outpost of the British Empire—the Canadian colonies. Here was where the later-life conservatism of Edmund Burke, which reflected the core judgement of a Québec Act that enshrined the Québec founded by the British in 1758, was very much alive and well. Burke was a parliamentarian born in Ireland but elected repeatedly in Britain. He was a Whig who defended serious devolution of taxing powers to the American colonies, but who later criticized the excesses of the French Revolution, thus becoming a conservative voice for reasonable democracy.

The Loyalist numbers essentially created what were then two new English-speaking colonies, New Brunswick and Upper Canada, while broadening the English and Tory presence in Québec and Nova Scotia. This influence essentially ended any uncertainty about Canada's ever-evolving identity within the British Empire. Revising this identity was always on the to-do list of "Manifest Destiny" Americans.

There is also strong evidence that American Loyalists (called "Tories" by the revolutionaries) did not agree with the arbitrary nature of British decision-making towards the colonies. Governor Hutchinson of Massachusetts, a strong Loyalist, went to the U.K. to protest the closing of Boston Harbor. Others, such as Daniel Dulany of Maryland, or Joseph Galloway, an American colonial lawyer, legislator and Loyalist of Pennsylvania, wrote in pamphlets about the British excess or mistakes in tax policy relative to the American colonies, some of which were quoted in the British Parliament. (An essay called "Consideration on the propriety of imposing taxes on the British Colonies," written by Daniel Dulany and read in Parliament by Pitt the Elder in January of 1766 in opposition to the Stamp Act, is one of many examples.)

Mob excess against disloyal Tories who would not switch allegiance from the Crown to American patriots—the revolutionary sacking of private homes, the tarring and feathering of respectable citizens—all helped swell Tory-Loyalist ranks. In the end, it was the clear dishonesty of American Whig leaders on the issue of independence that turned the tide. Almost half a year before the Declaration of Independence itself, American Whig leaders like Benjamin Franklin and George Washington disavowed any interest in breaking the imperial tie. On Christmas Day, 1775, any purpose related to independence was formally set aside by proclamation of the Revolutionary Congress of New Hampshire. According to W. Stewart Wallace, in *The United Empire Loyalists*, Benjamin Franklin is reported to have assured Lord Chatham that he had not heard one word in favour of independence in America, "from any person, drunk or sober."

The patriots' subsequent treasonous reversal was a solid contributing factor to Loyalist departure, as were the divisions along religious lines—with Presbyterians often becoming Whigs and pro-rebellion and Episcopal (Anglican) members becoming Tories and Loyalists. However, these were not ironclad divisions, as people from both denominations could be found on either side. Established classes were more likely to be both Tory and Loyalist, although many farmers joined the Loyalist migration, shocked by the mob excess of the patriots and discomfited by the break with Empire and established order.

Oppression and hounding of the Loyalists, sanctioned and encouraged by revolutionary and Whig leaders, made departure the only rational course. With the Declaration of Independence, Loyalism was now viewed as treason and subject to harsh prosecutions and penalties. Wallace's book is replete with stories of the mass imprisonment of those who would not take the oath to their state and set aside their allegiance to the Crown. Some were tried and hanged. Many had land confiscated, and many were prohibited from collecting debts, practising law and the rest. Americans hounded the Tories and Loyalists out of their newly independent colonies. America's beginnings were profoundly exclusionary, anti-communitarian and repressive of free speech!

These new conservative Canadian residents, who were loyal to the Crown, would help build our national identity in

English Canada, help influence our social, economic and political landscape, help defend the role of faith in society—not negate it—and help define Canada as a place different from both the United States and Great Britain. And their politically conservative, economically progressive and deeply-suspicious-of-American-populism tenor would become foundational for Canadian conservatism itself.

They would mould a conservative national identity that evolved towards responsible government and was very different from the American approach. They were not anti-democratic in their conservatism about Empire and stability; in fact, many had come from colonial areas with democratic local assemblies in which they themselves had participated and to which they had been elected. But their preference for the faiths, practices, structures and loyalties of Empire would define their contribution and the conservative Tory view for many decades to come.

There is an interesting debate among historians about how truly "conservative" the Empire Loyalists were on issues surrounding democracy and representation by population. To be fair, before Lexington and the outbreak of hostilities, the development in the American colonies of elected local assemblies, with a fair measure of local jurisdiction, did not evoke Loyalist protest or dissent within those colonies. It would be unreasonable to conclude that the Loyalist cause was, in any way, intrinsically anti-democratic.

But there is a difference between democracies with raw town hall intensity, filled with councils of elected "freemen," councillors, mayors, assemblymen and judges, and constitutional monarchies, in which responsible government evolves from the Crown. In constitutional monarchies, the state, as represented by the Crown, is above politics and has a distinctly broader reach than in situations where all are elected and are forever campaigning for re-election. The Crown, acting on behalf of all aspects of the present, historical and future state, speaks to the priority of community over individual political ambition. A Crown attorney, law officers of the Crown or a judge appointed by those who serve the Crown are very different vessels for justice and fairness than judges and state attorneys who constantly seek election and re-election and weigh all their deliberations against some future popularity contest. One is not better or worse than the other, but they are profoundly different.

There is also a difference between a society that is proclaimed on the premise of the separation of Church and state—and where a declaration of independence embraces "life, liberty and the pursuit of happiness"—and a society that has evolved through the joint rights (often hard-won) and mutual respect of established churches and the consistently applied British constitutional premise of "peace, order and good government." This phrase is found in various forms in many constitutions presided over by the Colonial Office in the late nineteenth century. The Empire Loyalists left what was a homogeneous American colonial society in revolution against a faraway British government—a British government overwhelmed by its over-taxing colonial bias and by its largely insensitive approach to colonial aspiration.

The Empire Loyalists came to the British colonies of the north that had already been fashioned by accommodation between English-speaking Protestants, French-speaking Catholics and First Nations, with Irish Catholics and Scots (both Presbyterian and Catholic) thrown in. They were leaving a society that was established with a founding promise, beginning with "We the people...," a society that would add to its already compelling wealth, productivity and trade, and a society that could speak to a new empire replacing and competing with the one it had violently risen against.

In the Canadian colonies, the Loyalists would both find and help build a loyalty to the Empire's constitutional nationality because of the guarantees that the Empire offered for French and Catholic survival and for stable British justice. These societies had the chance to evolve and to embrace their own sense of order, freedom, stability and representative democracy while protected by the often symbolic but on occasion, when it mattered, quite real reach of the Royal Navy and His Majesty's forces.

With the decision, by acts of omission and commission, of the French, English, Canadian and First Nations leadership to stay out of the revolution in 1775 and to warmly receive Loyalist refugees from the American colonies, a critical foundation of Canadian conservatism and Canadian national identity was formed. From the beginning of the post-revolutionary colonial evolution of British North America, the stability of the Crown and the balanced institutional and constitutional guarantees it offered (habeas corpus and the Québec Act) began to define the conservative mainstream and the reformer mindset. The Americans had chosen one route to sovereignty, independence, and the mercantile liberalism of pioneer expansionism; the Canadians had chosen another. And that choice would be inoculated with a blend of British Tory, French ultramontane conservative and American Loyalist sensibilities that would make the Canadian conservative brand as unique as the Canadian identity itself.

American democracy was built on the Jacksonian principles of expanded suffrage, such as extending the vote to all white men, not just landowners; Manifest Destiny, the belief that the U.S. had a divine right to expand from the Atlantic to the Pacific; patronage, wherein the rotation of political appointees in and out of office was not only the right but also the duty of victors in political contests; strict constructionism, which ensured most of the governmental power would remain with the individual states; and laissez-faire economics that favoured a hands-off approach to the economy. This winner-take-all promise of Jacksonian democracy—an approach that wanted all offices elected (including judges), a broader electorate, massive continental expansion and government posts and contracts to be won, or possessed—is at the root of the American sense of exceptionalism and patronage.

It has no place in Canada's political and national identity. The relative prominence in our history of minority governments speaks to that.

What was built between Champlain's arrival in 1603 and the American Revolution of 1776 reflected, in essence, not only a society where compromise became essential to sustained economic, political and social progress, but one whose host culture reflected the creative role of compromise as an instrument (often quite an activist instrument) for moving society ahead. It would be a condition of the Canadian political soul, shaped by the realities of geography and climate, the necessities of history and demography and the hard facts, dangers and opportunities of our particular political neighbourhood. In societal terms, compromise and accommodation became integral parts of our political culture. From the late 1700s, it became clearer, through the War of 1812 with the Americans and through the incipient growth of responsible government, that the policies of Tory and conservative caution and nation building would be traditions on the political spectrum that were reflective of their own Tory ethic of compromise. The core ethic was not so much a constraint as an enabler for spreading a new society and the Canadian ideal—the latter always being an amalgam of the aspects and particularities of the former. This would be very dissimilar to the Republican, federalist and democratic traditions in the U.S. colonies and broadly different from the common roots of the British Tory and Whig traditions.

In the first place, societies that evolve gradually in their democratic progress are far different from those that seize the next step through armed revolt. And, in the second place, Canadian political, business and rural societies were not homogeneous in the way that British society was then. As a result, our politics would always be distinct from both the British and American varieties.

Herein lies a vast demarcation between the pragmatism of the Tory world view that accepts established realities—culture, language, geography and religion—as givens that are inherited and with which a society must work, and the Whig or more liberal view that reason, optimism and positive purpose are a basis from which anything can be changed or improved. This view advances the dubious, if optimistic, notion that wherever one lives, or whatever the local realities, firm-willed central policy is always capable of changing things for the better. This universalist, liberal view has been responsible for much good in the world. But it has also, on occasion, been exceptionally shallow and unwittingly destructive and destabilizing. The Tory view that language, culture and identity, and geography are to be respected is vital to the way Canada was conceived and built.

This also meant that while conservatism in the U.K. would be, before the Pitt-Disraeli era transition, largely about Tory landed gentry, aristocratic privilege and constraining unruly change; in the U.S., it would be about Manifest Destiny and constraining the role of government. Whereas in Canada, as it entered the nineteenth century, conservatism would be about reconciliation, managing contradictions and sustaining a core civility. Loyalty, heart and hearth, soul and soil were at its essence. It was large "T" Tory in terms of stability and the institutions of the Crown. It was not "republican" or "radical" when compared to the emergent American political dynamic.

The skirmishes and battles between the Canadian colonies and the newly minted United States during the 1812–14 period were a component of transition and, as is often the case with armed engagement, a catalyst for both identity and nationalism. It was a war begun by the Americans allegedly because of the Royal Navy's arresting and boarding of American ships suspected of aiding the French in their war with England. The proximity of Britain's Canadian colonies made a responsive attack and a retaliatory American engagement apparently easy to achieve.

What American military and political leadership did not fully comprehend was how both the new post-1776 demographics of

Canada and the essentially Tory-*bleu* approach to society and governance would be ample reason for different parts of the Canadian colonial community to work together in resisting the U.S. The Constitution Act of 1791 had confirmed the clergy reserves for the French Roman Catholic clergy in Québec—not without controversy, but it was done. The Loyalists had received generous land grants, as did British officers who had moved north after the American Revolution. First Nations had working relationships and reasonably recent treaty and economic agreements with both the colonial and British administrations. While none on the Canadian side displayed much enthusiasm for war, and most hoped not to be embroiled in an event that would be a spillover between European empires, this did not mean that the simple expression of Manifest Destiny by the Americans would be allowed to go unchallenged when American troops marched.

If ideas and philosophies of government are shaped by geography and demographics, and not the other way around, then the geography and demographics of Canada, which had been the basis of our history and conservatism to that point in time, would prevail. While broadly outnumbered, British regulars, Canadian and Québécois militia and volunteers, and First Nations allies succeeded, through a better grasp of the geography, a more conservative and tactical approach on the ground, and a surprising tenacity, to make prospective U.S. territorial gains illusory or far too expensive to be worthwhile. The U.S. attacks were brought to an end.

But history conspired, in many ways, to influence and strengthen the joined-up Canadian response. Although the American declaration of war on Britain in June of 1812 as part of the Napoleonic Wars might, in view of Canada's French-English roots, have been a prediction of division in Canada, the hard truth was that France had deserted New France in its hour of need decades earlier, in the 1750s and 1760s. And the Québec Act provided protection and assurances to French Québec, a type of protection never before provided or defended in the history of the British Empire.

The Americans saw both the declaration of war on the British and the proximity of British colonies to their border as a ripe opportunity for annexation and expansion. Here again, the Crown and the British did not desert their offspring. Major General Isaac Brock repelled U.S. invasion efforts along the border territories from Niagara up into Québec. In Québec, General De Salaberry's repulse of an overwhelmingly larger U.S. force set the American cause back, and, firmly. Here again, Canadian geography inspired a battle plan that made preventing a division of Canada by an American incursion up the Champlain-Richelieu corridor—which would separate the Upper and Lower colonies— the critical priority.

In essence, when hostilities in the eighteenth and early nineteenth centuries among the English, French and First Nations had been replaced by workable, if not perfect, compromises, important defences were formed. These defences, reinforced by British regulars, Empire Loyalists and French Canadian militias were, in the end, a coalition the Americans could not overcome. And while the battle-tested experience of regular British troops made a real difference, it was the support of irregulars and volunteers, and local Canadian militias such as the Voltigeurs and First Nations allies that spawned the mythologies and war stories that shaped political life after the Treaty of Ghent in 1814. Whatever new borderlines had been agreed to, however many armed ships had been prevented from sailing into the Great Lakes without mutual consent, a new political reality and layer of national identity had come into being. A British North America, sustained by compromise and common cause between English, French, and First Nations inhabitants was now real and immeasurable.

An essentially conservative approach to society had now become embedded in the identity of the Canadian colonies. The blandishments of the Americans in 1775 and their invasion efforts of 1812–14 had been resisted, sometimes with force of arms. We remained part of the British Empire. We were custodians of British law, British due process and French language and civil procedure. We were protectors of the faiths that had come to settle and develop our part of the continent. The Tory values of Church, family, community, Crown and Empire were evolving in a way that reflected the climate, geography and community we shared. We had yet to develop our own approach to self-government, but we began moving towards responsible government utterly comfortable with who we were and very clear about who we were not.

If there was a philosophical message shared among Tories everywhere after the extremes of both the French and American revolutions, it was not the negative one often ascribed to them by chroniclers of the times. Of course, Tories were more cautious about change, more protective of established rights and the norms associated with order and stability. But considering where Tory conservatism in Canada had come from and how it had been born, that would not have been surprising. The most compelling message they shared, proselytized and defended (on occasion with muskets) was not the opposition to all change, but the need for balance in the process of change. From Edmund Burke's instructive analysis of the excesses of the French Revolution in *Reflections on the Revolution in France* (1790), in which he was anything but anti-democratic, to the Loyalists' views on the risks of revolutionary change within the British system of laws, governance and Empire, the Tory role was one of constructive caution. Avoiding the excesses of the American route was not so much about a different process but about a different country. The War of 1812 had established both our ties to Empire and our will to be different and unique; the Québécois have a wonderful expression for this: "conséquents avec nous-mêmes," or, consistent with who we actually are. Our larger, wealthier, stronger, and more populated southern neighbour created huge pressures for emulation just by its very existence. Some subsequent Canadian reformers

(William Lyon Mackenzie, Louis Riel), who took refuge with and succour from the Americans, tilted in that direction. Tory voices in Upper and Lower Canada and in the Maritime regions did not. On occasion, that made them less than popular, but it never made them less than right; the successful reformers possessed Tory "balance."

For better or for worse, a Tory nationalism had taken shape. It was about Canada and how she had come together, her origins, history, evolution and DNA. The Canadian way was to accommodate difference, respect diversity, tolerate dissent and build real citizenship. The American way was to build citizenship by banishing dissenters, using force and homogenizing diverse identities.

Our national identity situated freedom in the context of the earned citizenship that typified the relationship between residents, arrivals and the seigneurs in New France. It situated freedom within the context of responsible governments where, over time, elected legislators worked with the Governor in Council—essentially with the Crown, the prime minister and Cabinet—to ensure that only a government with the confidence of the popularly elected had the right to spend taxes levied on the people. This was remarkably more stable than the American (and French Republican) system of countervailing legislatures that allowed for a separate executive in the election of a separate president with his or her own countervailing powers, as well as an American Supreme Court with its own countervailing powers. The American design was very much about constraining government and reducing its role in the broadly mercantile hurly-burly of the American marketplace. The Canadian design, derived from the most appropriate aspects of Britain's unwritten constitution, was about responsible government able to act, with the support of elected parliamentarians chosen locally in their ridings and regions by Canadian subjects of the Empire and, ultimately, citizens of Canada.

The compelling imperative of compromise and accommodation was a sense of a fair and inclusive "order" that immigrants to

Canada found upon arrival in the modern era. They did not get off ships in Halifax, Montréal or Vancouver and find monolithic, melting pot cities. They found, instead, cities with cultural pluralism and linguistic dualism.

There was no lack, in the early days of immigration, of bigotry or antagonism towards foreigners. Canada can claim no ultra-high ground on that front. But the tensions were addressed by respecting differences under the Crown rather than crushing differences under the boot of an insensitive majority—a route taken in the U.S. From these roots, and under the rule of the Crown and parliamentary and constitutional democracy, emerged the balance between freedom under the law and respect for collective and individual identity. Here, the relationship between our First Nations and the Crown was very different from that between the American Indians and the White House, Congress and Senate. Whereas in Canada First Nations would be accorded reserved lands and continued status, in the U.S. the conquering of Indian territory and an approach favourable to assimilation would prevail. Canadian First Nations continue, by and large, to have what they themselves view as a special relationship with the Crown. That same difference can be found in the story of our evolution from being subjects of the British Crown to becoming Canadian citizens in 1947. The Oath of Allegiance in our Citizenship Act, which includes a pledge of loyalty to the Crown, reflects this. We not only pledge our loyalty to Canada, its laws and constitution, but to the Queen and her heirs and successors. This signifies the particular history and evolution of our values, practices and balances; it encompasses the Québec Act, the War of 1812, Confederation and all that has come since. It reminds new citizens that the country welcoming them developed and became democratic while working with the Crown, not against it.

Tories and Liberals believe in the advancement and preservation of full economic, social and human rights for so-called "new Canadians." John Diefenbaker's Canadian Bill of Rights passed

Parliament in 1960. The nationalist Union Nationale government of Daniel Johnson and Jean-Jacques Bertrand in Québec extended confessional school funding to minorities well beyond the traditional French-English divide in the late 1960s. Peter Lougheed's first bill in the legislature, upon being elected, was the Alberta Human Rights Act in 1972. Ontario established the first ministry of culture and citizenship under Bill Davis in the early 1970s. However, Tories differ from some Liberals by rejecting the notion that the Canadian identity can become whatever new arrivals chose to make it. The warm embrace of cultural diversity, which is a compelling national strength for any competitive society, is very different from allowing the migration trends du jour to influence or force the renegotiation of our own core identity. I tried to address this issue when I spoke in the Senate in March 2009 on a motion I had moved to keep the Oath of Allegiance to the Crown as part of our citizenship oath for new Canadians. I was concerned about litigation then proceeding through the courts (which has, to date, made little progress) in which a prominent civil liberties lawyer was seeking to strike the Crown out of our Oath of Citizenship, on the premise that the reference violated the Charter of Rights protection for prospective citizens who were being forced to swear allegiance to a monarchy he alleged had itself been racist and supportive of the slave trade. Without getting sidetracked by the particular take on history by the litigant, it struck me that the basis of our identity, our historical roots, our accommodationist legacy and our cooperative mix of loyalties to Crown, freedom, tolerance and order were not open to judicial reinterpretation and should not be, in any way, so diminished.

I put it this way at the time:

The question of Canadian citizenship must be inclusive, welcoming, warm and constructive, but it must also be firm. The core symbols of our citizenship, the core institutions of our society and the values they reflect and defend are not just another list of negotiable preferences to be chopped up in court challenges. Our French, English and First

Nation roots and history are not negotiable. Equality before the law, the trinity in the Parliament of Canada—the House of Commons, the Senate and the Crown, its agents and departments and laws—are not negotiable. One part of the Constitution, the Charter of Rights and Freedoms, should not be used, should not be allowed to be used, to crush another symbol, the Crown—as some might wish to do by using the Charter before the courts, even as we sit here today. Can the Oath of Citizenship never be changed? Of course it can, through Parliament, through petition to Parliament, through political campaigns and the election of people who wish to do so. Should elected parliamentarians choose to change the oath, should such a bill be introduced in the other place, pass with a majority of votes and do the same in this place and "ironically" be given Royal Assent—of course the oath can be changed ... I would oppose the removal of "Her Majesty" from the Oath of Allegiance, but I would respect the right of this Parliament to make that decision ... I support the Charter of Rights and Freedoms profoundly. It was my great privilege to be part of the team of officials, as Associate Secretary of Cabinet for federal-provincial relations in Ontario, to help with the wording and the structure of the Charter itself ... As a result of that experience, I know that there would be no Charter of Rights and Freedoms without the notwithstanding clause. If there had not been the notwithstanding clause, there never would have been passage of the Charter of Rights and Freedoms. I know that the clause was put into the Constitution to protect parliamentary sovereignty ... As for those who wish not to become citizens if it involves allegiance to Her Majesty, we should respect their right not to become citizens. We should respect their right to petition, campaign and advocate for the removal of that allegiance, however much we may disagree with that position. However, they should have no right to use one part of the Constitution to eradicate another through the use of the Charter in the courts. The bill before us today would ensure that travesty, that assault on the Crown, would not be facilitated in the future by the use of the Charter ... Honourable senators, we have a host culture in Canada. It is based on the evolution of responsible government, not

against the Crown but with the Crown… The Crown is a symbol of
our history, our roots and our future. It is both a diverse personality
of our royal and vice-regal constitutional heads of state and the laws
enacted, advanced and prosecuted in their name. It is the embodiment
of the clear sense that the society we share, when reflected by the Crown,
is greater than any elected politician or first minister du jour. They, as
we all know, come and go at the whim of the voters and the parties.
However, the framework of civility, due process, institutional memory,
fairness and the public interest continues through the Crown. That is
what the oath of allegiance affirms, that is what citizenship embraces
and that is how our society endures.

The great debate in the 1960s over the flag also needs to be
understood in historical and societal context as another chap-
ter in the evolving story of the Crown and identity in Canada.
In 2003, Lester Pearson was voted by a distinguished panel as
Canada's best prime minister among all those who served under
Queen Elizabeth II. The panellists included academics, schol-
ars and journalists such as Antonia Maioni, Alain Gagnon, John
English, Kim Nossal, Jean Paré, Tom Courchene, Desmond
Morton and Norman Webster in an evaluation done for the *Policy
Options* magazine of the Institute for Research on Public Policy.
Pearson received and deserves many kudos for his work on health
care, pensions and university financing. And, over time, I have
come to view his decision concerning the flag to be the right one.
The value to Canada of a unique and easily recognizable national
emblem has stood the test of time, whether the maple leaf is seen
on an exquisite embassy on Pennsylvania Avenue, over an ele-
mentary school in Athens, Ontario, or on the shoulder flash of the
men and women of our armed forces. At the time of the debate
in 1965, the divisions were on some levels partisan, on some levels generational and on some levels regional. Many in the Liberal
governing class dismissed Diefenbaker, who favoured retaining a
Union Jack in the corner, as a tired old man, overcome with nostalgia, clinging to a remnant of the past and bitter at not being in

office. While there may well have been some accuracy to the Liberal criticism at the time, the truth of the matter is that there was something to his opposition.

The Tory mindset, as a product of Canadian history, was not and is not about subsuming what was, or the identities that form who we are. In the same way, the debate about the flag was not only about the historical connection and roots of Canada, both at war and at peace. It was not only about the status of Canada as a parliamentary constitutional monarchy as opposed to a republic (although one must always be extremely vigilant when Liberals are in power on that front). It was about how our national emblem would reflect who we actually were. A flag to unify should allow all our constituent parts to see themselves reflected in it. Or so the argument went.

It is noteworthy that, of the many designs retaining a Union Jack in the corner, some featured the fleur-de-lys as the only prominent symbol anywhere else on the flag. Over the course of our history, some flags had portrayed all the provincial coats of arms in the centre shield; some, after World War II, had portrayed the harp, thistle, fleur-de-lys and maple leaf. The case for simplicity was attractive to new Canadians, Québécers, young Canadians and those who were part of the 1960s, post-JFK "all change is good" crowd. And for some, it was a change that became a proxy for the other debate: once the flag was changed, nothing more was necessary.

History has proven Lester B. Pearson, who proposed the new mono-emblem flag, absolutely right on the issue. Along with many other members of Parliament, including the Honourable John Matheson, a decorated war hero and long-serving Liberal M.P., who chaired the all-party committee on the flag, Pearson deserves immense credit for persevering in his support of the one-leaf design.

But Diefenbaker, who in his later years was a tireless promoter of an unhyphenated Canada, and whose pan-Canadian appeal, reach and vision were second to none, was, in 1965, really campaigning not against a new flag, but against a flag whose absent historic symbolism would do a disservice to the very unique history that sets us apart from the Americans.

It was the Honourable H.N.R. (Hal) Jackman cc, Lieutenant Governor of Ontario from 1991–97, who took and advanced the view that our constitutional monarchy-based parliamentary democracy—and all the manifestations and trappings of same— especially the role of the *Crown* as the embodiment of the institutions of the state *and* the people they serve, were and are integral to our sovereignty and unique identity in North America and the world. He remains right on this point today as he was when he served in the viceregal post in the 1980s.

It should not be surprising that the Maple Leaf was proposed, debated and launched at a point in our history when concerns about protecting the French language, establishing equal status and standing for both French and English as official languages and protecting and enhancing multiculturalism were emerging as parts of the national political discussion. As a symbol, the maple leaf picked no favourites between the English and French. It tilted towards no victor in our history. Mr. Pearson and the Maple Leaf prevailed, to the benefit of all Canadians, especially since a flag has to make a clear first impression that evokes the spirit of the land. And the Maple Leaf does that majestically and clearly.

But symbols provide both stability and continuity. They are intergenerational bridges that depict opportunity, sustain freedom, advance consistent values and help cement the order within which freedom can take root and prosper. The Crown—from its beginning in Canada under the French, from its continuity from 1760 on, from its support for responsible government and from its global reach and volunteer service—remains central and influential. It is a rock and a shelter, a reflection of common values and the instrument of a broader society and a spirit of inclusion and community.

The Crown in Canada, in all its viceregal, military, judicial, constitutional and emblematic reality, is often styled as the "Maple Crown." This reflects how the Maple Leaf and the Crown unite as deep emblems of who we are, who we once were and who we would be. The 2010 visit of Her Majesty to Canada, during which the Maple Leaf and the red and white national colours were always visible as a part of her wardrobe or setting, reflected how the symbols have come together to strengthen both Canadian identity and pride.

Those who see the Crown as simply an irrelevant part of the past, while perhaps well-meaning, misunderstand who Canadians are and where our forebears have come from. And if you get that wrong, there is little of our national identity you can possibly get right.

Liberal nationalism tends to be exclusionary of realities on the ground, such as Québec nationalism and Western pride. Often such Liberal nationalism is expressed through new central government institutions, laws or pronouncements making Ottawa and the central government the repository of our country's soul. This may well be done with the most positive and constructive intent. But it is almost perforce exclusionary of regional cultures, interests, identities and sensibilities. New Democrats will often be supportive of all this because they see government and government initiative as the sole enabler of social justice and economic fairness. They argue that the whole is greater than the sum of its parts—an inviting and attractive argument for many Canadians who are proud of our country and seek to affirm that which we share.

A Tory would argue, and often does, that the whole is greater than the sum of its parts, providing that the parts are not diminished or excluded from the identity that defines the greater whole. Hence the Tories are often described as the party of the British North America Act, which implies regional and federal balances, and the Liberals are often described as the party of the Charter of Rights and Freedoms, which implies from the Liberal perspective a central, judicial guarantee for the rights in the Charter, at the expense, if necessary, of provincial autonomy as expressed by elected provincial legislatures. This division in our mainline politics is healthy and important and, as a creative tension, is a far better one than a sterile debate over right versus left. But it is an important and defining debate nonetheless. Large components of this debate date back to the early and mid-nineteenth century, when two Governors General appointed by Queen Victoria's government would have very distinct and dissimilar views on who we are and how our future as a society should be shaped.

3

THE DURHAM-ELGIN DIVIDE

Ongoing Repercussions

Lord Elgin, former Governor General of Canada, in a letter to the British Colonial Secretary on May 4, 1848:

> I must moreover confess that I for one am deeply concerned of the impolicy of all such attempts to denationalize the French. Generally speaking, they produce the opposite effect from that intended, causing the flame of national prejudice and animosity to burn more fiercely—but suppose them to be successful and what wd [*sic*] be the result? You may perhaps Americanise, but depend upon it, by methods of this description you will never anglicize the French inhabitants of the province.
>
> Let them feel on the other hand that their religion, their habits, their prepossessions, their prejudices of your will, are more considered and respected here than on other portions of this vast continent which is being overrun by the most reckless, self-sufficient and dictatorial section of the Anglo Saxon race, and who will venture to say that the last hand which waves the British flag on American ground, may not be that of a French Canadian?

And from Hansard, the Right Honourable Stephen Harper, Prime Minister of Canada, November 22, 2006:

> I will be putting on the notice paper later today the following motion:
>
> That this House recognize that the Québécois form a nation within a united Canada.
>
> When Champlain landed in Québec, he did not say that this would not work, it was too far away, it was too cold, or it was too difficult. No. Champlain and his companions worked hard because they believed in what they were doing, because they wanted to preserve their values, because they wanted to build a lasting and secure country. That is exactly what happened nearly 400 years ago, when Canada, as a country, was founded.
>
> Québeckers know who they are. They know that they have participated in the founding of Canada and in its development and its greatness. They know that they have preserved their language and their unique culture, and that they have advanced their values and their interests within Canada. The real question is simple: do the Québécois form a nation within a united Canada? The answer is yes. Do the Québécois form a nation independent of Canada? The answer is no, and it will always be no.

Whatever differences may exist between Conservatives and Liberals on the spectrum of policies such as trade, fiscal and social priorities and the rest, the differences on the core issue of English and French duality, and how we reconcile and strengthen the partnership at the base of our existence as a country, are more profound. The past is truly a powerful telescope to the future on the Québec-Canada subject. This division can be seen in the essentially different approaches of Lord Durham, also known as "Radical Jack," who served as Governor General in 1838–39, and the Earl of Elgin, a Tory who served as Governor General from 1847 to 1854. Their views on how best to manage the duality at the heart of Canadian history differed as broadly as those of Bob Stanfield and Pierre Trudeau in the late 1960s and early 1970s. The Conservative view also explains why Stephen Harper, as prime minister, reached out to embrace Québécois and Québécoise as constituting a "nation" in a united Canada in November 2006. And for anyone interested in how Conservatives and Liberals will differ on this decisive question in the future, history is a compelling and revealing guide.

In Great Britain, Lord Durham was viewed as an aristocratic radical. He had been elected to Parliament in 1812 as a Whig and was called "Radical Jack." He was a solid orator and given to fiery outbursts. His arrival in Canada coincided with that of William Lyon Mackenzie, a rebel leader seeking responsible, more democratic government. Mackenzie had been travelling to the United States to encourage intervention and support on the side of the pro-democracy reformers against the authority of the Crown, even though the 1837 rebellions were over. Queen Victoria's government sent Durham to settle the local unrest, however modest by historical standards, in the face of the emerging American sense of the right to continue on the "side of freedom." "Radical Jack" felt he had to act quickly on many fronts to cement the British position in the face of the tensions created by the brief rebellions.

I have never agreed with those historians who have found racist intent underlying Lord Durham's famous *Report on the Affairs of British North America* (1839), which proposed the combining of Lower and Upper Canada and the gradual absorption of francophone Québec into an English-speaking mainstream, something Lord Elgin, as indicated earlier, summarily rejected. In this I am sustained by a very thoughtful and courageous Canadian academic, Dr. Janet Ajzenstat, who argued some years ago that Jack Durham was not driven by bigotry in his prescription for French

Canadian assimilation as the best way ahead, but by his intrinsic and determined liberalism.

Ajzenstat makes her point in a wonderful book, *The Political Thought of Lord Durham,* and does so in important and instructive ways. When critiquing those who call Durham a racist, Dr. Ajzenstat offers one of her many compelling analyses:

> When we approach the Report as a text in modern thought, focusing on the argument and the assumptions so implied in Durham's proposals, it becomes apparent that his position on assimilation is not peculiar to his century, his nation or his class. Rather, it is typical of what might be called the "mainstream of liberal thought." He will be seen not as a chauvinist, or an English nationalist, but as a philosophical liberal, as a universalist. He is indeed one of those liberals who supposes that particular traditions and particular loyalties must be discarded if liberal beliefs are to be sustained and liberal justice to prevail.

Her analysis sets aside the "racist" Durham in favour of something quite different: "He is arguing... that the French Canadian must adopt the way of life prevailing on the North American continent so that they can enjoy liberal rights and freedoms on an equal footing with English-speaking Canadians." She continues: "That the advent of liberalism depends on the assimilation of destructive ways of life is a central tenet of liberal thought..."

In her book, Ajzenstat concludes that Lord Durham's apparent chauvinism stemmed not from bigotry but from universalist liberalism, which assumes that who one is, what one's roots, language, culture and faith might be, count for naught when compared to some new, liberal good and the benefits it bestows. The Tory belief that the shape of any democracy and economy has always been and will always be a product of many factors, among which culture, language, civilization and history matter most, stands in opposition to the Durham approach. Russian "democracy," Canadian democracy and French democracy will always be different because Russian, Canadian and French peoples have different histories, different host and founding cultures, and different linguistic and cultural traditions. That the liberal Lord Durham got that so wrong speaks both then and now to the failure of liberalism to accommodate or reflect Canadian demographic, historic and linguistic realities. Interestingly, Canadian liberalism under Sir Wilfrid Laurier in the early 1900s became remarkably more accommodationist and reflective of the fact that "universal liberalism" unimproved by Canadian particularity would not work in Canada's politics. This was one of Laurier's most salient contributions to his party and country, and very much at odds with the Durham approach.

Lord Durham's approach in 1839 was anathema to who Canadians were. While some of his institutional recommendations were of value—such as his recommendation for a modified form of responsible government for the colony—many of his proposals subverted the Canadian idea. He shrank the gap between "high-minded" and "condescending." Fortunately, prominent Tories of his own and subsequent generations were not taken in.

Conservatism of the kind expressed in the same century by men such as Lord Elgin and Joseph Howe, and later by Sir John A. Macdonald, was never about crushing identities to achieve a universalist purpose. That was how, over time, the Americans chose to govern. And embracing that universalism led to the greatest American loss of life in any war: their own Civil War in the 1860s.

Lord Elgin, who was Governor General between 1847 and 1854 (and married to Durham's daughter), and who stoutly defended the Act of Union recommended by Durham that had united Upper and Lower Canada into one colony, defended French Canadian particularity, thus consolidating a tradition that began with the Québec Act in 1774 and would shape the framework of Confederation itself, and the Tory role within it. Moreover, the liberalism of Lord Durham created real forces of insecurity that would live on to challenge and sporadically threaten the survival of a distinct French Canadian nationality within Canada's multinational, "one country" future. In battles over everything from the structure of Confederation, the nature of divisions of power, the role of Ottawa versus that of the provinces, the patriation of the Constitution and even, in our time, the Meech Lake Accord, the Charlottetown Accord, the balance with Québec and the primacy of the Charter of Rights and Freedoms versus the right of Parliament and particular collective rights of Québécers, Liberals and Tories still differ along the lines of the Durham-Elgin divide.

It is important to contrast the Durham approach to the approach taken later, in the 1847–54 period that was so vital to the entrenchment of popular (elected) government and the balancing of critical French-English tensions.

James Bruce, the eighth Earl of Elgin, was born a year before the War of 1812 began. Elgin, very much of Tory birth and provenance—Eton, Christ Church, a master's from Oxford in 1835, elected on the Tory side for Southampton in 1841—subsequently accepted the hereditary peerage upon the death of his father and later his brother, the seventh Earl of Elgin, and set aside elected politics. He was appointed First Governor of Jamaica in 1842 and later took over the position of Governor General some years after the Durham-inspired Act of Union of Canada in 1840 (creating one Canadian province from Upper and Lower Canada). Elgin was a very correct and proper Tory who actually united reformers like Robert Baldwin and Louis-Hippolyte LaFontaine, who were anything but Tories, to jointly form a government. He recognized that winning a popular election was actually more than a passing matter of interest to the governor. It was, in fact, the fundamental determinant of whom the Crown, through the governor, should call upon to form a government.

On May 27, 1847, Elgin wrote Colonial Secretary Guy in London to update him on the progress being made in Canadian responsible government; in that letter to the Colonial Office he reported:

> My course in these circumstances is I think clear and plain— it may be somewhat difficult to follow occasionally, but I feel no doubt as to the direction in which it lies. I give to my Ministers all constitutional support, frankly and without reserve, and the benefit of the best advice, such as it is, that I can afford them in their difficulties ...
>
> That Ministers and opposition should occasionally change places is of the very essence of our constitutional support, and it is probably the most conservative element which it contains ... By subjecting all sections of politicians in their turn to official responsibilities it obliges heated partisans to place some restraint on passion and to confine within the bounds of decency the patriotic zeal with which, when out of place, they are wont to be animated.

That sense of democratic noblesse oblige, of the importance of balance, of support for French Canadians who had lost property due to rebellion damages and of respect for the French fact as an integral part of the emergent soul and identity of Canada migrated to a new generation of young politicians. One that included a young legislator from Kingston, John A. Macdonald.

He reduced the role of Governor General from "decider and arbiter" to one of certifier of the decisions, laws and directions chosen by the elected governments (here the "Governor in Council" notion) that had the popular support of the elected members of the assembly. When pro-British anti-rebel (and sometimes Tory) forces looked to Elgin *not* to sign an 1849 bill providing reparations for those in Lower Canada who had been part of the Rebellion of 1837 (the Rebellion Losses Bill), Elgin went against the Anglo opponents of the Bill and signed the act, which had been passed by the elected reform assembly, into law. The Elgin Riots, clashes on the streets of Montréal and Ottawa, did not deter him. He was a Tory, deeply and clearly to the manor born, but he defended the early stages of the government's development. If LaFontaine, Baldwin and their fellow reformers' agitations are rightfully celebrated on the path of early Canadian democracy and Canadian responsible government, then Elgin must be celebrated as the key nursemaid of Canadian responsible government. Elgin protected the infant of responsible government from the rioters and reactionary forces so that it could take its first steps and stride out under the protection of the Crown into an uncertain but promising world.

Elgin's reflection on the attitudes of French Canadians to possible U.S. annexation and his support of their democratic rights angered Anglo-Montrealers, who issued a manifesto in response to the reparations act Elgin had signed. In essence, he chose both democracy and the respect for French Canada's prerogatives and rights as the way ahead. His decision to sign the reparations act was the solid and determined choice of a Crown role. It was constitutional and symbolic as opposed to deliberative.

Prior to Elgin, the trend was constructive, if desperately incremental. Governors General between Durham and Elgin made some positive contributions. Sydenham had facilitated the union of the two colonies into one province with a capital at Kingston. And, thankfully, he had been weak and ineffectual in relation to any policy of anglicizing of the French-speaking population. Bagot had allowed Baldwin and LaFontaine to form a joint government, while not formally accepting responsible (as in accountable to any elected legislature) government. The Earl of Cathcart, who immediately preceded Elgin, had supported amnesty for the rebels and opposed forced anglicization. So, the trend was constructive, if desperately incremental. But in the run-up to Confederation it was Elgin, in the end, who put both a democratically accountable government and continued respect for French Canadian particularity into the core colonial DNA.

There were other Tory personalities who were involved in balancing and moderating the road to responsible government, but none as enduringly and intuitively Tory as the eighth Earl of Elgin and Canada's Governor General. He was, in fact, a Tory key to managing the rash pressures unleashed by the liberal universalism, however well-intentioned, of the earlier governor, Lord Durham.

The debates between reformers, who preferred more democratic legislation, and those Tories who were more cautious, are overblown relative to Whig-Tory differences in Canada. In reality, both sides moved towards a middle they could accommodate and engage. The so-called revolt in 1837 consisted of only a few riots and the odd whiff of grapeshot, but many historians have belaboured the truth in an effort to ensure we had something that looked and smelled like our own armed rebellion, when actually we had nothing very serious of the kind.

Such exaggeration is not unlike that associated with a group of young Communists and idealists who formed a brigade of volunteers for the Spanish Civil War in the 1930s and called it the Mackenzie-Papineau Battalion. That they chose this name does not, by retroactive presumption, make either Mackenzie or Papineau desperate, armed insurgents. But the differences over time between Lord Durham, a British un-Canadianized Liberal, and Lord Elgin, a British but Canadianized Tory, over how best to move Canada ahead speaks far more to the heart of the conservatism Canada's history and geography engendered.

To be fair to Durham on another front, he was dispatched with huge deliberative authority by the British Parliament and a young Queen Victoria. The British government was concerned that the rebellion, however meek and diminished, had put civil administration and order in the colonies at risk. The commander of the local British forces had asked for reinforcements. Durham was afforded dictatorial powers and was expected to decide quickly on reforms that would pacify and solve local grievances while also keeping the colonies loyal.

The Durham-Elgin spectrum reflects a range of both philosophical and actual choices. At one end, the universalist Durham option speaks to ideas of broad liberal reach shaping our society; at the other, the Elgin option speaks to Canadian demographic, geographic and historic realities on the ground that define who we are. But, essentially, all ideologies of the left or right need to be designed to serve a Canadian reality and context. Lord Elgin was true to the empire of the St. Lawrence upon which Canada was built; Lord Durham was not. Lord Elgin's singular defence of fairness for French Canada, specifically French Québec, was part of the political atmosphere in which John A. Macdonald began his career and later became shepherd of Confederation itself.

Donald Creighton's masterful 1952 work on Macdonald's early years (*John A. Macdonald: The Young Politician*) has a colourful citation from Macdonald's letter of January 21, 1856 (two years after Elgin's term of office), to Brown Chamberlain of the Montreal *Gazette*. In it, he castigates the Québec English for wanting to dominate and control, beyond their numbers and in a way that could do nothing but fuel a fury among francophone Québécois in Lower Canada:

> You can't and won't admit the principle that the majority must govern... lumping your judges of the Queen's Bench, Supreme and Circuit Courts, you have full one half British. More than half of the Revenue officers, indeed of all offices of emolument, are held by men not of French origin...
>
> No man in his senses can suppose that this country can, for a century to come, be governed by a totally unfrenchified government... If a Lower Canadian British desire is to conquer, he must stoop to conquer. He must make friends with

the French . . . he must respect their nationality. Treat them as a nation and they will act as a free people generally do— generously. Call them a faction and they become factions.

This was about more than respect for a separate language, culture and civilization. It was about setting a framework of respect for a people and a constituent foundation of the makeup of Canada itself. That many in the Anglo-business establishment, including local Tory swells, preferred assimilation and the idea of a single uncomplicated national identity, which would necessarily involve domination of the francophone majority in Lower Canada by an anglophone minority, is not surprising. It was a bias that would lead many to prefer annexationist U.S. options to a unique Canada. Fortunately, young leaders like Macdonald would have none of this. But this not uncommon, insipid condescension, which did not disappear from Québec, would serve to fuel the more negative aspects of strident Québec nationalism for many decades to come.

No understanding of Canadian history, from Confederation to conscription, from Papineau to René Lévesque, is complete without understanding this core Anglo bias. That key men, such as Elgin, Cartier and Macdonald, set this condescension aside is essentially why we have both a Conservative Party and a Canada in which founding partners have constitutional protection.

Translated into modern realities, this ideology very much explains the roots and origins of the Toryism that saw non-Québec-based Tories—including Macdonald, Stanfield, Robarts, Davis, Hatfield, Roblin and Lougheed—all seek to reach out to francophone Québec and build common ground. It explains why Stephen Harper, as prime minister, reached out to embrace Québécois and Québécoise as constituting a "nation" in a united Canada. It explains Robert L. Stanfield's cooperation with Premier Daniel Johnson and the emergence of a *deux nations* framework sponsored by Marcel Faribault at the August 1967 Montmorency PC Policy Conference near Québec City. (The actual idea was discussed at a workshop co-chaired by a young opposition leader from Alberta by the name of Peter Lougheed and a young education minister from Ontario by the name of William Davis!) In proposing this idea, they were being true to Elgin's legacy and to Sir John A.'s core sense of what Canada was and how it could be maintained. And in Pierre Trudeau's opposition to the idea, aided by a then out-of-office and terminally disgruntled Diefenbaker, Trudeau became very much Lord Durham's heir and acolyte espousing an intolerance to French Canadian particularity and the very Québec nationalism vital to a federal balance in ways that would have made Durham proud. Much of Trudeau's intolerance was portrayed in English Canada as the strength to "handle Québec" and keep nationalists in their place; as a result, Trudeau benefitted from the least attractive tendencies displayed by a certain part of the non-Québec population in 1968. Not even his stout and determined defence of official bilingualism, for which history owes him great credit, dilutes his impact on increasing polarization and enmity in Québec. It is as if Elgin's and Macdonald's worst fears almost came to pass under Trudeau's leadership over a century later, as they did when Chrétien's continued insouciance in the face of legitimate Québec particularity almost pushed the Séparatistes to victory in the 1995 referendum.

Universal liberalism brings with it, in its support of doctrines of unalienable rights and progressive social legislation, much substantive good. But when it is imposed in a way that threatens to erase established historical standing for a founding people with historic linguistic and cultural rights, the most illiberal of outcomes can emerge. The Tories in Canada understood this because Québec and Canada had moulded a Canadian conservative philosophy that was unique and reflective of who and what we were and how our geography and history had shaped us. It is not clear that federal Liberals (Lester Pearson notwithstanding) understand this even yet. Every time a Liberal threatens to dilute provincial jurisdiction, for whatever peacetime reason, Durham is alive and well! It is often purist scholars, such as Trudeau, who abhor the land of compromise because they feel it dilutes a compelling intellectual idea, who bring the country to its most perilous hours—however unwittingly. And on that Durham-Elgin divide, which is essentially about who we are as Canadians, much of the tension that characterizes the political contests of our own time is still defined.

The period of the two Governors General and those who served between them was one of huge consolidation and progress. Elgin, again presaging future Tory choices, negotiated the very best of trade reciprocities with the U.S. by gaining British authority to negotiate directly with the Americans and by persuading recalcitrant U.S. senators and congressmen. His deal was so good that, by comparison, those subsequently proposed by Laurier and others failed to match up and were consequently opposed by Tories. By 1854, the Canadian democratic context had been solidified. Canada's larger station as a binational country with democratic legislatures and responsible administrations was in place.

But the hard truth was that the "radical" liberalism of Durham almost brought the entire Canadian enterprise to an early end. The Tory sensibility and balance of Elgin sustained the Canadian enterprise and, through Tory principles of respect for identity, earned citizenship, linguistic protection and orderly progress, it shepherded Canada through its pre-Confederation responsible government period.

One cannot in any way understand the politics of John A. Macdonald—his masterful construction of coalitions that led to Confederation and beyond—without understanding his core respect for French Canada's legitimate aspirations and how this respect played on the vision that drove his remarkable capacity to build and shape.

One can track the road from the Rebellions of 1837 to the confederal agreement three decades later. It was more granular than any massive triumph or political sweep. It was a progress of minute rebalances, modest transitions and coherent accommodations that set aside small differences to achieve a compelling goal.

The Tory belief system—nurtured, for better or worse, by the Ancien Régime's roots in the seigneurial system, the role of the Church, the Québec Act, the arrival of the Loyalists and the excesses of the American and French revolutions—was, while not in any way perfect, unique to the Atlantic colonies and to Upper and Lower Canada. It had an institutional coherence that was intrinsically of and about Canada. It reflected our history, geography and demography, and was an indication of what had been built and shaped based on the traditions inherited two centuries earlier from the founding empires.

Tories believe in structure, obligation, history, proven stability and sustainability as pillars that form the institutions that matter. And Tories believe that, ideally, society, life and who we are as a people and a nation are sustained and nourished by these institutions.

In the context of the many seemingly token rebalances that would underline the Québec Resolutions (1864), the Charlottetown Conference agreement (1864), and the British North America Act proclamation in London (1867), Tory sensitivity to the interests of both French and English, both Upper and Lower Canada, both sides of the rebellions in both parts of Canada, east and west, actually established the quality of compromise that drove the nation-founding enterprise. Clear Grits, such as George Brown, had to overcome excessive anti-French, anti-papist bigotry in order to make Confederation possible. George-Étienne Cartier, who so ably led *les bleus* in eastern Canada (who were also supporters of an ultramontane clergy) allied to a Québec, nationalist-driven and Catholic-inspired view of society, brought a critical part of the Tory balance into national reality. Sir John A., who had stood in uniform with the Crown against the rebels of 1837, abhorred the radical, often pro-American reformist politicians who were gathered around the Clear Grit label of George Brown and others. Later, showing his conciliatory bent, Macdonald in fact defended rebel clients in court. Macdonald very much reflected the Elgin tendency to seek conciliation after battles had passed and the turbulence had subsided. In this way, bridges were not only built between disaffected parts of society, but between a past of divisions and a today of working together.

In Upper Canada, many Tory roots grew from the post-1814 Family Compact of royalist Anglican Church and business leaders who were cronies of the government and dismissive of the too-democratic proposition of any "elected" legislature. The *bleu* roots in Lower Canada, with a tradition of unelected governors, had similar provenance in the Château Clique group which was shaped by the predominant role of the Catholic Church, a church that was of the ultramontane variety. It saw the temporal and constitutional debate of secular society as beneath it and was subservient to the authority of the Pope and the Catholic hierarchy in Rome and beyond. Conservatism in Québec was not disconnected from the "natural constitution" view of early seventeenth and eighteenth century Tories who saw a natural order and divine right of kings as superseding any Whig fascination with what "reason" might convey. And when the Anglo establishment in Montréal, who were deeply offended by Elgin's championing of French Canadian rights, embraced the "Annexation Manifesto" in 1849, which advocated a union with the United States, it provided the young and emerging John A. Macdonald with more evidence of where anti–French Canadian bias unalterably leads and formed the basis of his next step in shaping Canada's identity and political evolution. Never mind that some of the great families—the Redpaths, the Molsons, the McGills—had led the pro-U.S. charge. John A. Macdonald would not sign that annexation abomination. His response was to establish a British American

League in 1850, which met with representatives from Upper and Lower Canada in Kingston; there they agreed on a partnership with the British mother country, a national commercial policy to promote trade and commerce between the loyal colonies, and a confederation of those colonies, and thus an end to the annexation silliness. John Macdonald did to the Annexationists what he did later to the radically anti-French and anti-Catholic George Brown and the *Globe* newspaper, which Brown ran. He withstood the blandishments of the easy hit against the papists and the French, supporting settlement on seigneurial lands and clergy reserves with equanimity and fairness.

Even the *Globe* newspaper itself had to admit on November 10, 1900, that "to all Conservatives who cherish the memory of Sir John A. Macdonald, we bring the reminder that no leader ever opposed so sternly the attempt to divide this community on racial or religious lines." Better late than never.

Sir Joseph Pope, one of Macdonald's biographers and a former private secretary to Sir John, summed it up this way in *The Day of Sir John Macdonald*, published in 1915: ". . . we find that at every step of his career, when the opportunity presented itself for showing sympathy with the French Canadians in their struggle for the legitimacy of their just rights, he invariably espoused their cause, not then a popular one." Brian Mulroney did the very same in 1984 in Manitoba in defence of minority French language rights—and while still Leader of the Opposition.

This indefatigable support for French Canada meant that John A., as Attorney General in the MacNab government of the early 1850s, could be a vital link to Québec. And when luminaries like Augustin-Norbert Morin, who had been MacNab's lieutenant from Québec in the formation of a joint government of reformed Liberals and Upper Canadian Conservatives retired to the bench, the newly elected George-Étienne Cartier, himself a former LaFontaine supporter in 1848, was now in a position to become Macdonald's vital Québec partner in the government of 1854.

That Macdonald-Cartier partnership, both a result of and symbol of the duality of our history to date, would in fact become the political cornerstone of a *bleu*-Tory alliance that would create Canada and form the basis of a multi-party coalition. This partnership would ultimately include Darcy McGee's Reform Party and would create temporary parking space for some Clear Grits. Such an integrated and cooperative Conservative alliance cemented the reality of French Canada's shared primacy at the essence of Tory roots and identity. The French fact and its accommodation are at the core of the Canadian conservative mission and soul. Canada is one country, but a multinational one, and we forget the exigencies of that reality at our own peril, as Conservatives and as Canadians.

This identity would not always work in the Conservative Party's favour. It is hard to assess Mr. Trudeau's electoral victories of 1968–79 or 1980–84 without noting the successful appeal of his radical disregard for legitimate French Canadian nationalism and his preference for pan-national bilingual institutions. His championing of a Charter of Rights and Freedoms, which (aside from provisions from the "notwithstanding clause," allowing laws to be passed without regard to the Charter for five years at a time) reduces the "collective rights" range of parliamentary freedom for Québec's National Assembly, was profoundly popular—and remains so, even in provinces like Québec and Alberta. The difficult battles over conscription in 1914–18 and 1939–45 found Tories, who were defending the military capacity essential for a meaningful war effort, very much on the wrong side of the "respect for French Canada issue," as was Macdonald himself in the treatment of the Riel Rebellion and Riel himself in 1885. And the victory of Sir Wilfrid Laurier in 1896 spoke eloquently to how Conservatives had mismanaged the Manitoba Schools issue, which was essentially about French minority education rights.

So, lack of competence on the Québec/French dynamic always means that a price has to be paid by both of our major parties. For Conservatives, the most damaging traps are usually set when conflicting senses of identity and fairness (such as on matters relating to conscription) do battle with each other across Canada's political and linguistic landscapes. For Liberals, the most damaging traps are set when undue centralization or condescending federalism is insensitive to legitimate local, linguistic or geopolitical aspiration. Both parties have often gotten the balance wrong, and Canada has always paid a price.

I recall running for office in the 1972 federal election as a twenty-one-year-old Progressive Conservative candidate in the forever-Liberal stronghold of Ottawa Centre. I was proud as punch at having won the nomination over the party headquarters' establishment corporate lawyer choice and prouder still of being Robert Stanfield's duly nominated candidate in the riding of civil servants, retirees, professors and small business people. I was particularly proud that Mr. Stanfield had supported the Official Languages Act, brought in by the Trudeau Liberals as a way of establishing language rights for both francophone minorities across Canada and the anglophone minority in Québec. As a graduate of the bilingual University of Ottawa, I felt good about the Macdonald-Cartier aspect of Bob Stanfield who, in his mid-fifties, had begun with immense determination to learn French. I recall as well how many doors were slammed in my face when I replied "Yes" to the question of whether I supported the Official Languages Act, which was actively opposed by other regional Tory candidates. Some were angry that I was supporting "something new." But what I was supporting was a core principle of Canadian duality that could be traced right back to the beginning of Canada. I didn't feel it should be allowed to perish.

Roots and history do not predict competence or cohesion. Competence and cohesion require discipline and focus and a considered and careful view of the central elements of the country's makeup and soul. Conservatives and conservatives have no way out when they get the French Canada component wrong. The best parts of our electoral history, including of course Mr. Mulroney's remarkable victories in 1984 and 1988, speak to how well the Conservative Party can thrive and be of national service—on Free Trade, on fighting apartheid, on the GST and on food aid to Ethiopia—when it gets it right. And sadly and clearly, throughout our history, when the balance is wrong, the results can be devastating. That too is a fundamental lesson of Tory roots and history that ought never to be ignored.

4

MACDONALD AND TORY "NATION AND ENTERPRISE"

*There can be no doubt that one of the purposes in creating
such agencies as the Canadian National Railways and the Canadian
Broadcasting Corporation was to keep them from detailed
political control and therefore from political interference.*
W.D.K. KERNAGHAN in *Bureaucracy in Canadian Government*

*The old order is gone ... If you believe things should be left as they are,
you and I hold contrary and irreconcilable views. I am for reform.
And in my mind, reform means government intervention. It means
government control and regulation. It means the end of laissez-faire.*
PRIME MINISTER R.B. BENNETT in a 1935 radio address

It is here, at the intersection of market freedom and public interest, that Canadian conservatism breaks ranks most directly
with the American free enterprise "uber alles" variety of conservatism. And the break goes far back beyond R.B. Bennett and
the creation of Crown corporations such as the CBC and the Canadian Wheat Board. The right balance here is the very essence of
a distinctly Canadian approach to communitarian conservatism
and national enterprise. It is a clear Canadian rebalancing of the
traditional relationship between free enterprise and private capital on one side versus public interest and social responsibility on

the other. It is about common interest conservatism as opposed to special interest conservatism, free enterprise for the poor and state-financed socialism for the rich. This kind of balancing is something I have always called the "nation and enterprise" stream in Canadian conservatism.

The "nation and enterprise" tradition is a continuous theme that runs from the Ancien Régime of New France to the subsequent granting of a royal charter by King Charles II to the Hudson's Bay Company in 1670, helping it to become the largest owner of land in the then known world. There was also the granting of licences by the French king in the early 1600s for everything from beer to construction, and the continuation of similar Crown practices throughout the British regime after 1758. These trends and events all spoke to the classic pioneer mix of public and private, of nation and enterprise.

This core belief in the required balance between public and private—and the required role of instruments of the larger community in maintaining that balance, through regulatory and other practices—is part of who Canadian Tories are.

Canadian Tory belief, nurtured very much from the Ancien Régime roots of the seigneurial system, the role of the Church, the Québec Act, the Act of Union, the arrival of the Loyalists and the excesses of the American and French revolutions was, while not in any way perfect, what took shape in Upper and Lower Canada. It had an institutional coherence that was intrinsically of and about the Canadian historical experience and geographic perspective. Tories believe in structure, obligation, and proven stability and sustainability as pillars that form trusted institutions. They also believe that who we are as a people, our very identity, is sustained and nourished by these institutions.

As a nation-shaping prime minister, John A. Macdonald saw the state as a guarantor of the railroad construction that would secure the West and British Columbia before the Americans got there to challenge confederal coast-to-coast prospects.

In a speech given in St. Thomas, Ontario, in 1860, Sir John A. Macdonald stated: "It is well known, Sir, that while I have always been a member of what is called the Conservative Party, I could never have been called a Tory, although there is no man who more respects what is called old-fogey Toryism than I do, so long as it is based on principle." That Sir John A.'s Tory conservatism had to combine with the more anti-establishment Clear Grit populism rooted in Canada West in order for Confederation to be made possible is not in dispute. What is important is to understand the many balances and trade-offs made by Macdonald, the ultimate symbol of the contemporary and the "progressive" conservatism of his era, and the role that Canadian conservative values would play in his decision-making.

Above all, the central unit by which and with which Sir John A. Macdonald built the new Canada was his progressive version of the Conservative Party as an evolving coalition translating the history of Canadian conservatism into a contemporary reality. It was a conservatism that did not reject all change but sought those changes that were purpose-driven in support of the national idea—the idea of Canada itself.

Ideologues often resent the practical accommodations that political parties have to make: accommodations that appear to dilute, if not pollute, the purity of ideological principle. John Macdonald rejoiced in those same practical accommodations, on everything from the new resolutions of Confederation to the reality of the day-to-day administration of the new Dominion's affairs. Ideology that hides from practical reality is not only in denial but is disconnected from the mainstream of society. It is when a party's principles meet and mesh in some constructive way with the reality on the street that the test of a party's ideals is met. Sir John A. became a master of this balancing act. And that is why for decades, from the mid-1840s to 1891, he dominated the politics and policies of the Dominion's affairs.

There was also the compelling value of his flamboyant and vulnerable style. A style that today's politically correct culture rejects, much to our collective loss.

One of sobriety's common meanings is to take a balanced, level-headed, down-to-earth approach to life. It implies not only the lack of impairment from drink, which is a good thing, but also the lack of impairment from passion, enthusiasm or emotion in the public decisions we make. Ours is a world defined, of necessity, by risk analysis, public and private auditors, management board guidelines and by journalists and politicians who are enjoined not to fraternize and never, ever have a drink or, God protect us, a friendship with each other. We are told that this careful approach is necessary because of ethics, the seriousness of the challenges we face and the need to respect both political correctness and the rational analysis of all things. Such behaviour, of course, is meant to produce policies that ensure prosperity, defer the economic cycle, provide for equality of everything and everybody, and put off death indefinitely. So, the question posed by all of this sobriety and rationality is clear. What has it done for our direction and purpose as Canadians? Is our sense of perspective really any greater than that of our predecessors?

I doubt very much if John Macdonald would view our prospects as Canadians with any great sense of either relish or fear. Certainly, if you visit Kingston and see the many places John A. Macdonald lived, drank, did business, slept and survived, stability does not appear to have trumped passion in his life. Based on what he confronted and the world in which he lived, his most overwhelming response to our present Canadian context would probably be boredom.

Even in response to the terror of September 11, 2001, Sir John A. would have reflected on the larger slaughter at Gettysburg, the clearly dominant story of mass violence in North America, and been understandably controlled, if still angry and troubled, by what happened in New York.

Before we dismiss John Macdonald's passion and intermittent sobriety as relics of an easier and less complex time, we would do well to reflect on the world events that occurred while he dominated our colonial, confederal and national politics. Between 1860 and 1891, the world in which Sir John A. and his interlocutors built the confederation of Canada experienced only the following events:

· The election of Abraham Lincoln as U.S. president
· The Second Maori War
· Garibaldi's Red Shirts taking Palermo and Naples
· The Warsaw Massacre of anti-Russian demonstrators
· The Emancipation Proclamation of 1863
· Civil war in Afghanistan
· The invasion of Holstein by Saxon and Hanoverian troops
· The assassination of Abraham Lincoln
· The end of the U.S. Civil War
· The destruction of the Italian fleet by Austrians at Lissa
· Russian occupation of Samarkand
· Disraeli becoming prime minister of the U.K. twice (and resigning in the first year of his first term)
· Spanish queen Isabella ii deposed by revolution and escaping to France
· The Franco-Prussian War
· The Suez Canal opening
· The British Parliament permitting labour unions under the Trade Union Act of 1871
· The Cuban Rebellion
· The Russo-Turkish War
· The Serbo-Turkish War
· Montenegro's declaration of war on Turkey
· The Transvaal Declaration of Independence

- The British occupation of Khyber Pass
- The massacre of a British legation in Kabul
- Chile going to war against Bolivia and Peru
- Chinese immigration banned in the U.S. for a decade
- The German annexation of Tanganyika and Zanzibar
- The failure of the Boulanger coup d'etat in Paris
- The German Social Democrats adopting a Marxist program at the Erfurt Congress
- The signing of the Franco-Russian Entente

I have enumerated these world events that occurred during Sir John A.'s time, any of which would have reduced the 9/11 tragedy in relative import, to help those people who are given to ahistorical and histrionic views of our present reality understand that Sir John A.'s times were as complex, as unpredictable and as full of challenge and jarring change as the times we live in. The absence of hand-held digital messaging devices, transmitting each and every second, did not make these events less tumultuous. Just as the presence of digital convenience does not make today's events more serious. Only our own narcissism and historical illiteracy could lead us to believe otherwise.

With all that was going on in his time, Sir John A. cajoled, organized, debated, expounded, invested, borrowed, spent, planned, cobbled, arranged, annexed, assured, consoled and hypothecated his way, our way, to a Dominion from sea to sea. In English Canada this was seen as the building of a new entity from various parts. In Québec, it was seen as the liberation of French Canada from the more populous, united Province of Canada, so that Québec could have its own status within Confederation. Since the Act of Union of 1841, which brought Upper and Lower Canada together in one Canadian province, Québécers had felt overwhelmed by the larger, Upper Canadian, English-speaking population and their rapid population and economic growth. The fear that Québécois in Lower Canada would be swamped was a pervasive theme of the politics of the time—and, in many ways, remains so today. The creation of the separate province of Québec in 1867, with the same constitutional Section 91 rights and powers as the other three founding provinces, was a response to this anxiety and became one of the core partnership provisions. It made Confederation possible. English-language newspapers proclaimed a "new dominion" on July 1, 1867. Newspapers in Québec, however, proclaimed Québec's liberation from the confining Province of Canada.

If Canada was born in the binding glue of ambiguity, this was probably because we could not have been conceived in any other way. Today, those among us who want all provinces to be the same are also those who profoundly misunderstand how we came to be and the underpinnings of our multinational country. Those who balk at Canada's capacity to accommodate the nationhood of Québec within a Canadian confederal union—some of the more extreme sovereignists and some of the more extreme centralists—deny the passion and practicality of Sir John A.'s vision. His vision was multifaceted, but sustained always by a profound belief in Canada as a special undertaking, a Dominion with unparalleled opportunity, reach and breadth. When he concluded that America would never embrace a true and open reciprocity and would always offer less than Lord Elgin had negotiated on our behalf a decade or so earlier, he shaped a national policy to maximize Canada's east-west market and to advance our economic, agricultural and industrial growth. When it became clear that, without a compelling national enterprise, what our Québécois friends would call "un projet de societé," the Union would be in peril from American expansionism, the railway happened. Not without pain, some corruption and much debate... but it happened.

We would do well to ask ourselves today, as Sir John A.'s great achievement approaches the adolescent age of 144, what is it that we are truly passionate about? What is the "projet de societé" that drives our vision and sustains our determination to keep building a unique Canadian reality on the northern half of this continent? If it is not enough to define that purpose as simply to be something other than Americans, then it is also essential to define a mission, both at home and abroad, that is both the source and object of our national passion. At some level, there is a Canadian sensibility about diversity, freedom, identity, quality of life and society that reflects who we are and the history from which we have come. Asking how every generation can preserve, advance and enhance that unique Canadian reality is a question that every Throne Speech and budget, every piece of legislation and new initiative should engage.

The thing about passion is that it is not about how others see us but about how we see ourselves. That is what Sir John A.'s Dominion, and the passion that drove it, were truly about. At that time, in those circumstances, we wanted a national Dominion to replace our sense of colonial dysfunction and to withstand American Manifest Destiny pressures. In view of the trends in Europe and the war of succession in the United States, Sir John A. was creating his own trend, shaped by the reality of Canada, rather than by forces originating from abroad. And while that reality may not have been without flaws and tensions, it was our reality, as indigenous to Canada as our First Nations people and as ubiquitous as changes in the weather.

Sir John's passion was to overcome those divisions, not by crushing them, not by making them illegal or *ultra vires,* but by accommodating the different threads in a new fabric, one that was strengthened by diversity. Above all, he wanted to ensure that the political, military and economic might of British North America was not diminished, which meant including a Québec that was protected initially by the Québec Act and then, later, by the provincial jurisdictions enshrined in the Constitution Act of 1867.

In the end, today's vision and passion will define our national purpose and will distinguish Canada among nations. The absence of that vision and passion, that compelling Canadian purpose, renders all decisions we face little more than balance sheet transactions, some "on balance" and some "off." Let me put it another way: if "Canada" is the answer, what is the question?

Drifting into a union with the United States only becomes inevitable if we offer ourselves no better alternative. If we set no goals, if we embrace no higher purpose, if Canada is simply about muddling through, then joining the United States has always been and will always be the more efficient answer. As Janice Stein articulated so clearly in her 2001 Massey Lecture entitled *The Cult of Efficiency,* there is more to life than efficiency, and in the area of public good, efficiency is, at best, a truly ambivalent if not contradictory value.

Canada did not come about through an uncompromising focus on small initiatives, a sort of housekeeping *über alles* governance mindset. Conservative successes have, since Macdonald's days, been about reaching out to more broadly define tomorrow based on compelling values and enduring goals. There would have never been a Canada had housekeeping and the myopia of tiny steps been the dominant Tory frame. Incrementalism is a methodology, not a goal. Compromise is a tactic and means of inclusion, not a sign of weakness. Being excessively uncompromising and ideological limits a government's purpose and dilutes its reason for existing. Being ambitious for one's economy, for one's people and national prospects, and being prepared to compromise in order to achieve that ambition was the Macdonald formula for both party and country. It is still the only inclusive and efficient way forward today.

And our war efforts, while not always efficient, have been about defending Canadian values; in fact, I believe Sir John A. Macdonald would approve of even the Liberal government's deployment decision concerning Afghanistan, and that he would heartily wish the troops well and want them to stay until the job is done.

Sir John A.'s passion strengthens our own because his was the passion of a builder as comfortable with compromise as with any other tool in his kit. He understood its creative potential as an instrument for nation building and strengthening the Dominion. Compromise is a tool that we have discarded over the last decade, both in terms of arbitrary federal and provincial actions and in terms of the courts—where, in the past, political compromise and debate were seen to be more effective and responsive.

This lack of creativity or lack of the will to compromise is sometimes blamed on incumbent governments. Most incumbent governments seek to manage the public agenda in support of the ultimate public benefit, namely their own re-election—which, to be fair, is essential to the competitive structure of our parliamentary democracy. In a perfect world, this effort is not driven only by partisan zeal, but from a sense that the overall balance and mix of what they want for Canada's future is a far better and more substantive choice than the world view and domestic priorities offered by the opposing political parties. Opposing political parties often get caught in the "oppose for the sake of opposing" cycle, avoiding substantive policy commitments that give voters a real choice. Both sides use a lot of tactics, but from the voter's perspective the lack of an overarching view of well-articulated national priorities reduces the struggle to one between competing partisan interests, and not competing views of how society might best be served. If they did not honestly believe that their own re-election was ultimately in the public interest, political parties would have no reason to exist. That incumbent governments are not forced by creative, competent and truly competitive opposition parties to aim higher is not their fault; it is the fault of the opposition. And if opposition parties continue to avoid expressing their passion through wide-reaching policy goals, through well-conceived national visions, preferring narrow minuets aimed at self-preservation, it is still unfair to blame the government.

In Upper Canada particularly, Canadian conservatism was about ensuring the survival of a society that saw itself as very different from American society in terms of economic, social and political structures. Tories were anxious about the clear-cut, willy-nilly embrace of popular and wholly elected government that brought with it the excesses and extremes of American politics, replete with immigration riots, crime and corrupt political machines. As the distinguished Canadian historian S.F. Wise so aptly put it in *Upper Canada and the Conservative Tradition*, "... the cities of the United States, swollen by non-British immigration, torn by crime and violence and governed by corrupt machines kept in power by demagogic appeals to mass envy and greed," did not arise in Canada.

Professor Wise reflects with immense insight on the confluence of Tory economic policy and nation-building institutionalism. This is a stream not found in any other conservatism to the same extent. Whether it was the Rideau Canal built by Colonel By to protect Ottawa or the fortifications at Kingston built after the War of 1812, or the proposed public ownership of the Welland Canal or the public financing of a coast-to-coast railway, Tories saw "nation and enterprise" as linked to the survival and identity of Canada itself. This approach has been a hallmark of Tory governments from the 1850s to the present. It is alive today and can be seen in Bill Davis's joint funding of the early oil sands project initiated under Premier Peter Lougheed in the 1970s; Mike Harris's creation of the Ontario Family Health Network in 2001; and even Stephen Harper's refusal to allow Alliant Techsystems Inc., a U.S. company, to buy Macdonald, Dettwiler and Associates Ltd. in 2008. It is a strain that cuts a wide swath of difference between American neo-conservatives, who embrace a "marketplace, *über alles*" approach, and Canadian Conservatives, who never have.

From the seigneurial roots of Canada, from the public borrowings for core infrastructure, from the role of the governors in enterprise and exploration—under both the French and the English—this mix of public and private has been essential to the growth of Canada and to its ongoing economic development.

Some of this spirit came with the Tory-Loyalist settlers who were refugees from the republic to the south in the late eighteenth century; many of them had commercial, legal, small business, farming and local government experience. This experience was of immense value within government and within business.

The Family Compact, however closed and self-interested, with its foreign-appointed governor, ran Upper Canada. Loyal to the Crown and to the institutions of the Empire, it was connected, through the granting of licences, favours, grace and contracts, to the economy on the street. It lacked and even abhorred the radical, often pro-American reformers, politicians who were gathered around the Clear Grit label of George Brown and others. For better or for worse, many Anglo Tory roots, as I mentioned earlier, grew from the Family Compact. And the *bleu* roots in Québec had similar provenance in the Château Clique. In both groups, established interests had been clustered around the unelected governors and their councils.

John A. Macdonald's conservatism excluded none of these groups completely but put them into a pragmatic context that could embrace more than just the true believer or anti-change establishment, or the "to the manor born," self-reverential aristocracy. His was a more inclusive version of conservatism than that which dominated America after the revolution. In jailing or expelling the Loyalists, American Patriot conservatism had excluded the Tory sensibility, fostering in America the disconnected, exceptionalist self regard that has spread like a virus to American liberals over the centuries.

American conservatives had long championed the notion that working industry, private businesses, farms and individual enterprise would produce the goods, services and resources that formed American well-being. They also believed that government, constrained by a mix of countervailing federal authorities and states' rights, should be rendered sufficiently powerless to get in the way. The Canadian conservative view was that, despite the importance of all the great work of companies, farms, small businesses and large enterprises, there was a distinct public interest to be defined, not by the accidents of the free market exclusively, but by the public interest choices of ministers of the Crown responsible to parliaments elected by the people. In the Canadian view, public interest as expressed by government and the private interest as expressed by companies and investors could often, if not always, do better through cooperation. This is not a U.S. view, in peacetime. Instead, there is a very strong bias that, outside the exigencies of wartime politics and production, American companies have one sole purpose: to generate return for their shareholders, and create wealth which, by its creative force, serves the broader American interest. The public interest is the result of separate government and private sector actions. It is a passive result as opposed to an intended outcome. Recent events like Enron's collapse and the 2008 credit meltdowns that severely diluted American and global financial capacity have changed this perspective, but up until the last few years, the American approach was very different from Canada's. The substantive praise now given to the Canadian financial regulatory structure really reflects the development over decades of this "nation and enterprise" form of early conservatism.

In fact, the very design of government in the U.S.—conceived by the Whig establishment that led the revolution and expelled the Tories—reflected the desire to render government largely ineffective and incoherent: two houses of Congress that could countervail each other; a judiciary that could countervail all the rest; a separate executive branch headed by a popularly elected leader who could not act without financial resources approved by two legislatures; and a federal structure that, at the outset, could appoint senators to the upper house. The structure involved feuding power cliques and a dominant role for private enterprise and market interest.

It is, in some ways, deeply understandable. American political and state-based leaders did not want a government in Washington that could do to them what the British government had done to them. They had other choices, such as giving more power to the individual states as an offsetting force. But the choices they made—with the perfect conceit of the Whig bias that only rational design, and not faith in tradition, can create structures of immense value and worth—would lead to an inefficiency in government. Gordon Giffin, a former American ambassador to Canada and a sophisticated lawyer, political strategist and senior Democrat in the Clinton years and since, has often responded to any criticism of the intrinsic contradictions of America's structure of government with the admonition that "American democracy is about process and not results." He is, of course, spot on. On the other hand, the British parliamentary system as adapted in Canada is about a blend of results and process, which a mixed private and public enterprise economy like Canada's has always required. And this difference of opinion as to the role of the state, whether it be about National Policy tariffs or building the Canadian Pacific Railway, became a seminal divide in Canada between the Clear Grits and Macdonald's "progressive" Conservatives. America's larger economy and teeming population has always created more market solutions. Canada's huge geography and smaller, less concentrated population has always required more intervention and initiative from Crown and country—public enterprise of one form or another. Clear Grits aspired to an American reality; Tories saw reality as it was in Canada.

In *Canada's First Century, 1867–1967*, Donald Creighton summarizes the emergent differences between the Liberals and the Conservatives after the Tory victory of 1878. Railways, tariffs and Macdonald's protectionist National Policy were all on the table for that campaign. Creighton put it this way: "The Conservatives had espoused the National Policy of protection and a national strategy for all Canadian railways. The Liberals stood by the doctrines of international free trade and the sensible economies of continental transport. The Liberals believed that Canada was and should remain a low cost country, a cheap place to live in, where government should intervene as little as possible on economic matters and stick firmly to retrenchment..." To the Conservatives this seemed a tame, spiritless program for a young and vigorous people to adopt. In Creighton's view, the 1878 election saw the Tories win the debate once and for all.

And in that victory, Sir John A.'s "progressive" Conservatives also established that the legacy of historical conservatism they had inherited, from Champlain through to Lord Elgin, was very much its own brand. It was different from both the British and American forms. It was not about "private" versus "public" or "aristocrat" versus "commoner." It was about a conservatism of economic ambition and political inclusion. It was about the inspirational leadership of Sir John A., who always reached out to those from other parties and other factions to get the support he needed to sustain the government in which he and George-Étienne Cartier served.

Cajoling and discussing his vision of the country with the elected members in bars and restaurants was what he did best and he was an absolute dynamo at it. He understood the difference between the bureaucrat and the politician and he preferred to be a politician. If it took many drinks to get someone on side, it was a sacrifice he was prepared to make for the cause. I like to call this approach "glass by glass for a better tomorrow." If he had stood on ceremony about party names or labels, or let the Women's Christian Temperance Union get in the way, well, we might all be Americans today. What he understood viscerally was that the public good was more important than any party's narrow partisan interest. What he understood is that a party campaigning solely for its own survival and not for broad public policy purposes that are clear and understood is of little national importance.

Later, in 1891, when a Liberal administration, yielding to the reasoning of the Whig disposition on what did or did not matter in society, proposed "reciprocity" with the Americans, it was a deeply flawed idea. It was far less advantageous than what Elgin had negotiated. At this point in history Macdonald fought his last electoral battle. He won it handily, extolling the benefits of Canadian independence from the United States: an independence best expressed through fealty to the British Empire, to the British form of government and to the civilization of which the newly independent Canada was clearly a part. His famous battle cry "A British subject I was born, a British subject I will die" echoed his resistance of the great Montréal families who sought annexation with the U.S. in their anger over Lord Elgin's noblesse oblige in the rebellion reparation cycle. In reaching out to the Northwest, in facilitating the construction of the railway, in putting down the Riel revolt—despite the toxic politics on both sides of that challenge—Sir John A.'s statecraft embraced a mix of order, enterprise, conciliation, common purpose, strength of will and human decency. It is easy to say that he "forged a nation." It is perhaps more accurate to say that he let his conservatism be a bridge as opposed to a barrier among people of good will who had never before been invited to look beyond language or class, geographical or partisan divisions, and build something better. The history of Canadian conservatism deployed in this way had depth and a texture of compassion. Not till Sir John A. Macdonald of Kingston did an elected Conservative leader have the humanity, intensity, good humour and likeability to make much of the practical politics of inclusion. The debt he is owed by Canadian Conservatives and Canadians generally is simply indescribable. And throughout his tenure as leader, Macdonald used the twin calls of nation and enterprise as a framework for national expansion, economic growth, political consolidation and country building in general.

We can, as we go forward from that era, summarize the critical effect of his time and his "nation and enterprise" leadership. Under Sir John A. Canadian Conservatism became an instrument for national development and patriotism—local, national and imperial loyalties were all integral parts of its heart and soul, and the narrow, aristocratic landed gentry who opposed all change and who came from another time and place were who Macdonald sought to leave behind. Macdonald's Liberal-Conservatives were progressive and understood the appeal of reaching out to a broad section of men of good will in order to build working coalitions. "Nation and enterprise" meant that national policies had to respect, advance and protect economic and social interest at the same time. Perhaps Sir John's most famous campaign poster says it all: "the old flag, the old policy, the old leader," which stressed the identity of Canada as a Dominion within the Empire while rejecting reciprocity with the Americans and extolled Sir John's resolute identity as a Canadian. It featured Sir John being carried by a working farmer and factory worker and was captioned as a poster of "The Industrial League." This was not about the mansions of the lumber barons or railway moguls of Montréal, Ottawa or Toronto. This was about working men from the country and the city being seen to endorse an "everyman" conservative who put the nation first and its working class at the top of his political priority list. To this day, working class sections of less wealthy regions—rural eastern Ontario, "le Québec profond," the Maritimes and Saint-Henri in Montréal—have Conservative strongholds among them.

While the union of the colonies might have benefitted from more central powers (as Macdonald himself pointed out) consistent with a unitary state, the hardscrabble truth was and is that the union of the colonies would not have been possible without a strong division of powers between the roles of the colonies and that of Ottawa. This accommodation, something Liberals especially find hard to accept as fundamental and non-negotiable, reflects the respect for local linguistic and political traditions, which are essential to Canadian conservatism.

How would Sir John A. view today's Canada, and what might we learn from him in a non-partisan way? He would surely be puzzled by all the political correctness in our political system; he would be especially sad to know that most politicians, bureaucrats and media would rather drink mineral water than alcohol, and that some among the media would see having a drink with a politician as fraternizing with the enemy. It must also be said that he would see much of today's Canada and be quite proud. The survival of the union, the durability of Confederation itself and the continued existence of a northern country from sea to sea, and its diversity and economic capacity, would surely give Sir John A. a great sense of how all that drinking in Charlottetown and Québec City and all the hard work and relationship building in the 1860s were what built the connections that really mattered— those between people. Those relationships and connections built a country that has lasted and prospered.

While he was the most Toryest of Tories—someone who had stood up to the armed rabble at Montgomery's Tavern as a member of the loyal militia—John Macdonald was a man of ideas. And while his principles were well expressed in the progressive conservatism of the day, he was a person who built coalitions in support of ideas. When a coalition was formed in support of a large idea that would serve his countrymen well, he would invariably succeed. When the fight was for the survival of a hapless government for a few more days, he would be dramatically less successful.

In fact, while it may pain today's purists, the origins of what is the Progressive Conservative Party really came together from a strange amalgam of different groups in 1854. While Allan MacNab became the premier of the Province of Canada, it was John A. Macdonald who collected and united the pieces of the new government. As Don Swainson of Queen's chronicled so well in

Sir John A. Macdonald, *The Man and the Politician,* assembling the other parties and their leaders was key to his success. Uniting with ultra-Tories like MacNab and more moderate Tories like Sir John A. were French Canadian reformers who had been loyal to LaFontaine and Liberals from Canada West (or reformers from Canada West, as they were then called) who had been loyal to Baldwin and Hincks. If there was a left-right spectrum in the Province of Canada, the new coalition government represented all of that spectrum, and John A. assembled the best of it for the MacNab government.

The Confederation coalition, formed a decade or so after the 1854 government, was headed by Étienne-Paschal Taché and had in it reformers such as Thomas D'Arcy McGee and George Brown and old Québec Conservatives such as George-Étienne Cartier, along with Sir John A. and Alexander Galt. In fact, it was almost 140 years ago, in the great by-election in Leeds South, that John Macdonald campaigned with McGee by his side in a crucial electoral contest and the Tory, Jones, won against the favourite from the other side, Fredenburgh. The two of them, McGee and Macdonald, Catholic and Protestant, reformer and Tory, campaigned together, and spoke and sang to crowds throughout the hinterland to elect the Tory. Originally they had been from different provinces and on opposing sides. Now they stood, campaigned and drank together, for the forces of light. The *Globe* was less than happy with this outcome, calling Macdonald a "pretended Orangeman" and McGee a "pretended Roman Catholic." But the message to our generation is that two people who had once fought each other bitterly served on the same side for a greater good. That was the majesty of McGee and Macdonald. That was the lesson of Leeds South, and that, I submit to you all, is the core message of Sir John A.'s career.

You turn foes into allies by reaching out, not closing in. You embrace tomorrow by refusing to be a prisoner of yesterday. You leave being mean to others.

John Macdonald understood that politics was both the art of the possible and an endless debate, a series of moving coalitions that existed for specific public purposes. Those who want to use the banner of the party label not as a platform for working with others but as a shield against change or openness misunderstand what political parties are. They are not private clubs with crests and membership restrictions. They are public trusts, which belong to all Canadians, and they are made real and relevant by citizens of good will in the public interest.

Sir John A. understood the public interest of his day. His National Policy—higher tariffs, the rapid construction of the CPR, heavy immigration—became the policy he developed to regain power while in opposition. It was a policy that built the foundations of Canada. This was a man unrestricted by left or right, even as they were defined in his day. Reformers, ultra-conservatives, those who had been on both sides of the barricades in the rebellions decades earlier, all were welcome when the cause was Canada. While in government, the same man who afforded the CPR such a wide corporate franchise to open the West and unite the country also approved the first legislation allowing unions for the printers in Toronto. Excess sobriety ranked right up there with narrow partisanship as tools of little value and less import to John A.

When, in the 1990s, there were competing conservative parties, he would have said to his own successors in the old Progressive Conservative Party: "first, tend to your knitting, pay off your debts . . . strengthen your organization . . . build a solid policy plan for all Canadians that reflects your history and your principles . . . fight for a better Canada, one where social progress and economic performance progress together . . . a Canada that has paid its way, can discharge its own defence obligations with honour and capacity, and where any Canadian who fell behind through no fault of their own was one Canadian too many . . ." When the Progressive Conservatives under Clark (1998–2003) failed in these tasks, he would have encouraged Mr. MacKay and Mr. Harper to create a new national party. And I believe that any assessment of John A. Macdonald's career would argue that when his Conservative party had strengthened its resolve, paid off its debts, focused its policy priorities and rebuilt its organization and team, he would expect it to reach out to find allies with whom to pursue a common cause. It would do so from strength. It would do so from principle. It would do so for Canada.

And even from a non-partisan perspective, it strikes me that Sir John A. would have a point. He would offer a firm "fiddle faddle" to those who said that all differences between parties of the right were irreconcilable. "They are only irreconcilable if you want them to be," he would say. Any Tory who understands the true essence of Sir John A. understands that if the cause is right, if the policy is required, then making a new coalition, reaching out and up, is the right course.

So what is the message of Sir John A. for the Canada we love and the party he created? There can be no competitive democracy unless two or more possible governments face each other across the floor of Parliament, and across the country. And he would remind us that just as the whole spectrum mattered then, it matters now. Ideally, he would want a Conservative Party that had no fear of being both progressive and conservative as the social or economic issues and priorities dictated. A national Conservative Party to the left of Liberals on income security and assistance to the farming communities—that is, fundamentally more humane and caring—and more to the right on defence, on reducing waste in government, on moderating taxes and on foreign policy priorities would have the kind of balance required, were we to be true to his approach to progress and victory.

Sir John's core legacy is that compromise is in the national interest and that creating division for narrow gain is short-sighted and ultimately unproductive.

5

BORDEN, BENNETT

and Twentieth-Century
Tory Nationalism and Internationalism

W hat Robert Borden inherited when he was elected in 1911 was a Canada that had been shaped by the "progressive" conservatism of Macdonald. Borden's immediate predecessor, Sir Wilfrid Laurier, was a stout and loyal supporter of the Empire and had created our first coastal defence system: the Canadian navy was inaugurated in 1910. Laurier was a moderate trade innovator who embraced creative imperial preferences with Great Britain and reasonable tariff improvements with the United States. In many ways, his achievements were a continuation of Sir John A. Macdonald's. It's worth noting that Laurier's first budget extended a more expansive trade preference to the United Kingdom than any Tory ever had to date.

But, in the end, although he supported Laurier's modestly constructive nation-building initiatives, Borden would come to power in the same way Sir John A. stayed in power: by opposing Liberal continentalist excess, an excess that threatened the survival of any "nation and enterprise" approach to the future.

Laurier, having been engaged with U.S. President Taft in a triangulated tariff negotiation to balance preferential tariffs already given to France, found himself tied politically to a reciprocity agreement in 1911. This became Borden's unbelievable opportunity. He could let the success of Sir John A.'s final campaign slogan, "the old flag, the old policy, the old leader," become the new party mantra. The perils of American continentalism, the excesses of American republicanism, the corruption of American politics and judicial campaigning all reaffirmed, as was the case in the days of the Empire Loyalists, that the core Tory intellectual and emotional commitment to a different society on the northern half of the continent remained right and true. Laurier's mismanagement of reciprocity was to Borden's advantage. It appeared that the moment Laurier fell out of the Macdonald mode, a mode that had preserved his electoral prospects, his political success collapsed.

A prosperous Ontario, for which immigration, industrialization and Laurier himself deserved equal credit, became a bulwark against reciprocity. Deserting the covering fire of the Tory "no truck or trade" posture on reciprocity of 1891 (Sir John's last great victory) left Laurier vulnerable to major Tory and nationalist gains throughout Québec and Ontario. In 1911, Ontario only gave thirteen seats to the Liberal Party. In the same election, Robert Borden's successful candidates numbered seventy-two in Ontario and, as a result, a new Tory nationalism was born.

Borden led Canada through the Great War of 1914–18, fought for independence for Canadian forces during the war and for an independent voice at the treaty negotiations at Versailles in 1919. He also shaped critical parts of a new "nationalist" infrastructure absolutely vital to Canada's Great War and postwar needs. And he attracted young candidates, such as R.B. Bennett from Alberta, who had their own very strong "nation and enterprise" principles. Tory nationalism, from the Borden and Bennett era onward, became synonymous with a "nation and enterprise" social conscience, which defined order in terms of equality of opportunity. In fact, Tory nationalism became part and parcel of the "nation and enterprise" mix on freedom and order.

Borden took the unspeakable sacrifices, victories and setbacks of the Somme, Ypres, Passchendaele and Vimy battles, which had left few Canadian families unscathed, and turned them into a national identity and emergent international independence. The old Empire was being turned into a Commonwealth of equals, and Robert Borden was doing the heavy lifting on Canada's transformation.

Borden became the father of modern, twentieth-century Canadian Tory nationalism and internationalism. National instruments such as income tax (to pay for the war) and the National Research Council were created during his leadership. The War Measures Act (for better or for worse) and the employment of troops to control the Winnipeg General Strike of 1919 were also his doing. The Tory principles of a compelling nationalism and a focus on statecraft, order, stability and Canadian sovereignty were implicit in his very Canadian conservatism.

The hundreds of thousands of Canadians who had joined the allied war effort did not do so to address only those "issues that directly affected them"; they went to engage in a battle about the future of Europe and the British Empire, the future of the world, and they made huge sacrifices in defence of the freedom and survival of all of the above. To limit Canada's voice and role once the future of the post–Great War world was being sorted would have been a monstrous denial of the sacrifices made by the dead, wounded and living who constituted the Canadian expeditionary force, as well as the political convulsions and controversies Canada's democracy had navigated to support that deployment. Borden had secured the independent right of Canada to ratify, through the Parliament of Canada, the treaties it would sign as an individual Dominion. There had been some in his cabinet and beyond who worried that Borden had pushed Canadian independence too far, and had done so at the expense of the much-valued diplomatic unity of the Empire, both during and after the war. But Borden's nationalism was neither timid nor petty. It was founded upon a deep conviction that Canada was making an autonomous contribution to the war effort and that this independent presence, sacrifice and determination merited separate standing and a Canadian voice proudly articulated.

The wartime innovations that shaped the particular nationalism at the heart of Borden's Toryism became central to the Canadian idea under both Conservatives and Liberals. The Wheat Board, corporate and personal income tax, the War Trade Board, a business profit tax and domestic borrowing by the state all underlined wartime exigencies that Canada and the federal government embraced in defence of the national interest. But as not all of these instruments were terminated at the end of the war, they became the muscular structure of the modern Canadian state. Macdonald had created the skeleton and the brain, Laurier had extended the reach and shaped the heart, and Borden added the muscles that gave the political and fiscal body politic the ability to move forward of its own volition. And through his war and postwar efforts, he had achieved clear Dominion status for Canada. The public ownership of the Grand Trunk and Canadian Northern railways, which came as the result of a Royal Commission into the mismanagement and incompetence that typified railway construction under Laurier, added to the sinews of federal strength—as did the war effort itself.

But not all of these measures proved popular when the unavoidable postwar recession hit large parts of Canada's economy after the brief war-based expansion. The growth of agrarian protest and political organization; the use of force during the 1919 Winnipeg General Strike; the strong opposition among organized labour to the Union government as a result; the coalescence of rural angst into and through "Progressive" or "Farmers'" parties in Ontario and the West all sowed the seeds of a postwar realignment of Canadian politics that would itself influence the tenor and form of "nation and enterprise" Canadian conservatism.

The broad and far-reaching nature of the war effort—of the domestic, industrial and technological focus it helped unleash; the labour pressures; the political impact of the conscription crisis and the fault lines it would embed—led to the maturity of a country whose identity and existence beyond Empire was affirmed and established and whose political system was formed by the foreign and defence experience.

Indeed, from World War I, three seminal principles of foreign and defence policy emerged as clearly Conservative:

· Canada will match, and should match, diplomatic values-based principles with actual engagement in defence of those principles with its allies, when either is attacked by hostile powers and realms.

· Internal controversies and domestic political divisions are not an excuse for timidity or for the failure to carry our weight and engage the military when all else has failed.

· Canada, even when in alliance with other nations with similar priorities, values and geopolitical interests, has its own views and priorities based on its current and historical realities and will assert that Canadian voice whenever necessary.

These new nationalist and internationalist principles, along with universal suffrage (brought in first at the federal level by Arthur Meighen, Borden's justice minister, for spouses, mothers, sisters and grandmothers of men serving overseas), also unleashed in Canada, as was the case in other mature or maturing modern industrial democracies, a more heated division of opinion about resources and economic fairness. While out of office, Liberals, such as Mackenzie King, would build their individual career prospects by serving American industrialism and creating tame in-house trade unions. (Later, King would shamelessly run as an anti-conscription Laurier Liberal candidate for the 1917 election.) This classic Liberal hypocrisy—pursuing corporate interests between elections and then running to the left at election time—began with Mackenzie King and, in some measure, is still with us today. When the articulate, hard-working and supremely rational Arthur Meighen, who had done so much of the domestic heavy lifting for Borden during the World War I, in the pre-Unionist and Unionist Party period, was chosen party leader after Borden's resignation in 1920, the forces of realignment were already underway. But if Robert Borden had been the father of twentieth century Tory nationalism and internationalism, with all its "nation and enterprise" implications and innovations, it would be R.B. Bennett who would face the Depression head-on and who would argue for many of the key elements of the future "nation and enterprise" agenda for Canada, an agenda that was profoundly about social justice, social change and a more economically inclusive Canada.

R.B. Bennett had one of the most complex careers of any Canadian prime minister. By the time he became prime minister in 1930, he had been a lawyer, an independent member of the territorial assembly in Canada's northwest and, after Alberta became a province in 1905, both leader of the provincial Conservative Party in Alberta and a member of its legislature. By 1911 he had been elected to the federal House of Commons; he then returned to provincial politics in 1913. When that effort did not succeed, he served for a short time in the brief Meighen administration as its finance minister (having not resigned his federal seat while provincial Tory leader). After the King-Byng manoeuvre and the defeat of the Meighen administration in Parliament, he was chosen as national party leader at the 1927 general convention of the Conservative Party in Winnipeg.

It is not clear that Mackenzie King, seen by Tories and others as the trimmer and prevaricator, actually knew there was a depression on when he lost the election of 1930. Bennett, by focusing resolutely on jobs and economic suffering during his successful election campaign, indicated that he did. R.B. had been a stout campaigner for a more robust and socially just public-interest presence for government ever since he was first elected to the House of Commons in 1911. Many decades before Liberals would discuss social justice at the famous Grindstone Island meeting near Kingston, Ontario, in 1961, R.B. was espousing universal health care, protection for workers, generous unemployment benefits, pensions and broad measures for equality of opportunity.

Bennett also used his broad political experience, strong personality and compelling capacity for hard work to out-campaign, out-manoeuvre and out-policy Mackenzie King in the 1930 election (the date for which King characteristically chose with the help of a Kingston fortune teller).

While King seemed determined to ignore the Depression and its effects on people's lives, Bennett proposed explicit measures to address the challenge head-on. Bennett was very much a traditional Conservative: he believed in hard work, family, thrift, faith, community. These were the pillars of a strong and prosperous society. And that ramrod-straight clarity connected in 1930 with a public that was frightened and needed the assurances of a level-headed leader.

R.B. Bennett had shown his Red Tory credentials well before the Depression and his election as prime minister. When first elected to the federal House from Calgary in 1911 with the Borden majority, he moved the Speech from the Throne—often a "first-up" privilege awarded a newly elected, promising M.P. In that maiden speech he spoke in favour of trade unions, government-owned grain elevators, regulation of prairie freight rates and workmen's compensation. He punctuated his core concerns in that November 20, 1911, speech with this central declaration: "The great struggle of the future will be between human rights and property interests; and it is the duty and the function of the government to provide that there shall be no undue regard for the latter that limits or lessens the other." In its Canadian incarnation, robust conservative nationalism was not only about "nation and enterprise," but also about civility and compassion.

Bennett was a maverick. In 1927, long before becoming first minister in 1930, while working with Labour politician A.A. Heaps, he supported pensions and unemployment insurance. And, when he did form a government, one of his first measures was an emergency Relief Act to help the unemployed. With it, he answered the pleas he had heard earlier during the prairie drought of 1913–14, for aid to farm families.

Within six weeks of the writ being returned, the new Conservative-led Parliament not only met, but moved on protective tariffs and historically large amounts of money for social relief, unemployment aid and job-creating initiatives. Bennett also continued extending Canada's international reach, after the Statute of Westminster established foreign policy sovereignty for Canada and other dominions in 1931. He further championed Canada's independence and Canada's separate voice while plagued by the crushing social, economic and regional challenges of the Depression and the rank protectionism of America's Smoot-Hawley laws, which raised import duties to protect American businesses and farmers.

Bennett took these measures very much in the Sir John A. National Policy mode while the inquiry into the Beauharnois power scandal revealed a trail of Liberal benefit-seeking, even implicating Mackenzie King personally for taking a Bermuda holiday financed by the Beauharnois Light, Heat and Power Co. This company stood to benefit enormously from a King government decision on a St. Lawrence River diversion for power generation. The scandal became public between June 1931 and April 1932, when committees of the House of Commons and Senate investigated allegations that the Beauharnois company had made contributions to the Liberal Party in return for permission to divert the St. Lawrence River thirty kilometres west of Montréal to generate hydroelectricity. Company director R.O. Sweezey testified that Liberal senators W.L. McDougald and Andrew Haydon had personally received Beauharnois funds, and that the company had paid approximately $700,000 into the campaign fund of the federal and Québec Liberal parties.

While this diversion was not unhelpful to the Bennett side of the debate, his early days' discomfort with overly direct economic intervention in the private economy meant that, despite tariff action and support for relief, the depression waves did hit most parts of Canada. Provinces were also unwilling to coordinate relief efforts. The study of what Bennett failed to do, or of what he failed to do enough of, would not have been lost on Canada's twenty-second prime minister Stephen Harper. Harper's increases in public spending in the 2009 budget—mostly for job-sensitive infrastructure investment and renovation tax incentives—contributed, despite the angst of those on the fiscal far right (let the markets decide), to Canada getting it more right than others in staring down the U.S.-based credit crisis that threatened us all.

In 1935, influenced by Roosevelt's New Deal, Bennett introduced a series of then quite radical measures for Canada, including a minimum wage, health and unemployment insurance benefits, tighter regulation of banking and trade, and other vital measures. In much of this, he was urged on by H.H. Stevens, a British Columbia cabinet minister who had headed a Royal Commission on trade—the Royal Commission on Price Spreads and Mass Buying—and who concluded that radical measures were vital. Despite Mr. Bennett's initiatives, Minister Stevens was convinced that much more had to be done. As a Tory, he wanted policies to be a stronger reflection of social justice and populism. The level of suffering, unemployment and relative poverty was very high, and trade-based areas such as B.C. and Ontario suffered from protectionist efforts elsewhere in the world, just as agriculture and commodity areas across the country suffered from severe demand collapse and price deflation. Stevens created a breakaway Reconstructionist Party that reflected his frustration with the late nature of Bennett's conservative engagement on poverty; he carved off enough votes in the 1935 election (eight percent nationally and as high as fourteen percent in Atlantic Canada) to hand Liberals victory, despite the taint surrounding Mackenzie King. Conservatives fought amongst themselves about social justice and how far one could realistically go in one policy surge, and all the while social justice was at the centre of the public debate.

Before his defeat in 1935, Bennett had sought a sea change in our national politics. In 1932, he acted to create the Canadian Radio Broadcasting Commission, the forebear of the CBC, so as to keep U.S. radio from occupying all the space available on the Canadian spectrum. And he did so via a Supreme Court reference and legislation. He also brought in the Farmers' Creditors' Arrangement Act in 1934, to help folks stay on their farms during very tough times. His views were radical—even today, some in America and the U.K. would still see them as radical.

According to James H. Gray, in his book *R.B. Bennett: The Calgary Years*, Sir James Lougheed—grandfather of Peter Lougheed, who would become premier of Alberta in 1971— employed Bennett as a young lawyer when he first moved from New Brunswick to Calgary. In the young man, Lougheed could already see signs of his future greatness: "Bennett can solve any problem he puts his mind to. No man is quicker to strip a problem of unnecessary verbiage and translate it into a simple and understandable language. Some day Bennett will be called upon to solve the greatest problems in Canada. Some day Canada will turn to him to get the country out of its difficulties."

In the end, R.B., a Red Tory at heart, modernized the economics and social policy of Canada to address the changes of a fresh and more demanding age. He fought for a new relationship between Canada and the Empire and launched, in all serious respects, Canada's first foreign policy and diplomatic corps, after the 1931 Statute of Westminster afforded Canada formal foreign policy sovereignty.

Even in the launching of that statute, the balance of rights essential to the moderate balance of Canadian conservatism was evident; Bennett had had significant influence on the content. But the statute repealed prior legislation under which provinces had made, over the years, separate agreements with London. To appease Canadian provinces, Bennett sought and received exemption for Canada so that prior agreements between the provinces and the U.K. government within provincial jurisdiction were not snuffed out. The ability to amend the BNA Act still rested with Westminster, as did the right to appeal beyond our own Supreme Court to the Law Lords and the Privy Council at Westminster. Compromise here was vital in part because R.B. needed provincial cooperation to combat the Depression and, in 1931, it seemed counterproductive to make that cooperation more difficult. Change and its benefits had to be measured against respecting provincial jurisdiction. Moreover, he acted to protect the Tory principle of collaborative nation building—a principle that was generally ignored or opposed by Liberals from Durham to Trudeau. One builds the country with and alongside the provinces and regions, not despite them or in opposition to them.

Bennett was an activist and a compassionate conservative. He was a hardscrabble, self-made man with a heart of gold and endless compassion and time (not to mention personal financial help) for those less fortunate. In many ways, his persona spoke eloquently to the complexity of the unique Canadian conservative brand. A "high finance" and "pro-business" conservative, his Red Toryism (a term not yet invented then), made him an unreconstructed proponent of social justice and fairness. Suspicious of the size of government, its spending and bureaucracy, he created new public bodies to protect and balance the public interest. A native-born Maritimer and then Calgarian, he ended his political life as a viscount in the British House of Lords, defending Canada's interest in a more collegial and consultative Commonwealth. Conservative policy in Canada, because of our complex geographical, demographic, linguistic and geopolitical realities, can only be simple and unidimensional for those who prefer simplicity to reality. The reality is that our conservatism stands alone in its unique mix of accommodation and social justice, which underlies the rock-ribbed Tory belief in tradition, institutional strength and the balance between freedom and order.

In the modern era, R.B. Bennett's successes and defeats speak as eloquently as any one man's might to the complexity and demands of Canadian "nation and enterprise" conservatism. And despite the difficulties he faced within a country ravaged by a depression that began elsewhere, his Toryism was one of genuine learning and growth. He was not unmoved by suffering. Instead, he was shaped by its dimensions and depth. He acted personally, often while avoiding media notice, to help many who wrote to him with great and serious financial challenges. He confronted the traditionalists of his own party and the Bay Street and Rue Saint-Jacques business elites to reach out to the poor and suffering. He may not have been as relaxed or contemporary an orator as FDR, but he was genuine in his passion and determination. Although a recently published R.B. Bennett biography by John Boyko certainly helps to rebalance the historical record, history has yet to give him the full credit he deserves. In the toughest of times, he sought the right balance with remarkable courage.

6

MR. MEIGHEN BUILDS THE BRIDGE

to Modern Progressive Conservatism

A rthur Meighen was a "minister of everything" in the Tory government of Robert Borden but would not attain the same electoral success as R.B. Bennett. However, he would very much keep the theme of "nation and enterprise" conservatism alive and well. Arthur Meighen served briefly as prime minister in the post–World War I era but his defeat by King, through the manipulation of the King-Byng Affair, would end his prime minister days for good and would lead to the Bennett ascendancy and R.B.'s 1930–35 government. But Meighen would serve his party and his country long after R.B., in defeat, moved to the United Kingdom. In essence, Meighen became a rock-ribbed pillar of Tory nationalism.

There were many "firsts" associated with the ninth prime minister of Canada, Arthur Meighen. He was the first prime minister born after Confederation; the first to represent a Manitoba riding; and the youngest to hold that post up to that point in history. He had both a mathematics degree and a law degree when he became prime minister. He was intellectually acute and rigorously logical with a rhetorical style that was both fluid and compelling.

Arthur Meighen, who had been a senior minister for Borden and who had established women's right to vote and sorted through the railway mess inherited by Borden from Laurier, also made a vital contribution to the Canadian voice in the world. Some might say that he made a virtue out of necessity. There is considerable evidence that the virtue was not reactive but engrained and meaningful. As prime minister, he had, after all, been like Bennett and Borden before him: a stout proponent of a Canadian world view that refused to be subsumed by British condescension and American exceptionalism. Rather than speaking in support of two-country alliances such as the U.K.-Japan alliance that was up for renewal, Prime Minister Meighen spoke eloquently for moving away from two- or three-country alliances because they were exclusionary and merely spawned more of the same. He preferred embracing a new multilateral approach to international organization. A renewed U.K.-Japan alliance would needlessly alienate the Americans and Chinese; it would be neither helpful nor constructive. Meighen's articulate and focused argument on the issue convinced both the British and South African first ministers, and ultimately other Commonwealth members of the Imperial Conference, to agree with him. Subsequently, an Empire position was sustained and a multi-country Pacific agreement was born. The Canadian Press piece dated June 27–28, 1921, on Arthur Meighen's leadership for Canada at the conference in London was headlined: "CANADIAN PREMIER STIRS CONFERENCE; Meighen Demands Wide Authority for Dominions on Foreign Policy of Empire. WITH TREATY VETO POWER Canada's Decision to Be Final in All Questions Between Her and United States."

Meighen's defence of moderated tax protection in opposition to the anti-tariff views of rural and Western voices, as well as his identification with the nationalization of the railways, which infuriated the moneyed interests who were profoundly pro–Canadian Pacific in Montréal and elsewhere, was more than enough to cause him political grief. He was the ultimate Tory nationalist with a strong belief in the balance essential in the "nation and enterprise" equation.

His Toryism was austere and direct. It was tied to innovation and independence for Canada in imperial and international affairs, but also to classic conservative economic protection, social structure and economic fairness at home.

And while his political setbacks and victories led to a mixed series of electoral results (prime minister from July 1920 to December 1921, and from June 1926 to September 1926; leader of the opposition from 1921 to 1926 and again from 1941 to 1942) he had a decisive role in critical disputes and events of his time. And when the time came for the Conservative Party to take a more humane and creative stance on social and economic policy, Meighen would be the key facilitator of that step ahead. In victory, government, opposition, the House and the Senate, his contributions over half a century were overwhelming.

Meighen's was a career whose conservatism was buffeted by many issues, including the post-conscription tensions, Mackenzie King's hateful but effective misrepresentation of Meighen as anti-Québec and the arrogance of King, who would not see losing an election to Meighen as any reason *whatsoever* to consider resigning as prime minister. Mr. King lost the 1925 election and Mr. Meighen won the largest number of seats in the House of Commons by a fair margin, but King insisted on his right to meet the House. With some support from the "Progressives" in the House, he governed with the express understanding of the Governor General, Lord Byng, that, should he be defeated in the House, His Excellency retained the right to call on Meighen to govern. When corruption defeated King (motions of censure of the government and various ministers passed three separate times in one late sitting, the King government having had a problem with scandals of one form or another), King, who had snuck over to Rideau Hall to seek dissolution and an election before the votes could take place—and who was justifiably rebuffed in his electoral request by the Governor General—actually resigned by letter (again secretly) before the House resumed the next day and before Arthur Meighen visited Lord Byng at the Governor General's invitation. Meighen was asked by Lord Byng to form a government, which, sadly, did not survive. The subsequent general election saw Mackenzie King given the mandate again.

As trimmers and tacticians, the Liberals have, since Mackenzie King's day, been more effective than the Tories. Meighen helped rebuild the Conservative Party after the realignment defeat of 1922 (Liberals, Progressives and others ate into the Tory-Unionist vote) in a most impressive fashion. He rightfully criticized Mackenzie King for saying different things at different times in different parts of the country, on everything from transport policy to Senate reform. This remarkable tendency of King to say whatever seemed to work at the time—without a shred of policy coherence—was seen by some critics (perhaps a little unfairly), as the true genesis of the Liberal capacity to become the national and natural governing party for a majority of terms and years in office. (Thankfully, today's instant digital media loop would make the Mackenzie King approach utterly suicidal!) The largely pro-Liberal biases among the Canadian establishment have confused tactical flexibility with competence and integrity. To be fair, winning more elections than your opponents is one of the core goals of any political party in a competitive democracy, and it is both unjust and churlish to be critical of Canada's Liberals for doing just that. But when purposeful dilution of policy integrity (and appealing differently to different regions and linguistic groups) is often at the base of that success, it is absolutely legitimate to blame past Liberals for the costs of their approach to Canada. (In the same generation, promoting "French Power" in Québec, while campaigning in 1968 as the one leader who could "handle" Québec, tied Mr. Trudeau quite directly to this Mackenzie King tendency.)

The unchallenged father of this brand of "flexible" politics for some modern-day Liberals in Canada is Mackenzie King. That he succeeded as he did politically, despite his obvious contempt for democracy, his dislike of his fellow provincial Liberals, his rather sad and strange personal life, and his early admiration of Hitler, speaks to how successful he was at maintaining a card player's tactical intensity—and how little about him the press of the day knew or, worse, cared to share with the public. He does deserve credit for his agile tip-toeing through the broken glass of conscription politics during the war years, but there is little to commend him beyond that.

In the 1925 election, the popular vote for the Meighen Tories exceeded Mr. King's by more than two hundred thousand. This was a great Tory comeback, after having been thumped by the Liberals in 1921. In the words of his biographer Roger Graham, for Meighen, Toryism embodied the "standards of private and personal conduct in which he believed among which frankness, honesty and consistency ranked high. He tended to idealize politics as an intellectual competition, a continuous great debate which performed an educative function essential to the proper working of democracy..." According to Graham, Meighen also believed that the "duty of... indeed the purpose of the party system, was to define and clarify issues in such a way that the electorate, when the time came, could make an intelligent decision." Clearly, his was a pan-national conservatism of principle, clarity and understandable logic.

But, in the King-Byng Affair, King was more tactically nimble than Meighen and was able to win the 1926 election after the defeat of Meighen in the House. (Meighen had reluctantly accepted Governor General Byng's invitation to govern, more out of respect for the Crown than political opportunity.) The Tory, straight-ahead on principle and right, was walloped by the Liberals' superior tactical sense. It was clear throughout that

Meighen was torn between party advantage, duty to the Crown and anger at King's relentlessly manipulative and anti-democratic bias. That a prime minister could lose an election by hundreds of thousands of votes and cling to office by promising one thing to the Governor General, then, do another, and subsequently win an election by claiming to support democracy, speaks eloquently to Mackenzie King's tactical skill. This brought into sharp relief the straight-laced Tory world view versus the devious and nimble whatever-seems-to-work Liberal world view. That King would be defeated by R.B. Bennett a few years later would only suspend King's tactical liberalism for a time.

Sir John A.'s dexterity, minus the sense of a larger purpose, had found its acolyte in King. The Liberals under King became the apostles of tactics without principle. The more straight-laced, rock-ribbed Toryism of Borden, in whose government Meighen had served with such distinction, had found a clear, articulate and compelling promoter and advocate in Meighen. But Meighen's lofty philosophical coherence had become principle without tactics. To survive and be a relevant player in the narrative of Canada, Conservatives would have to master both.

The King government's electoral defeat by R.B. Bennett in 1930 and Bennett's remarkable period in government greatly affected the tone and nature of modern conservatism. But just as Meighen, during Borden's years, had played a key role in shaping many of the vital instruments of government, so too did Meighen, in opposition, play a key role in capitalizing on the successes of R.B. Bennett, who was defeated in 1935. Understanding that contribution in defeat is essential to understanding the magisterial contribution of Meighen to the modern Conservative Party.

Meighen was of the "nation and enterprise" school of Toryism. Echoing aspects of Macdonald's vision, he brought in the seminal legislation, the most substantial in Canadian history, that created the Canadian National Railway, which remained a Crown agency until privatized by the Liberals in the 1990s. Meighen was very much a nation builder while serving in the governments of other Conservatives, in cabinet and in the Senate. This talent formed a clear preparatory and supportive basis for the proposals that R.B. Bennett made both as part of the earlier Borden government's caucus and when running his own government later.

Much of the "nation and enterprise" conservatism of R.B. Bennett would, after his defeat, become part of Liberal dogma. Part of the problem was that the Tories had faced the brunt of the early Depression. With Bennett's defeat in 1935 and the return of King, the Liberals would put into place many of the proposals on which Bennett had campaigned. This would foreshadow an interesting pattern between Liberals and Conservatives, a pattern that wasn't part of Canadian history until 1935—namely that Tories propose, engage and face the brunt and political cost for national and necessary policy innovation, while Liberals sort out how to more expertly profit politically in terms of seat totals and electoral outcomes. There is no particular evil in the latter, just as there is not endless virtue in the former. But there is a core and defining difference. Think of Stanfield's wage-and-price-freeze proposals in 1974, opposed by Trudeau at election time and then later implemented; think of Liberal opposition to Free Trade, which was proposed by Mulroney in 1988, and Chrétien's joining of the "three amigos" on NAFTA and Free Trade in 1993; think of the GST, proposed by Mulroney in 1991, and the end of the GST promised by Chrétien in the 1993 campaign and how he sustained and advanced it in the years following his election.

Arthur Meighen was in the Senate in 1935 when Bennett was defeated. Meighen had been appointed in 1932 by Prime Minister Bennett, who had used him not a jot in the successful 1931 campaign, although Meighen had been a tireless campaigner against Liberal scandal (the Beauharnois scandal being front and centre). And while more cautious in his social reforms than the Red Tory Bennett had now openly become near the end of his term, Meighen ensured the passage of Bennett's reform package in the upper house, albeit with numerous amendments. While some could have seen Prime Minister Bennett's famous radio address on ending laissez-faire and engaging to help the people as his finest moment, Meighen, who supported the legislation and was artful in getting it through, was unimpressed with the alarmist nature of the radio address itself.

The radicalism in Bennett's now-famous radio address reflected, at some level, his buying into the New Deal radicalism of Franklin Delano Roosevelt, very much an upstate New York Democrat. This sort of departure from the traditional conservative belief in markets, as the only instrument for wealth creation and broad-based progress, is not atypical of a Tory response to market failure. In essence, it could be seen in the past by initiatives in canal and railway construction and would be reflected in the future by initiatives like Diefenbaker's "roads to resources" program. This involved the construction of the Trans-Canada Highway and other provincial Tory initiatives in Québec, Ontario, New Brunswick and Alberta, in everything from power company nationalization (with compensation), educational television, nuclear power, airline acquisition and oil sands development. All of these were state interventions, made by priming the pump, critical mass consolidation, innovation and/or new development of which the private sector was not yet capable or in which it was not yet interested. And, to be fair to Americans, another Roosevelt, Teddy, had, at the turn of the century, responded to undue monopolistic economic control by large and broadly unregulated economic trusts (like Standard Oil) while serving as a nationalist and not-all-that-modest Republican president. And while many in the media are desperate to dismiss Prime Minister Harper as a neo-conservative in Conservative clothing, his government's investment in new carbon-capture technologies, assistance to automobile manufacturers and stimulus spending since 2008 is very much in the same tradition. R.B. Bennett's vision reflected economic activism from the Canadian conservative past. It helped to establish a legacy since taken up by Conservatives such as Diefenbaker, Drew, Frost, Davis, Lougheed, Hatfield, Mulroney and Harper. It is an entirely appropriate and deeply Canadian strain of conservatism shaped by Canadian reality.

The long period of Liberal government (1935–57) that saw Canada through World War II was a time when the Conservative Party sought leaders from outside the usual herd. Leaders like Manion, Bracken and Diefenbaker, with deeply Western and more populist economic and agrarian roots, would become dominant, and their politics, which had little to do with American-style capitalist excess, and more to do with community and populism, would shape a basic "nation and enterprise" Red Tory presence for Conservatives going forward.

As the country joined in support of the United Kingdom after the Germans invaded Poland in September of 1939, and just four years after R.B. Bennett's defeat, the exigencies of war, the debate over conscription and the mobilization for the emergency effort were dominant political themes.

During the war, opposition Tories were broadly pro-conscription in principle and had a challenging period. Jack Granatstein's seminal *The Politics of Survival: The Conservative Party of Canada, 1939–1945* presents the best analysis of this period. The challenges were both tactical and substantive. In an effort to modernize its platform, the Conservative Party held a Port Hope policy conference in 1942 that embraced some new economic and social directions.

Meighen did not agree with all of the resolutions from the 1942 Port Hope Conference, which included support for free enterprise, conscription, full employment, low-cost housing, trade union rights and a government-financed medicare system. Meighen was cautious but focused on the need to oppose, with competence and vigour, the Co-operative Commonwealth Federation (CCF) and its "paradise on earth" socialist promises in a way that was effective. The chosen candidate (and answer, from

Arthur Meighen's perspective) was the Progressive premier of Manitoba, John Bracken. Meighen would reach out to bring the unlikely Tory into a position of leadership.

An agriculturalist by training, Bracken had no early interest in politics and certainly none in the Conservative Party. His Manitoba roots were not far removed from the "anti-all-party" biases that energized the various protest movements on the Prairies during the Depression. Old party governments, Tory and Liberal, fell on the Prairies during the late twenties, thirties and forties to new groundswell coalitions: CCF, Social Credit and United Farmers. The United Farmers had replaced Manitoba's ruling Liberal government in 1922, and then turned to John Bracken, the president of the Manitoba Agricultural College, to become provincial premier. He was seen as straight and true, incorruptible and decent as well as humane.

A decade later, in 1932, Bracken and his party had merged with the local Liberals to form the Liberal-Progressive government. But in the process they had come face to face with the crass insensitivity, post-1935, of Mackenzie King, most especially to the needs of the West and the farmers who were suffering horribly. Confronted with King's disregard and an economically devastating Manitoba grain surplus, as well as Ottawa's (that is, King's) mean-spirited disdain for Bracken's 1940 decision to have, after the outbreak of war, an all-party coalition in Manitoba, Bracken turned away from King's Liberalism. Bracken had built a solid, if not convivial, reputation as a people's premier connected to real suffering on the Prairies. He did not see his own future as a Mackenzie King Liberal. In fact, if anything, he was more open to futures elsewhere.

Bracken was courted by Meighen as a potential leader and Meighen was not deeply troubled by Bracken's interesting terms: no convention fight; a name change to Progressive Conservative; and the adoption of the humane, forward-leading, communitarian Toryism of the "Port Hopefuls," as those who attended the 1942

Port Hope meeting were called. The names of other potential leaders were also circulating: John Diefenbaker from Saskatchewan, who was a caucus member; Murdoch MacPherson from Saskatchewan, who had been the favourite of many at Port Hope; Howard Green from B.C., also a caucus member; and Sidney Smith, president of the University of Toronto. Even the Honourable H.H. Stevens, who, as leader of the breakaway Reconstructionist Party that had garnered just enough votes to help elect Mr. King in 1935, had declared a candidacy, doing the "prodigal son returning" two-step, but he was not seen as a serious player.

Bracken's conditions, when shared with the delegates at Winnipeg in 1942, about changing the name of the party and adopting the Port Hope principles, seemed presumptuous—not so much in content but simply because the party was being asked to change in order to accommodate him. With Meighen's encouragement, various procedural motions to keep the Port Hope ideas and the prospective "Progressive" name change alive until after the new leader was chosen. But in the end, Bracken had to be nominated in the usual way and have his candidacy submitted to the whole convention for open choice. (Bracken's initial desire to avoid all this pre-dated the Ignatieff approach to leadership assumption by more than six decades!)

Bracken was successful on the second ballot. And then, as Canada's pre-eminent historian, Jack Granatstein, described it in *The Politics of Survival*, "The victorious Bracken, freed from the anxiety of the past week, then proceeded to deliver a magnificent acceptance speech calling for team work and reiterating the progressive principles upon which he would base his leadership. Following the address, Allan Cocherham, the leader of the fight against the name change, came to the platform and announced that although he had not voted for Bracken, he wished to move the adoption of the new party name. And, the motion creating the Progressive Conservative Party was approved without debate by a resounding chorus of ayes from the floor." It was then that the formal Progressive Conservative era in the "nation and enterprise" saga of Canada's Conservatives began. Progressive Conservative became a brand, and not just an adjective defining a noun. The long Tory march from horrible defeat after defeat was almost over. The lights of the next town, while not fully apparent or even straight ahead, were discernible through the blizzard and almost within reach.

The divisions over conscription, where Tories rejected the "conscription if necessary, but not necessarily conscription" stand of Mackenzie King, had diminished Tory prospects. A huge price was paid by Tories in Québec. While the wartime referendum on conscription would, in its different results in English and French Canada, be less than decisive, Mackenzie King successfully manipulated public opinion, while unreinforced Canadian soldiers took substantial casualties.

The Bracken period (1942–48), made difficult by the conscription crisis, would start as most new leaders' early days and months usually do: it was disorganized, financially irresolute and filled with a certain amount of tension between the caucus and the new leader. But in economic and political terms, the Progressive Conservative brand would continue its advance, aided by the stunning provincial Tory victory the very next year in Ontario.

George Drew's surprising Ontario PC minority electoral success in 1943 was the first Tory victory anywhere in Canada in over a decade, and this added equity and heft to the new Progressive Conservative brand. Drew's list of proposals involved profound social justice and expansionist policies, namely: increasing the government's share for public education spending from fifteen percent to fifty percent; promising such radical reforms as free dental care and universal health care; and proposing an ambitious $400-million plan to enhance Ontario Hydro's electricity grid. His proposals were clearly of a Red Tory, "nation and enterprise" interventionist variety. Interestingly, Bracken had campaigned successfully in rural Ontario, helping to deliver seats for Colonel

Drew (just as provincial PC leader John Tory visited thirty-three ridings in Ontario in 2008 in support of Stephen Harper).

By the end of the war, there was a federal Progressive Conservative Party under Bracken alive and well and in reasonable financial health. With a leader in the House and a gain in seats, the party was finally emerging from the long night of King duplicity and Liberal domination. Arthur Meighen had inherited the party at its weakest and most vulnerable and he had brought it back to life. He left it inspired, progressive, stronger and awash in new prospects for victory. As Granatstein has so dramatically pointed out, this transformation was more about survival than victory. There were times, especially as the corporate world flocked to the already-flush-with-taxpayers'-cash Liberals, when Tory survival hung by a thread. That thread was often Meighen himself, and the strength of his personal resources and business network. It is clear that without Meighen there would not have been a Conservative or Progressive Conservative Party for John Diefenbaker to lead.

[7]

RED TORY PRAIRIE
POPULISM AND
MR. DIEFENBAKER

The more populist side of "nation and enterprise" would come from the leadership of John George Diefenbaker. In 1956, when the Progressive Conservative Party chose Diefenbaker to take the party forward, it stepped firmly outside the Toronto circle to embrace a populist who had tried to win the leadership before and who had been rebuffed many times in Saskatchewan before winning Prince Albert in 1940. And Mr. Diefenbaker would take on the leadership at a time when the Liberals, in a postwar economic and victorious blush, seemed simply undefeatable, when the central government-business partnerships made large industry and government each others' primary clients and key de facto shareholders. In essence, the war effort had fused corporate and private into one massive government-industry consortium, as wars often do. This was not "nation and enterprise." This was nation and enterprise as each other's "subsidiary," with no serious accountabilities for either. But what this Liberal corporatist approach meant for the future was more problematic, especially because the war had been over for a decade.

The end of World War II, the selection of George Drew as national Progressive Conservative leader after his successful government service to Ontario, the succession of Liberal Louis St. Laurent from minister of external affairs to prime minister in 1948, spoke to some changing of the guard in national politics. But the change in our political masters was really trailing far behind the changes in Canadian society. In fact, we wouldn't begin to catch up until 1958. And, as I have argued from the very first chapter, ideas and political philosophies do not change the geography, demographics or ethnicity of a society. It is profoundly and clearly the other way around. And the core changes that the end of World War II would bring to Canada would not only change the generic makeup of Canadian politics, but greatly affect the character and reach of Canadian conservatism.

The nature of the war effort had greatly empowered women, who stepped up to occupy the industrial jobs left vacant by the men who had gone to war. Large and expansive female naval, army and air force membership served and supplemented the war effort in a host of vital ways. At the same time, the concentrated development of aerospace, armament and related munitions industries once again turbo-charged the forces of urbanization, increasing the pull of people away from the rural and agricultural communities.

The returning veterans and the growing demand around the world for Canadian natural resources and manufactured commodities such as steel and aluminum quickly began to inject new life into the economy. By the end of the 1950s, positive cash flow from exports and related royalties began to pour into government. But there was another sea change as well; a sea change that cut right across Canada, the United States, the United Kingdom, Australia and other Western countries. It was a product of the attitudes of the surviving and burgeoning postwar population and their experience of the war itself.

In Canada, hundreds of thousands of new veteran families would require the government to invest in vital new services—housing, education, infrastructure, health and financial—in order to ensure that the brave men and women who had saved Canada, Europe and Asia from civilization's worst enemies to date could now build their own lives and Canada's fortunes at home and in peace. This same social pressure was happening in the United States, Australia, New Zealand and other countries whose territory and infrastructure had largely not been touched by the ravages of the war. Yet even in the U.K., there was a mood that had developed near the end of the war, a feeling that the core assumptions about society and its welfare needed to be very different. Hence the defeat in 1945 of Mr. Churchill and the progress by the new Labour government towards universal health care, council (public) housing and more red brick universities.

In the United States, instruments like the G.I. Bill, which facilitated university education and low cost mortgages for returning G.I.'s, had broad bipartisan support. The core pressure of President Roosevelt's New Deal had been ramped up by the war effort, and it continued after the war, when demands generated by returning servicemen and servicewomen were intense and dramatic. The general postwar feeling of optimism and faith in the potential of "can do" nation-building was very much a motivating political force.

There were frankly two underlying attitudes shaping public opinion. The first was driven by the compelling conclusion that the positive outcome of the war had produced, namely that no problem was too difficult. And the second was that we could solve any problem by throwing at it all available people and reserves. After all, it had worked during the war!

Although the Allies had won the war, fifty million human beings had perished on all sides. Canada's per capita war losses were the highest among Western allies. The anti-democratic Axis powers, replete with their insanely rigid bureaucracies, advanced war machinery and rigid and narrow corporatist agendas that subsumed the individual, had taken an early and compelling lead. Ethiopia, Korea, Singapore, parts of China, Austria, Czechoslovakia, Poland, Norway, Denmark, Belgium, the Netherlands and France had, among others, all fallen under the Axis's power. Japan's attack on Pearl Harbour had been a source of genuine and palpable fear in North America.

The multinational menace that from 1938 to 1945 was at times so intense, evil, inhumane, totalitarian and cruel had, in the end, been stopped by the forces of freedom and civilization. Even the Soviets had come around, changing sides after the Nazis attacked them in 1941 and joining the fight against evil, and taking huge civilian losses in their brave resistance to the Nazi invasion of their homeland.

While much of the popular mythology about good and evil invested in "the last good war" is undeniably true about World War II, it was the design of the 1919 peace agreement that contributed to the forces that led, in Germany, to the Nazis' electoral success. There was mismanagement of the Great Depression by the Americans and others, with Smoot-Hawley trade restraints in particular adding considerable strain to the international economic climate and contributing to economic decline worldwide. This succeeded in closing markets and reducing the liquidity of trade flows.

The rapid decline from deep financial recession to job-destroying depression produced political instability around the world. That kind of instability generates a mixture of fear and meanness, scapegoating and finger-pointing about which no one who cares about society can be naïve or complacent. Whatever the cause, collapsing demand, massive joblessness and the eradication of investment flows mean that certain pressures cannot be easily managed, even in the most developed of civilizations and societies, of which Germany was one. While the classic debate between left and right about the role of the state is always relevant, it is a superfluous self-indulgence when the number of hungry, displaced and hopeless people rises in broad and stark dimensions. The descent to broad levels of poverty and collapsed prospects often leads to racism, revolution and war and has always ended up costing far more than intervention for economic stability. (Joys in our world's history such as the Ku Klux Klan, the National Socialists and similar destructive movements tied to racist scapegoating often use abject poverty to gain the footholds they need to spew hate and division.) The "freedom" to be poor must be weighed against the debilitating impact of mass poverty. This was a notion R.B. Bennett clearly captured.

Whatever guilt the United Kingdom and France shouldered for not having confronted Hitler militarily in Austria or in the Czech Sudetenland, or not confronting Mussolini in Ethiopia or in Spain, the collective sigh of relief in 1945 sucked all the air out of any "multiple cause" popular narrative. Hitler was the incarnation of evil and brutality, the anti-Christ and cruelty, and he and his Japanese and Italian allies had been stopped.

And how? By the simple decision to throw all the money, resources, people and technology civilization possessed at the time against the Nazi and Axis threat. This is exactly what Canada, the U.S., the U.K., the USSR and others did. And this most dangerous of threats to freedom, individual rights, liberties, democracy, sovereignty and peace—indeed, civilization itself—was defeated on the land, in the air and on and under the seas.

If one could fight and win against such odds, surely challenges such as education, housing, health care and infrastructure would only require serious investments of cash, people, programs and policy in order to function. This postwar can-do social engineering and social-build school of government was not about any policy debate of substance between left and right, certainly not in North America. In fact, Progressive Conservatives in Canada and Republicans in the United States frequently supported new and expensive measures in these areas. Often, they pushed Liberal or

Democratic administrations to do more and to do it more quickly. In the United Kingdom, Mr. Churchill, in opposition, supported the British Labour Party's national health care engagement. The broad sense of "we can solve this social challenge or that infrastructure need together" was robust and infectious.

In Canada, there was also a flood of new immigrants. This included a remarkable workforce of economic immigrants from England, Scotland, Wales and Ireland (Tory premier George Drew in Ontario set up offices in the United Kingdom to help encourage immigrants to come to Ontario). A similar workforce of economic migrants seeking a new life from eastern and western Europe, Poland, Ukraine, Yugoslavia and other areas came as well. All of this transpired at a time when fatigue with the war, memory of the economic deprivation before the war, unemployment and poverty for millions in the U.S., U.K. and Canada—including many veterans of WWI—formed the policies and ideas of the democratic socialists: the CCF and later the NDP in Canada, the left wing of the Democratic Party in the U.S. and the Labour Party in the U.K. So the pure competitiveness of the political dynamic saw Liberals and Conservatives in Canada tilt to the progressive side of the spectrum to compete with the socialists, or at least make them politically less singular and attractive. And largely, Liberals and Conservatives succeeded, as did their proposals for student financial aid, enhanced seniors' pensions, huge hospital and university construction programs, new primary and secondary school construction, serious public housing and programs for veterans, and one of the largest highway construction initiatives in the history of the world.

Many of these ideas first appeared in Colonel Drew's provincial Progressive Conservative campaign of 1943, which established a minority Tory government in Ontario against great odds, and which led to the Ontario Tories holding uninterrupted power for nearly half a century. Many of the most progressive and humane "nation and enterprise" concepts that would build Canada over

the coming decades would come from the provincial governments of Drew, Kennedy, Frost, Robarts and Davis. At the same
time, other provincial premiers such as Hugh John Flemming
in New Brunswick, Robert Stanfield in Nova Scotia and Duff
Roblin in Manitoba would advance similar progressive causes
around labour codes, public housing, post-secondary education, health care, seniors' pensions, employment insurance, rural
development, hydroelectric and nuclear expansion, microwave
networking and large-scale flood control. Louis St. Laurent, who
dominated federal politics in the early 1950s, before Diefenbaker,
was a very Laurier-like Liberal. He modernized and invested
heavily in national defence and launched great projects like the
St. Lawrence Seaway. In Québec provincial politics, Maurice
Duplessis governed as a nationalist conservative. Remember that
the roots of his Union Nationale Party were the Québec Conservatives and the left of the Québec Liberal Party. They had come
together to nationalize the private electricity-generating monop-
olies and create Hydro-Québec—hardly a right-wing agenda.
The entry of Newfoundland into Confederation in 1949 was an
act of nation building and one that genuinely affirmed an ambitious Canada. Here it is important to remember that Liberals in
power in Newfoundland and in Ottawa helped make the case for
"union" in many ways, and extending Canada's fiscal capacity and
social safety net to Newfoundland was a vital and integral part of
their argument. Liberals were, to their credit, the main promot-
ers of this new arrival in Confederation, a Newfoundland that had
recently been a stout participant in World War II and deserved
great credit for its service and sacrifice. (Tories, it pains me to say,
were mostly supportive of the "team up with the Americans" or
"stay independent" political schools in Newfoundland.)

In the West, populist movements were also on the ascendancy.
From roots in H.H. Stevens' Reconstructionist Party, the Social
Credit Party's "Bible Bill" Aberhart and the radio broadcasts of
Ernest C. Manning, who was another compelling prophet of the

Social Credit Party, held sway in Alberta and B.C. with their anti-establishment prairie populism and the "social gospel" of making a better world, which informed the politics of all prairie politicians. This was the case from the worst days of the Depression to well into the 1950s. While there was a healthy dose of anti-establishment opposition in the East, focused on bankers and others who appeared to be the source of all economic evil during the Depression, anti-establishment populism has always been more intense in the West. And this political turmoil melded with the ascendancy of the Co-operative Commonwealth Federation (CCF)—and its successor in the 1960s, the New Democratic Party (NDP)—who began, near the end of the 1950s, to reach out to broaden their base and advance on provincial government power, despite the rapidity with which their ideas and more attractive suggestions were being gobbled up by Liberals and Conservatives alike. (Interestingly, it would be Tory philosopher George Grant, Québec intellectual dilettante Pierre Trudeau and future president of Carleton University Michael Oliver who would work with others on the NDP's founding manifesto.)

The populist, anti-establishment stance of the West grew, in part, out of its immigration history. While western Canada had received waves of European immigrants, including those from eastern Europe and the British Isles for decades before and after the war, the largest single in-migration to the West ever was the huge American settlement of the 1890s. Americans had come to the region looking for affordable, high-quality grazing land. The frontier mindset of post-reconstruction America—of a society less deferential to authority, tradition and, for that matter, government itself—became deeply ingrained in the political ideology of the West, right, left and centre. And the Conservative populism that would finally emerge to take over the Tory legacy and make it a more compelling political offering would be that of an iconoclastic people's Conservative, John George Diefenbaker.

The changing Canada that postwar immigration, demographics and aspirations created was a challenge for the Progressive Conservatives. The postwar Liberal social policy consensus and can-do spirit did not immediately set Mackenzie King's expedience aside. John Bracken's modernization of the Progressive Conservative Party and his appeal as a Manitoba-based progressive did not serve the Canadian Conservative cause badly. But it was not enough to dilute the Liberal western roots that remained from Clear Grit support for reciprocity and Tory national policy preferences. Protectionism on trade and continuing Québec discomfort over the two pro-conscription Tory campaigns of 1914–18 and 1942–45, which Liberals like Mackenzie King were able to exploit mercilessly, helped Liberals retain their dominance politically. When John Bracken was succeeded in 1948 by Colonel Drew, prospects brightened. But Louis St. Laurent's general popularity, the remnants of anti-conscription sentiment and lingering anxiety over the prospect of having a prime minister so resolutely a champion of Ontario prevented Drew from taking the Tories to government and saw the Liberals glide back to victory in 1953.

Colonel Drew's relatively stiff demeanour, the geniality of "Uncle Louis" St. Laurent and the strong Liberal brand in Québec helped to sustain Liberal hegemony through the mid-1950s.

It was only when Conservatives broke out of the frame of the R.B. Bennett, Arthur Meighen, George Drew ("establishment men") hierarchy and went to someone so clearly not of that frame that the broader electorate responded. Diefenbaker also brought expansion beyond the party's largely British Isles–rooted, inter-generational base. In many sub-regions this base was large, but not dominant. The Liberals, however, through their "cost-plus" (albeit autocratic and clubby) approach to industry during the war, and through their "minister of everything," C.D. Howe, for some years thereafter, continued to shape a support base tied to the establishment. While significant Conservative business, financial, manufacturing and media interests were present and engaged, most of Canada's business elite, especially the continental business elite, were deeply pro-Liberal. Key organizations such as the *Toronto Star,* the *Montreal Star,* the *Winnipeg Free Press* and CBC all advanced the establishment cause. The dynamic was not much different from that of the pre–responsible government era of the late eighteenth and early nineteenth century with the Family Compact in Upper Canada and the Château Clique in Lower Canada, when established interests clustered around the governors and their councils. These unelected officials had the power to award licences, dole out regional business franchises, appoint suppliers, approve loans and grants, and even find jobs for children, neighbours and business associates.

In those pre-1970 years, the absence of even a scintilla of campaign financial transparency or of any codes of conflict regarding crossover between business and government really made industry and government subsidiaries of one another. Whether this scenario reflected a mutual hostage-taking or a mere intermingling of elites and reciprocal interests is a debate for another time and place. But, fortunately, the cooperative mindset around the war effort blended easily with the expansive growth of government in the postwar years to blur the difference between public and private. The success of the war effort and the isolation of the Iron Curtain countries created a rationale for impressive defence spending. The adoption of "CCF light" policies and politics by the left of the two major parties diminished and diluted any mainstream debate about the distinction between public and private prior to the mid-1950s. Canadian big business was, naturally, okay with that. There had been no long postwar recession in Canada; construction and investment were booming. And one other thing: the postwar desire for change and new beginnings, which saw Labour replace the Tories in the United Kingdom in 1945, had clearly *not* happened in Canada. And in the U.S. Mr. Truman became president, following Mr. Roosevelt's death before the end of the war, and his Missouri-style, homespun

Democratic approach was sufficiently different from FDR's rather imperious manner to also give America a sense of change and new beginnings.

In Canada, the dynamic of regional biases, the huge advantage of our first-past-the-post system—in which you need only the single, largest vote total as opposed to a majority of the votes cast in any one seat to win (making twenty-six percent a potential winning number in a four-candidate race)—and the fact that parties were consolidated by region, coalesced to keep Liberals in office and the business-government enterprise very much in place. (It was quite the opposite of the "nation and enterprise" balancing of different interests.) And, as standards of living were improving for most Canadians and as immigrants pouring in under Liberal governments were coming largely for the related economic opportunities, there was little to disturb the Liberal's perpetual government machine. It was a machine that bred a deeply Liberal public service, with the great men of Queen's University— O.D. Skelton, W.C. Clark and later J.J. Deutsch—being central to the process through the early and mid twentieth century. The overall notion that no public service or business leader would ever meet someone in power they did not like or agree with created a remarkably deferential and "courtier" mindset that continued into later decades, as has been so ably documented by leading academics like Donald Savoie of the University of Moncton, in *Governing from the Centre* and other works.

In the Macdonald, Borden and Meighen days, debates about important and divergent policy views—on railways, the navy, reciprocity, minority rights, the war effort, the imperial connection, federal-provincial roles and Depression-era economic policy—were commonplace, heated and of genuine import. They took place within cabinets, sometimes producing rifts (such as the one between H.H. Stevens and R.B. Bennett), and also within Parliament and the media. Back then, political parties had newspapers formally committed to their respective causes.

Most ministers and M.P.'s came to Parliament after having built their lives as farmers, teachers, lawyers or businesspeople, which afforded them a living independent of their parliamentary honorarium (which was tiny in those days). Many continued as local citizen and community earners, going to Ottawa only when necessary. Their real lives were in their ridings with their fellow citizens and neighbours. They were from rural B.C. or small-town Saskatchewan, from downtown Halifax or the fishing village of western PEI, and they represented the interests of their communities.

The war, Mackenzie King's "whatever seems to suit at the time" approach to public policy, a government by and for the civil service and the erosion of de facto provincial powers all conspired to remove much of the debate and challenge necessary to the government's consideration of large ideas, undertakings and initiatives. And after the 1935–57 era of uninterrupted Mackenzie King and St. Laurent liberalism, the civil service was unquestioningly Liberal. Ottawa was a place of Liberal ideas, postwar triumphalism and big business cooperation. It was not a place for big debates that mattered. Not until John Diefenbaker.

John Diefenbaker's sense of what it meant to be excluded from the charmed circle, of being outside the mainstream, of being primarily among the outs, reflected not only where he was from (first rural Ontario and then, in terms of his education, professional life and politics, rural Saskatchewan), but also his serial defeats for provincial, federal and party office, which preceded his final victory in 1956, for the party leadership. As his ultimate success came (after losing twice before, to Mr. Bracken in 1942 and Mr. Drew in 1948), it was clear that Mr. Diefenbaker would not be easily discouraged. Some mainstream liberal historians dismiss him as a hollow, flamboyant orator who happened to come along when Liberal judgement and political sensitivity flagged. (This school of historian always views a Tory victory as an aberration and, historically, this view has often become a compelling self-fulfilling prophecy for those in the media and civil service who profoundly wish it to be so.)

John Diefenbaker did not just "happen to be there" at the right time and place and get chosen as a result. John Diefenbaker confronted the Liberal supporters of St. Laurent and later Pearson about the central question they and other Canadians had not really asked during periods of great Liberal hegemony. His question was not "what should government do?" It was, more importantly, "for whom does government work?" (This was a question Mr. Harper would ask with great success in the 2004 and 2006 elections.) His real underlying question was the one asked by Tories when at their best: "who should government serve?" It was the principal question posed in their day by giants like John A. Macdonald, Robert Borden, R.B. Bennett and Arthur Meighen. And it is always the right Tory question. It is the question at the root of the "nation and enterprise" answer. But it was never before asked with the populist heat employed by Mr. Diefenbaker.

What he came upon in Ottawa was a smug establishment of businessmen, civil servants and all those who relied on government—Crown corporations; suppliers, financiers and others, including some media—for whom a mutually beneficial Liberal-established consortium served its internal constituents and connected benefactors very well. If you were part of that system, you prospered. If you were not, you did not. (Part of what attracted me, as a member of a working-class family, to Diefenbaker's conservatism was the sense that he was an outsider who welcomed other outsiders to the Conservative Party; his populism included all those liberals that soft corporatism left out.)

The famous pipeline debate of 1956–57, where Ottawa sought authority for a precise pipeline route and project, was about more than what route a west-east energy pipeline should take, or how that route should be approved. Increasingly, it was about how decisions were being made and who in Canada got a say in vital infrastructure choices. To be fair to Liberals, during the war and postwar eras making decisions by fiat was often the route that governments in the U.K., the U.S., Canada, Australia and elsewhere took to facilitate the war effort. The war was a time of heroic productivity; rubber, nylon, steel, aircraft and munitions all rolled off Canadian assembly lines because of superb government-industry cooperation. In Canada, the usual source of opposition (Québec notwithstanding)—the provinces—was relatively benign during the war and the immediate postwar years. But a head of steam was being built up, a sense of "we will decide" within the Liberal Party and the civil service, which the St. Laurent administration inherited and expanded and which was seriously exclusionary. There was a growing sense that the Liberal establishment had become restricted and deeply self-reverential.

In politics, when the government drifts beyond the parameters of relevance, becomes disconnected and loses a sense of common touch, the government is usually the last to "get it." Bad editorials or unhappy stories in the media are dismissed by the government as biased. Classically, prime ministers and ministers complain that the "communications people" aren't "doing it right." Actually, the problem is rarely any of these, and usually it takes a defeat or near defeat for a governing party to figure that out. Often, the Ottawa bubble of agreeable civil servants and obsequious lobbyists does not generate push-back. M.P.'s desperate for cabinet promotion, or ministers desperate to stay in cabinet, can insulate governments and prime ministers from reality on the ground. And in the 1950s, polling was in its very early and primitive stages and the media was far less investigative than they are today. The crucible of debate was parliament and, on occasion, the provincial-federal dynamic would show its head.

The Diefenbaker victory, which created a surprise minority government in 1957, and the relentless parliamentary debate on the pipeline that preceded it, are facts of public history and electoral achievement. Essentially, Diefenbaker and the Tories were able to make the promotion of nationalism and the combatting of arrogance key themes of their victory. The 1958 Tory landslide that followed was Canada's response to a confidence vote proposed by Liberal leader, Lester Pearson. He felt, as all Liberals did, that the minority Diefenbaker government should simply give the keys back to the Liberals, who governed as a matter of right. It was an opportunity that allowed Canadians to vote, in huge numbers, for change.

In this massive Tory victory, which included the support of a whole new generation of voters—most of whom had either never voted before or had never voted Tory—we find the seeds of the central populist challenges of today's "nation and enterprise" Canadian conservatism. The broad and compelling nature of Diefenbaker's 1958 majority—it was built in part by changing the perception of who the main shareholder and beneficiary of government should be—unleashed economic and social programs that deepened the nation and enterprise focus of prior conservatives and reflected the new Canada. It was the broadest mandate ever given to a new administration in Canadian history.

So, the specifics of the Diefenbaker government initiatives should surprise few when they are viewed in the context of the stakeholders who brought about his rise into power: the substantial increase in pensioners' and veterans' allowances; the formulation of a Canadian Bill of Rights; the creation of the Agricultural Rehabilitation and Development Act (ARDA); the arrangement of massive sales of prairie wheat to eastern Europe and China; and the opening of de facto trade relations with the People's Republic of China without regard to U.S. angst. All of these initiatives reflected a populist "nation and enterprise" approach. There was also the creation of the Board of Broadcast Governors, distinct from the CBC, allowing the opportunity for network competition; the expansion of the Wheat Board; the Hall Commission on health care, which essentially translated Tommy Douglas's health insurance in Saskatchewan into a nationally endorsed universal health care mandate for Lester Pearson to inherit in 1963 and take to completion; and the creation of the National Productivity Council to advance trade efficiency. Diefenbaker, along with India's Jawaharlal Nehru, led the plan to facilitate apartheid South Africa withdrawing from the Commonwealth. He appointed the first female minister of the federal Crown (ever!); initiated a focus on levels and purposes of foreign investment in terms of reporting and analysis; provided serious investment for the North, including the development of Frobisher Bay in what was then the Northwest Territories; and created the Ottawa Valley line energy policy, forcing all consumers living west of the Ottawa Valley in Ontario to purchase their oil (albeit more expensively) from Alberta. Mandated by a National Energy Board analysis and other recommendations, this last policy did more than any other to provide fresh cash flow, investment incentives and exploration cash for Alberta's traditional oil basin. (Québec and Atlantic Canada could buy substantially cheaper energy supplies from the Middle East and Venezuela.) He began the building of the Trans-Canada Highway, built the South Saskatchewan Dam, appointed the first aboriginal Canadian to the Senate and gave First Nations members the vote for the first time in Canadian history.

These populist, progressive and pan-Canadian initiatives showed Mr. Diefenbaker at his best. And they added a "nation and enterprise" thrust to the Toryism his administration had inherited from Colonel Drew. His focus also became the foundation for the kind of Progressive Conservatism of later Tory first ministers including Stanfield in Nova Scotia, Shaw in PEI, Frost and Robarts in Ontario, Roblin in Manitoba and former Conservative Bill Bennett Sr. in B.C. This focus would continue as well with the Hatfield, Peckford, Buchanan, Davis, Lougheed and Bennett Jr. administrations that would follow in New Brunswick, Newfoundland, Nova Scotia, Ontario, Alberta and B.C. in the 1970s, long after Mr. Diefenbaker's administration was defeated in 1963.

The role of provincial conservative forces—Progressive Conservatives in the Atlantic, Manitoba and Ontario, and Union

Nationale forces in Québec—should never be underestimated. The hard, day-to-day realities of education, roads, health care, municipalities and the rest largely defy narrow ideological prescription. So when Conservatives from provincial government move into the federal Conservative Party, or when provincial Conservative organizations are vital to federal election planning and success, the pragmatism of local conservatism not always, but often, strengthens the practical and GROUNDED nature of "nation and enterprise."

Ontario's approach to road construction, education expansion, health care and attracting skilled immigrants in the 1950s and 1960s; Liberal Québec's movement towards *maître chez nous* in the pre-1962 period; and the Union Nationale's victory in 1966 (defending the crucifix in the classroom) and subsequent early 1970's defeat would all leave that imprint on Conservative challenges and priorities. This mix of initiatives, competent people, causes and commitments at the provincial level within Conservative administrations, would be helpful in the federal arena in terms of people and talent but also, on occasion, problematic in terms of conflict and differing agendas.

Diefenbaker's defeat in 1963, after a minority win in 1962, reflected the Liberal capacity to capitalize on difficult economic times and the coming apart of the Diefenbaker cabinet over the Bomarc missile issue. It was after this crisis that George Grant's infamous treatise *Lament for a Nation* was published, grieving the end of Canada as a separate country and the ultimate victory of what Dwight D. Eisenhower called the "military-industrial complex." Grant, a respected philosopher and professor, evoked a sense of Diefenbaker as a heroic clarion for Canadian sovereignty and the British connection who was beaten electorally by U.S. industrial, political and military interests—headed in Canada by Lester B. Pearson, the Liberal leader.

Grant, who was a magnificent writer and polemicist, made a compelling but flawed case. (As a teenager, I consumed his view and embraced it without an ounce of doubt, as young people often do.) It cast Diefenbaker as a lonely hero defending peace, non-proliferation and sovereignty. It cast the Americans as so driven by modernity, technology and the east-west Cold War psychology as to be almost beyond reason. This was and is, of course, a wild overstatement about both Diefenbaker and the Americans.

The Americans thought they had an agreement under the provisions of joint air defence that anti-bomber missiles at La Macaza, Québec, and North Bay, Ontario, would have the requisite nuclear warheads. The Diefenbaker government was divided on the issue. Some ministers believed the missile threat replacing the bomber threat obviated the anti-bomber Bomarcs. Others believed that a promise made should be a promise kept. Diefenbaker dithered, his cabinet became divided, and some members, including defence minister Harkness and transport minister Hees, resigned. The result was that the Liberals won an election in the face of Tory division. That some American media (*Newsweek* magazine) and others may have wished for his defeat is neither here nor there. What Grant, who was not a historian or political scientist, simply missed is that there is no heroism or nobility in division or incompetence.

Mr. Diefenbaker brought his own intellectual and emotional focus to the "what kind of Canada in what kind of world" challenge. Tory global engagement and Diefenbaker's nuclear disarmament bias and suspicions of a too-powerful United States were and remain profoundly positive. Some traits, like the lack of facility with the dynamics of Québec politics (thereby failing the "what kind of Canada" test) and an erosion of Sir John A.'s critical belief in a Québec-Canada partnership through the Tory party, continued to plague and dilute. It was Diefenbaker's political lieutenant in Manitoba, M.P. Gordon Churchill, who argued that one could win Canada without winning Québec. In the same way that Mackenzie King's decades of politics without principle and world view that was, except when pushed by events, devoid of engagement with or sense of obligation to Empire or international responsibility, continue in some ways to impact Liberal dynamics and policy struggle, so too would Mr. Diefenbaker's seven years come to profoundly dictate, for decades to come, both Conservative struggles and opportunities.

John Diefenbaker's secretary of state for external affairs, Howard Green, had cut new and important ground on disarmament within Conservative and Canadian foreign policy. This did not, however, make up for the relative incompetence of Mr. Diefenbaker in holding his cabinet together on the nuclear warhead (Bomarc) issue or during the Cuban missile crisis when the installation by the USSR of missiles on Cuban soil was deemed a threat to North America—and when Mr. Diefenbaker declined to put Canada on "alert" status. And despite Joe Clark's short time in office as prime minister (June 1979 to February 1980), his failure of judgement on the embassy in Jerusalem caper should not be allowed to dull the leadership he showed in bringing the Vietnamese boat people to Canada through the efforts of his immigration minister, Ron Atkey, and his foreign affairs minister, Flora MacDonald. This initiative was courageous, humane and the right thing to do, for those refugees and for Canada. And the Canadian government's clandestine hiding of and escape facilitation for six U.S. Embassy hostages threatened by Iranian extremist mobs, with Canadian ambassador Ken Taylor playing a central role, reminded the world that Canadians knew who their friends were and stood by them.

Prime Minister John Diefenbaker's down-to-earth connection with the people struck a nerve for a time with Canadians. It was 1946, in the House of Commons, when he first stated loudly: "I believe the time has come for a declaration of liberties to be made by this parliament. Magna Charta is part of our birthright. Habeas corpus, the bill of rights, the petition of right, all are part of our traditions . . . freedom from capricious arrest and freedoms under the rule of law, should be made part and parcel of the law of the country." Tom Axworthy, Pierre Trudeau's principal secretary during the constitutional negotiations that led to our Charter of Rights and Freedoms, once wrote: "In 1982, the Constitution was finally amended and the Charter came into force. But this would never have happened if John Diefenbaker had not lit the way with his life-long dedication to human rights." And upon Diefenbaker's death in 1979, it was one of his successors who summed up the prairie populist's greatest achievement. "I was struck," Pierre Trudeau said, "by his vigorous defence of human rights and individual liberties. The Bill of Rights remains a monument to him."

Diefenbaker's moment was one of nationalism tinged by a populist distrust of those within the charmed circle of bureaucratic power and self-perpetuating wealth. And to some extent, however annoying this may be to the powers of Bay Street, Rue Saint-Jacques, Howe Street or the Petroleum Club, that remnant of popular distrust continues still. Conservatives in government often seem more Main Street than Bay Street; more driven by populist aspiration than public-service inside advice. This is, of course, a two-edged sword, depending on the times and the circumstances. And while his successor as leader, the Honourable Robert L. Stanfield, formerly the urbane and successful premier of Nova Scotia, would never become prime minister, he would add a new level, an important one, to the "nation and enterprise" policy framework, one that underlined his core civility and compassion.

8

STANFIELD, CLARK
AND MULRONEY

The Long Road to 1984

etween 1967 and 1984, the balance that served Tories well
in the past would be, on occasion, quite elusive. But it
would not disappear altogether. In fact, the mix of Stanfield's decency and urbanity, Clark's sincerity on Québec and the
emergence of a party united behind Mulroney, as had not been
the case under Stanfield or Clark, would preserve the right balance, despite early setbacks and defeats.

Robert Lorne Stanfield was in many ways the opposite of
Diefenbaker. Of wealthy birth, editor of the *Harvard Law Review*
and a dollar-a-year employee of the Wartime Prices and Trade
Board, Stanfield was suspicious of high-blown rhetoric and overblown visionary excess. His balance, moderation and independence from politics, with politics for him being neither a way to
live nor a way to make a living, made him more temperate and
dispassionate and remarkably less self-obsessed than Diefenbaker.
His conservatism was classically of an incremental and modest
nature. He tolerated no excessiveness in either government or
ideology.

Stanfield knew Canada's business elite personally and was neither intimidated nor overly impressed by them. He had revived Tory fortunes in Nova Scotia after a long drought through his steady-minded pragmatism, inclusive politics and coherent and frugal approach to public administration. After winning the Tory leadership federally in 1967, his commitment to rebuilding the party with and within Québec reflected his sense of realism and fairness. He learned French from a zero base in his mid-fifties and surrounded himself with bright, experienced aids and staff, including Graham Scott, Lowell Murray, Rod McQueen, Bill Grogan, Marjory LeBreton, Joe Clark, Françoise Morissette, Finlay MacDonald, Murray Coolican, Tom Sloan, Richard Le Lay and John Rolf. These people brought journalistic, legal, economic, political or communications expertise to their tasks. To speak figuratively, it's as if Stanfield sensed that the excesses of Diefenbaker had broken eggs without ever making an omelet, and on everything from Canada-U.S. relations to Québec, from the Bomarc missile problem to the early run on the dollar, there was much to be done.

It is important to remember that Stanfield was as much about sustained and even-handed balance in the affairs of government as Diefenbaker was not. A sense of balance and calm as one sorts through issues and challenges is an essential ingredient of governing. Lurching back and forth or launching new initiatives without consultation does not advance the national interest as much as it devalues the modest and positive role government can and should play in society. Stanfield's conservatism was characterized by its equilibrium, which is far more important than narrow ideologies of the right or the left. These elements of equilibrium were reflected in his approach to federal-provincial relations, economic policies, French-English relations and Canadian foreign policy.

Stanfield visited China in his official capacity as Leader of the Opposition long before Mr. Trudeau recognized the People's

Republic. And when he did so, he was able to critique the Chinese for their criticism of Western involvement in Vietnam. He pointed out to the Chinese that their complicity in the prolonged struggle was unhelpful; later he admonished the Americans on the same issue when he visited Henry Kissinger in Washington. His approach to Québec was to recognize that two peoples, English- and French-speaking, had formed a partnership when Confederation was cobbled together in the 1860s and that those two "nations" were at the foundation of Canada.

In this way, Stanfield's conservatism and Conservatism not only reflected provincial-federal balance but also the central role of Québec in the ongoing Tory legacy and mission. This harkens back to the Lord Elgin, Sir John A. Macdonald, George-Étienne Cartier frame. And beyond this sense of partnership between French- and English-speaking Canada, Robert Stanfield also had a strong and abiding interest in the cooperative federalism envisioned by the original constitution. In this way, he was opposed to the "unlimited" federal spending power approach of Liberals like Trudeau. And on one level, the two problems of undue federal centralization and the anti-Québec notion of special status intersected. He worried that the Trudeau Liberals feasted on crises in Québec and actually helped to generate them with their dismissive and inflammatory approach to legitimate Québec nationalism. Québec nationalism, in its federalist or confederalist form, is not seen as negative by Canadian conservatives.

For most conservatives, federalism is not a hierarchical structure with Ottawa at the pinnacle and the provinces at the bottom, treated either as junior partners or as wholly owned subsidiaries. Being a Tory, Stanfield tried to erase that imbalance. In neither section of the British North America Act is there a reference to a division between important or less important powers. Section 91 of the BNA lays out federal powers. Section 92 lays out provincial powers. And, in reality, for the vast majority of Canadians, the Section 92 powers and responsibilities of the provinces—roads, civil law, education, administration of justice, local policing, health care, natural resources—are far more important on a day-to-day basis than the Section 91 federal powers, such as foreign and monetary policy, or weights and measures.

Stanfield's economic policies were profoundly centrist, but in the 1972 election he tilted to the "progressive," or "nation," side of the traditional conservative position. In his Hamilton speech in the final weeks of the October campaign, he called for a Canada "where the accident of where and to whom one was born would not limit one's prospects or future." A few years earlier, at a Tory policy conference, the idea of a Canadian basic income floor for all had been advanced. While in opposition, during the ensuing 1972–74 Liberal minority government, Stanfield railed against an income tax system that made the government into profiteers at the expense of taxpayers during times of inflation—and how that same inflationary effect reduced the value of fixed income to pensioners. He advocated indexing pensions to the rate of inflation and de-indexing taxes—a policy John Turner, as finance minister to Mr. Trudeau, actually accepted and implemented in its early form.

This same Stanfield concern about the impact of inflation on middle-income earners, low-income earners and seniors led to the price-and-wage-freeze proposal (a ninety-day freeze to break the inflation cycle) of the 1974 election campaign. It (and Tory disagreement about it) helped Mr. Trudeau win his 1974 majority. Trudeau himself opposed and ridiculed the Stanfield proposal. At the heart of the matter was Stanfield's determination to confront forces like inflation, which enriched the tax coffers of all governments while oppressing the most economically defenceless. For a Tory to stake his career on that kind of social justice was a profound statement of the "nation and enterprise" premise at the core of Canadian conservatism. That Stanfield would rather lose an election than abandon this principle is a seminal indicator of the difference between Canadian and American conservatism.

That Trudeau essentially implemented a form of price-and-wage-freeze through the Anti-Inflation Board less than twenty-four months later no doubt contributed to the cynicism about Liberals that helped Joe Clark win his minority victory in 1979.

What Stanfield also achieved was an urbanization of the party, to the extent that seats in big cities could be won by compelling figures who had earned a certain degree of renown and respect before their political days as Tory candidates. And because his policies were very much of the balanced variety, academics and young people were attracted to the party under his leadership. This was no mean feat in the face of the charisma juggernaut that Trudeau and the Liberals used effectively at every turn. Stanfield may not have been, in his thoughtful and prudent demeanour, a great "television age" communicator, but he was a man of ideas and reflections. And he expanded and developed the party through his special sense of equilibrium in ways that would benefit subsequent Tory leaders.

Bob Stanfield survived and brought the party through the Trudeau age as the saviour of the national fraud that was the War Measures Act. That FLQ cells had engaged in violent kidnapping or murder was not at issue. That Pierre Trudeau saw his popularity soar to remarkable heights (reducing the Tories at one point to sixteen percent) is understandable. The promise that the Liberals had made quietly, beneath all the diving-board gigs of their candidate in the 1968 campaign, was that Trudeau was a French Canadian who would "handle" Québec. There were many ways the government could have proceeded in October of 1970 that did not require the suspension of all civil liberties, as the proclamation of the War Measures Act did, or that did not require the arrest in the middle of the night of hundreds of French Canadians, not one of whom was ever charged. (Pierre Marc Johnson, then a student, but a future premier of Québec, minister of justice and PQ leader, was arrested five times in several days.) Instituting short-term martial law, using the sections of the Criminal Code under sedition or even the Coroners Act, which afforded wide latitude to the Crown, would all have been better instruments. But Trudeau took the mallet approach and the media went along with nary a question, save for George Bain at the *Globe and Mail*, Tim Rafe of the CBC and Peter Reilly of CTV. The Tory rank and file was not for questioning the federal government's authority except for a small band clustered around David MacDonald, the M.P. for Egmont, PEI. Among others, this group included Wally Fox-Decent in Winnipeg; Nate Nurgitz, then vice-president of the Tory Party; Tom Hockin in Toronto; Roy McMurtry, Dalton Camp, Norman Atkins, Gordon Fairweather in New Brunswick; John Meisel of Queen's University in Kingston; and Flora Mac-Donald in Kingston. Along with David MacDonald, Flora Mac-Donald had been a moving force in organizing a protest booklet called *Strong and Free—A Response to the War Measures Act,* with essays attacking the War Measures Act directly. Even H.H. Stevens from Vancouver and Bill Macadam, then on Stanfield's staff, joined the small group of balance-seeking Tories. George Grant in Hamilton, Roger Graham in Kingston and John Carter in St. John's, Newfoundland, had supported this small effort. And to their credit, some Liberals, such as Lloyd Axworthy in Winnipeg and Brian Flemming in Halifax, joined to help publish the booklet. But they (and myself as a student of twenty, then on David Mac-Donald's staff) were vastly outnumbered within the Progressive Conservative Party and the country as a whole. Had Mr. Trudeau brought in an amendment for pretrial sentencing, I suspect it not only would have passed, but been defended by long memoranda from our distinguished civil service and leading editorialists.

But the fact that Mr. Trudeau was nearly defeated a year later, in 1972, at the hands of Mr. Stanfield, speaks volumes to how assiduously Mr. Stanfield had worked to rebuild and reshape the Tory party. He gave the government the benefit of the doubt during the War Measures Act period, but he peppered them with daily questions, in essence doing what opposition leaders have a duty to do during a crisis. Later, long into his retirement, he very much regretted not defending civil liberties more intensely and not causing Mr. Trudeau more grief during this period and after. The Liberals never produced any proof of the "apprehended insurrection" they proclaimed in the middle of the night on October 16, 1970. But on election night, the unbeatable and unassailable Mr. Trudeau came, in two ridings, within two seats and seven votes of being defeated by the Stanfield Tories. Bob Stanfield's decency, his competence as a campaigner and his coherent policy had put the party to the left of Trudeau on social issues and to the right of Trudeau on fiscal and defence issues. In the end, he had almost carried the day. A remarkable feat.

Trudeau persevered with the support of the David Lewis New Democrats and moved to the left, easily winning a 1974 rematch by galvanizing unions and voters against the price-and-wage-freeze of the Conservatives—which he promptly imposed after the election, making Mr. Clark's victory in 1979 far more likely.

While the short Clark interruption, from June 1979 to February 1980, would not be known for any deep economic achievement, Clark's basic decency and political tilt to the Red Tory side of the debate kept the "nation and enterprise" part of the Tory vision very much alive. In terms of economics, his ill-fated mortgage interest deductibility proposal and his budget proposal to raise the excise tax on gasoline eighteen cents per gallon were both flawed. The former proposal was politically sensitive but fiscally imprudent and the latter fiscally responsible but politically insensitive. But the failure that caught him and, in the end, destroyed his electoral prospects in the 1980 election was his inability to find the "nation and enterprise" balance between Ontario's consuming role on the energy front and Alberta's role as a pre-eminent oil producer. That both governments were led by largely centrist premiers who were themselves Tory did not help. Neither Mr. Davis nor Mr. Lougheed was deeply ideological. Loads of public funds had gone into creating TV Ontario, the Urban Transit Development Corporation, the Ontario Development Corporation, and the Ontario Energy Corporation in Davis's Ontario. And Lougheed had no difficulty using taxpayer funds to purchase Pacific Western Airlines or allowing the Alberta Heritage Fund to become a serious investor in largely fixed-income instruments across Canada.

But Clark's inability to find the common ground and show national leadership sent Ontario voters to Mr. Trudeau in droves in 1980, opening the way to the National Energy Program, which, under Trudeau, fiscally attacked the Section 92 natural resources rights of the provinces while establishing a "fill the coffers" tax strategy for the federal fiscal framework. This, in turn, created the opportunity for Mulroney to win in 1984, with a firm commitment to respect provincial resources and jurisdiction. In other words, history reveals that incompetence at the "nation and enterprise" task by the Tories inevitably leads to Liberal victory and excess—which, in turn, defines the next Tory "nation and enterprise" mission as one of rebalancing.

Mr. Mulroney's victory at the Tory leadership convention in 1983 was, in a sense, a decision of the party to reconnect with the roots and soil of the Tory party of Sir John A. Macdonald and George-Étienne Cartier. The partnership with French Canada would become central once again. The Sir John A. approach to assembling a broad coalition from many disparate pieces—a coalition that would be purpose-driven—would re-emerge. The Conservative Party as a reflection of the national will, as opposed to an artificial imposition upon that will, would become the dominant force for a decade. A nation-building party that had a long view and a courageous intention would be offered to the public.

Mulroney waged a masterful campaign for the leadership. Clark, having received a remarkable two-thirds endorsement at the party's annual meeting in Winnipeg months earlier, used that endorsement as an excuse to precipitate a convention he could not win. The fact that former ministers of his, including John Crosbie and Mike Wilson, announced their own leadership plans made it clear how difficult his position was. Bill Davis came very close to entering the race but eventually decided against it, although there had been substantial national pressure and specific representation from a Québec delegation for him to do so. His decision opened up many key delegates in Ontario and Québec to Mulroney, whose momentum was obvious as soon as the convention was announced. Even in a process in which Clark started with sixty-six percent of the delegates, he had been overcome by unnecessary hubris when Davis's potential candidacy was first advanced. He quickly dismissed it as "regional." Mulroney, on the other hand, welcomed it as a "national voice for a strong Canada." When Davis eventually declined, his supporters did not forget where civility had emerged and where condescension had resided.

Within seconds of winning, Mulroney began the process of assembling a truly national team by calling on Erik Nielson (the M.P. for the Yukon), a long time Diefenbaker posse member and Clark caucus supporter, to become House Leader. Within hours of his convention win he also quickly reached out to the organizers of the Big Blue Machine by hosting them for brunch at the Château Laurier. The organization was a group of pollsters, volunteers, organizers and policy and logistics people who had served Mr. Stanfield in 1972, and helped elect Bill Davis in 1971, 1975, 1977 and 1981. (Many of the Big Blue Machine people had been purposefully left out of Clark's 1979 campaign efforts.) But as Mulroney proceeded to assemble a team of candidates and organizers that reflected different factions in the party and different voices across the country, the Liberals decided to do to him what they had twice done successfully to Stanfield. They decided to try and trip him up on language rights by helping to precipitate a crisis. And it would be their most ill-fated mistake.

During the 1968–74 minority period, Liberals twice introduced motions affirming the Official Languages Act, long after the act itself had been passed. This was a way of deepening their support among francophone voters and causing the Conservatives difficulty. Trudeau and Diefenbaker got along well. Diefenbaker could be counted upon to sew disunity on this issue, which he obligingly did on more than one occasion, leading seventeen Tories to vote against their own leader (Mr. Stanfield), and allowing Liberals to crow once again about their rightful role as minority French-language protectors. In a sense, the Liberals, flush with the Big Red Machine dominance of Québec federal politics, sought always to sever the Tories from their Macdonald-Cartier roots, knowing that to do so was to potentially reduce them to one third of Parliament's seats.

Liberals intended to do to Mulroney what they had done to Stanfield. Here was this fluently bilingual son of an electrician from Québec's North Shore purporting to give the Tory Party a foothold of hope among francophone voters. As the Liberals manoeuvred with the same old bear trap in the month leading up to the 1984 election, they miscalculated in two ways. They had failed to account for the burden that would be lifted from the Tory caucus in this third round by the fact that Mr. Diefenbaker had passed away years earlier during the Clark administration. They also underestimated Mulroney's visceral engagement on this issue—the extent to which he had internalized, at a young age, the French-English alliance and its central role in the success of Confederation, and, indeed, the country. They had either forgotten or, in that Liberal-centric way, never noticed that Brian Mulroney, as a young law student at Laval University in 1958, had organized a conference on the future of Canada focusing specifically on the French-English dynamic. Others involved in its organization included Lucien Bouchard and Michael Meighen (also law students), Bernard Roy and Paul-Arthur Gendron. The conference attracted law students from across the country. Ironically, half a century later, in 2008, Senator Meighen's son Hugh, a law student at McGill and great-grandson of Arthur Meighen, combined with Adam Daifallah, a law student at Laval and frequent centre-right conservative columnist and advocate, to organize a similar event. From the Québec Act of 1774 to today's young Tory law students, the French-English partnership is seen as essential.

Rather than avoiding or diluting the debate, Mulroney embraced it. He went to Manitoba, where resistance to official bilingualism was still a key element of conservative angst, and, at a large and challenging public meeting, nailed his colours and those of the Progressive Conservative Party of Canada to the official bilingualism pole. In so doing, Mulroney established his bona fides in every francophone riding in Canada. He established a common bond with Conservatives like Bill Davis, who, as minister of education and premier of Ontario, built what was then the world's largest non-denominational French-language school system outside France. He forged a common bond with Richard Hatfield, the Tory premier of New Brunswick who had continued the remarkable work of Liberal Louis Robichaud in making New Brunswick the only officially bilingual province in the country. He did the same with Premier Lougheed, who had waited in a long line with other Alberta parents to enrol his own children in French immersion schools. He created a common bond with the Stanfield wing of the party, which had seen their leader fight on the right side of this issue against both the cynicism of the Liberals and the ego-driven, divisive self-reverence of Diefenbaker. And, of course, this set him apart in the Québec media and among nationalists in Québec as someone who, whatever else he may stand for, would not be small-minded on the issue of minority language rights for francophones throughout the country. In a sense, while other Liberal miscalculations—TV debate missteps and patronage excesses—would make Mulroney's well-crafted campaign and personal intensity unstoppable in English Canada, this cynical Liberal attempt at a pre-election ambush gave Mulroney his greatest opportunity.

And while history tells us how well he seized it and turned it to the Progressive Conservative Party's immense benefit, the truth is that he faced mixed advice at the time. The senior caucus leader figure from Manitoba was not at the fateful public meeting in Manitoba. Conservative provincial leadership in that province was less than enthusiastic on the bilingualism front. And some in Ottawa counselled caution—a euphemism for not letting oneself get carried away by principle. Mulroney cut through all this and showed the heart and courage that would contribute to him winning the largest Tory majority in recorded electoral history. And that courage would set the tone for his administration, in the sense that large structural issues facing Canada would not be set aside for the sake of simply muddling through. He would confront the excesses that the essentially uninterrupted Liberal government from 1963 to 1984 had imposed on Canada. He would reconsider centralist and excessively statist policies that cried out for rebalancing, such as the National Energy Program imposed by Trudeau. He campaigned openly on this, as well as on traditional Tory themes of lower taxes, a stronger national defence system and more competent and engaged relationships with our allies, including the United States. He campaigned from the centre of the Tory spectrum, or just centre-right of the mainstream spectrum. His was a campaign that harnessed the disaffection with Trudeau and the seeming discomfort in office of Mr. Turner, despite Turner's early surge in the polls. Mulroney was aided by a Liberal campaign that seemed never to come together and that eventually retreated to a hard-left nationalist position (always the Liberals' primary redoubt), one that contradicted their prior pro-business and pro-American stance.

The National Energy Program was dismantled by Mulroney and replaced with a series of regional energy accords that underlined provincial mineral and resource ownership. His new system of accords eliminated the confiscatory and market-distorting regulations and taxes that the Trudeau administration had imposed. It actually respected the terms of the British North America Act. Pat Carney, the bright and strong-willed economist from Vancouver, was the minister of energy, mines and resources in charge of this engagement, ably assisted by her chief of staff, Harry Near, who himself had done superb work as operations director of the successful 1984 campaign, and deputy minister Paul Tellier, who was known for taking on tough jobs for Liberal governments and doing them well (like the internal group to address "new challenges to national unity" of 1977). Those accords helped cement the fact that the Conservatives as a party, unlike the Liberals, actually believed in Sections 91 and 92 of the British North America Act. They also believed that there actually was a constitution and that there were civil liberties in Canada before the Charter of Rights and Freedoms of a few years earlier. Mulroney reconnected the party and the government with his respect for regions, provincial rights and local identities, a respect which had been Macdonald's strength and Elgin's legacy. He exposed the Durham-Trudeau Liberal philosophy of "Canada by centralist design," and defeated it clearly and effectively.

The party unity that Mulroney championed after becoming leader would serve him well as he dealt with large issues such as Free Trade, constitutional reconciliation, post-1988 GST tax reform, NAFTA and the Meech and Charlottetown accords. But party unity could not insulate him from the recession in the early 1990s, anti-GST anger, post-Charlottetown fatigue and a loosening of his coalition in Québec. I have written extensively about the dynamics and dimensions of the fracture and rebirth of the Conservative spectrum and party between 1992 and 2003 in two other books, *No Surrender* and *The Long Road Back*. But what was relevant to Canadian Conservatism and conservatism bears underlining here.

Mr. Mulroney's base of policy development—the energy accords and the various negotiations concerning the Meech Lake

Accord, which almost brought Québec back into the constitution as a full signatory—were all positions on which he campaigned and on which he received encouragement from all the provinces to advance. And that coherence was part of the economic and political strategy that made the great leap to Free Trade negotiations with the Americans possible. This was the ultimate political and policy initiative for "nation and enterprise" conservatism.

At a premiers' meeting in the summer of 1986, chaired by Don Getty of Alberta, those in attendance agreed that, as the Parti Québécois had been defeated by the federalist Liberal Robert Bourassa in Québec, it was now time to have a Québec round and clear the "deep hole" of Québec never having signed the 1982 constitutional agreement that had repatriated the Constitution from Westminster and amended the Charter of Rights and Freedoms. They had seen the reality of a popular Lévesque sovereignist government, aided by Trudeau intransigence, and knew that the election of a federalist nationalist Liberal like Bourassa was an opportunity one could ill afford to miss on the constitutional front. Leaving Québec permanently out of the constitution could only mean trouble ahead. The costs of doing so could well have been far too high. Essentially reasonable premiers were joined by partisans on the other side, including Jean Chrétien and Trudeau's former clerk of the cabinet, Senator Michael Pitfield, who urged Ottawa to begin a Québec round as soon as possible. And when the negotiation proceeded, not without controversy or difficulty, it was a serious step forward for Confederation. The Trudeau faction in the country and in the Liberal Party, with many supporters in the media, could not accept the extent to which the original spirit of Confederation had been enshrined in Meech Lake—in terms of the balance between Sections 91 and 92 (federal and provincial powers). They bristled especially at the notion that Ottawa's previously unilateral power to appoint the entire Supreme Court and the entire Upper House would be bracketed by an agreement that formalized both consultation and provincial say, essentially opening the door to a democratic Senate. Liberals then and now have been largely untroubled by the fact that we are the lone federation in the world whose constitutional court and Upper House only has appointees from the central government. The notion of shared appointments to government bodies, where both sides are respected, is an important one—one that Liberals who are more centralist do not like. This runs to the core of the confederal balance—the Mulroney approach was to broaden it in a way that reflected the intention of the founding confederal negotiators, circa 1864–67—and had been left unaddressed during the 1981–83 negotiations around the Charter of Rights and Freedoms and repatriation.

One did not have to be a radical provincial rights advocate to understand that provincial autonomy, established in 1867 and at the very heart of Confederation itself, would be diluted by the judicialization of rights and freedoms with a federal Charter of Rights ultimately arbitrated by a federally appointed Supreme Court. For that arbitration and resolution process to be limited to a court, appointed by solely the federal side, compounds the problem. Canada is the only real federation that appoints its Supreme Court with no formal provincial input. It was that very problem that necessitated the "notwithstanding clause" of the Charter of Rights, which underlined the right of any province or Ottawa to enact legislation "notwithstanding the Charter of Rights and Freedoms" for a limited duration of five years. This was a small way of protecting provincial jurisdiction and the parliamentary sovereignty of provincial legislatures and Parliament from the full monty of American-style judicialization.

When the notwithstanding clause was adopted in 1982, none of the provinces saw it as falling into immediate disrepute. Some might have held the view that the provinces were a necessary evil, not a strength—not an engine for managing and embracing diversity, social experimentation, and developing local best practices of benefit to all. At their core, many centre-left Liberals and New Democrats would delight in a large central government with wide-ranging powers. Whatever benefits such an arrangement might engender (and to be fair, there might be some), that is not Canada and that is not the Conservative or conservative view of the rational balance of powers that a large geography, small population country like Canada needs. Mulroney's approach ran right back to the historic alliance between the Tories and *les bleus,* right back to Maurice Duplessis's *coopération toujours, assimilation jamais* and embraced the careful balances that leaders like Bob Stanfield had fought for in both provincial and federal office. This Tory-Liberal discrepancy concerning the provinces is directly connected to the differences between British universal liberalism à la Lord Durham and the more conventional and respectful of identities approach of British Tory Lord Elgin.

In the sweep of the Trudeau centralist assault on Meech Lake (not unrelated to Mulroney having achieved an agreement with all the provinces, and Québec, which Trudeau had been unable to accomplish), otherwise decent and thoughtful premiers like Frank McKenna in New Brunswick, Gary Filmon in Manitoba and Clyde Wells in Newfoundland began unwinding the Meech Lake Accord (either through acts of commission or omission and often, but not always, in the best of faith) in a way that would contribute to the 1995 Québec referendum, a near-death experience shared by the entire country. In the case of McKenna, who held every seat in the New Brunswick legislature, his position was hard to fathom. In Filmon's case, as he held a minority government in a legislature where Sharon Carstairs, the Liberal leader, held a balance of power and supported the Trudeau-Chrétien-Wells view, the weakness of his stance was at least explainable, if not justifiable. As this dynamic played out, Mulroney also faced the negotiations on Free Trade, a window of opportunity occasioned by the Reagan-Mulroney relationship of trust and, on the negative side, increasing protectionism in the American Congress.

The demands of these two quests, Free Trade and constitutional renewal, and the remedial Charlottetown round from 1991 to 1992 in response to the failure of the Meech Lake Accord (which was not put to a vote in either the Newfoundland or Manitoba legislatures, despite formal agreements from the respective premiers to do so), removed options from Ottawa that would subsequently be available to the post-Mulroney Chrétien government. While it is doubtful Ottawa would have ever cut transfers to the provinces under Mulroney, as Chrétien and Martin did, the absence of the option and the concurrent growth of the deficit, largely because of the cascading interest costs on the inherited debt from the Trudeau regime, combined to help fuel the growth of the Reform Party. Reform had nowhere to go in 1988 during the Free Trade election but everywhere to go in 1993, campaigning against a high deficit, high debt and what many Canadians considered a Québec-centred government.

Mulroney staked his career and government on the Free Trade proposition. It was a profoundly enterprising thing to do. It also had the remarkable virtue of uniting Québec and Alberta voters, in a way that allowed for the election of an historic second Tory majority in 1988 and ratified the negotiated Free Trade agreement, including the vital dispute resolution provision. This back-to-back majority had not happened for Tories in electoral terms since Macdonald's leadership in 1871. That Mulroney also increased pensions, brought in the child tax credit to replace family allowance, negotiated mineral rights and revenues for the provinces and signed more land claim agreements with the First Nations than any other Canadian prime minister before or since reflected the full nature of his "nation and enterprise" vision. The GST, when introduced, reduced the government's popularity from thirty-two to seven percent in the 1990–91 polls, yet it was a compelling piece of public policy.

Brian Mulroney had been weakened in the polls and, with his departure, the Conservatives chose a virtually unknown minister from British Columbia, Kim Campbell, as its new leader. In the election of 1993, the Lucien Bouchard nationalists disappeared from the Tory fold, the prairie populist conservatives broke away for Preston Manning, the GST anger was still present and Prime Minister Campbell's Conservatives were reduced from 157 parliamentary seats to two, ushering in Mr. Chrétien's thirteen-year easy run.

During his time as prime minister, Mulroney preserved the intrinsic Tory balances of provincial rights and economic and fiscal prudence. (The operating side of the government, excluding the Trudeau debt-based interest costs, operated in the black for the first time since before John Turner became finance minister in the late 1960s.) Mulroney led the fight against apartheid and for Nelson Mandela; he also began the rebuilding of the military and set aside reciprocity for secure trade access to our largest export market. He unwound confiscatory Liberal tax regimes (NEP) and kept to core terms of Confederation that had been ignored for decades (the bridge to PEI), while opening new fronts such as the appointment of more women to cabinet, agencies, boards, commissions and diplomatic posts than ever before in Canadian history. He also engaged fully on the environmental file with the help of the remarkable leadership of Minister Charest. In fact, in 1992, when Petro-Canada pulled out of the Newfoundland offshore oil exploration and drilling opportunity, Mulroney's intervention, encouraged with intensity by John Crosbie, saw federal investment and back-stopping keep the initiative alive. That involvement helped set the groundwork, with the Atlantic Accord of 2005 (which replaced the confiscatory Trudeau National Energy Program), for the remarkable economic rebirth we have seen since in Newfoundland. Dismantling the National Energy Program was not about reducing the nation-building role of the state in collaboration with the private sector, begun by Macdonald with the CPR. It was about diminishing the central government excess, in violation of the core values of Confederation, so that provincial mineral rights could be used to encourage strategic investment and growth. This is the growth that ultimately builds economies, jobs and private and public revenues and capacity. It is not perfect as a formula, but, in some contexts, it is vitally necessary and deeply productive. It also reflects the perfect balance between a confederal partnership and "nation and enterprise" policies and investment.

Mulroney's ambition for the country was compelling and has not been repeated in any way since. That ambition perhaps broke another Conservative rule: that it can be folly to overestimate what any government can or should try to do. Both Conservatives and conservatives see a more modest role for government, a role that is premised on government knowing its place and not assuming that it is the central actor in society. There is a basic tenet to conservatism that sees what happens at the family table and in school rooms, laboratories, farmers' fields, small businesses, campus lecture halls, churches, mosques, temples, synagogues, volunteer community groups, hospital operating rooms and militia regiments as more important than what happens in Ottawa. When Ottawa is top of the news all the time, in part because the Ottawa media presence has no other choice (regardless of whether what is happening in Ottawa is newsworthy or not), and in part because the government of the day is pushing, advocating, changing, risking, reorganizing, negotiating and campaigning on one issue or another of high intensity or contrived controversy, voters tire and turn away. Conservatives and conservative voters do so first, and others retreat to regional focus. Mr. Manning and M. Bouchard had the perfect vehicles for fragmenting the Mulroney coalition, and in the process sending the Progressive Conservative Party into oblivion for more than a decade.

9

THE FIVE STEPS
TO CONSERVATIVE REBIRTH

Manning, Day, Charest, MacKay, Harper

For Preston Manning, there was more involved in his 1993 surge than simply capitalizing on the retreat of Western voters from Clark and Mulroney Tories. After Diefenbaker, westerners had stayed loyal to Stanfield—the conservative easterner—and after Stanfield to Mulroney. In some measure, these voters saw the Tories as a way to right the imbalances of decades of central Canadian myopia as represented by the allegedly Québec- or Ontario-centric Liberals. They had stayed loyal because they wanted to end the injustice of unrepresentative institutions like the Senate and put a stop to the minimization of western Canada. They distrusted the civil service; they wanted a serious return to fiscal sanity, with fewer taxes and no pillaging of their natural resources, as had been attempted by the Liberals. With the Meech Lake and Charlottetown excursions, the CF-18 maintenance contract awarded to Québec and the increase in the deficit, many westerners, who were by definition conservative and Conservative voters, began to embrace the notion that there might not be all that much value for them in the current

Canadian political experience. No matter that elected politicians from Alberta, the Prairies and British Columbia held sway in the most important Mulroney cabinet posts or that critical issues vital to the West—such as doing away with the National Energy Program or successfully negotiating Free Trade—had been achieved by the Mulroney-Tory administration. The Tory brand lost popularity as Mulroney began to wear on westerners and as the wildly unpopular GST and related measures took their toll. There is a case to be made (which I would not have appreciated when I served as Mulroney's chief of staff from February 1992 to April 1993—mea culpa) that, had Preston Manning and his policy guru, Stephen Harper, not come along to shape the Reform movement, a more divisive, truly separatist Western movement might have occupied the political vacuum created by the collapse of a Tory vote that would never go Liberal.

In reflecting on my own disconnection from any understanding of the Reform "The West Wants In" option and how much more positive that was than "The West Wants Out" alternative, the paralytic and destructive haze of the Ottawa bubble has emerged over the years as an important factor. Extreme partisanship on all sides produces its own distorting "fog of war." Intensive media coverage of trivial divisions or partisan excess combines with those excesses themselves and unites with the endless and often trivial (but no less intense) anxieties and micro-manoeuvres of the civil service to produce a deeply unreal world quite disconnected from life beyond the bubble, where people go about their day-to-day activities. The amount of time M.P.'s now spend in Ottawa and the ever-increasing number of conflict-of-interest strictures cut them off even more from real life on the ground. The days when citizen farmers, teachers, haberdashers, small business owners and the rest went to Ottawa for only a few weeks of the year to represent their communities are long gone. This focus on Ottawa always makes it easier for insurgent political movements to gain momentum, while those in the bubble fight their own internal pettifogging partisan engagements. Many political capital cities have this problem, and one of its impacts is that those near the centre of the fray do not see, sense or hear what matters in the real world as they get consumed by the skirmishes that have no meaning outside of their own tiny universe of partisan to and fro. That the national media covers most of this activity in Ottawa as competitive news of objective value only magnifies the distortion. I have been no less susceptible than others caught up in the bubble and no doubt I've done my share to contribute to the distortion on more than one occasion. Having, along with many others, passionately campaigned for the "Yes" side on the Charlottetown Accord, my focus on the Québec threat had clearly dulled my understanding of the western dynamic around a similar axis of inclusion and exclusion.

Reform, as a grassroots movement, campaigned on the theme "The West Wants In." Another movement could have just as easily campaigned on "The West Wants Out." While the effect of fragmentation and the easy Liberal majorities (achieved essentially by · just showing up in 1993, 1997 and 2000) were the short-term price to pay, it may very well emerge, across the broad sweep of Canada's history, that the Reform movement saved Canada in the same way Jean Charest's shift to provincial politics did in 1998, and how the taming of the immensely popular Lucien Bouchard administration in the post–1998 period kept Québec inside the confederal Canadian family.

The search for balance during the Stanfield, Clark and Mulroney eras had seen successes and failures. With the changes brought in by Mulroney—GST, FTA, NAFTA, ending the National Energy Program—Tories had rebalanced the federation away from the judicialized, overly centralized Trudeau vision. Stanfield's inability to break through in Québec, despite immense efforts, and Clark's hubris and isolation had awarded Trudeau the platform and time he needed. Mulroney had successfully reconnected the Tory Party to its roots, in particular to the legacy of

Sir John A., but the ambition of his reach, along with the party's self-indulgent choice of Kim Campbell (who could not be blamed, as Senator Lowell Murray has said, for winning the leadership or "not knowing what she didn't know") over Jean Charest at the 1993 leadership convention, was itself an imbalance of a kind that would take the conservative spectrum in Canada some time to sort out. And throughout all this, Preston Manning built up a coherent back-to-basics conservatism that would tilt away from the many assumptions of the Ottawa bubble.

When Prime Minister Campbell was defeated in 1993, by a mix of forces that pre-dated her winning of the leadership of the party as well as some she launched herself, the party was in desperate shape. Its former ranks in Québec and the west had largely moved to other parties. Jean Charest, who had been the youngest M.P. elected in 1984 (in Sherbrooke, Québec) and who had been a successful environment minister in the Mulroney cabinet, became, as the inheritor of the leadership after Campbell's resignation, absolutely essential to its survival in the same way Meighen had been decades earlier. That he brought the party back to official party status, winning twenty seats, was a compelling victory for him. That he did it as a clear proponent of balanced conservatism is forever to his credit and an essential part of the process that saw a new Conservative party subsequently emerge.

The conservative spectrum is and always will be much larger than the Conservative Party. The latter's success electorally is usually defined by its ability to expand, not simply to occupy, the former (to ninety percent at least, in electoral terms). And if governing is the goal, they must also acquire a reasonable piece of the centrist spectrum usually dominated by the Liberal Party when that party expands to eat the electoral lunch of the New Democrats. Paul Martin's success as a deficit-slashing Liberal finance minister not only served the Liberal Party, and Canada's fiscal balance (albeit at the expense of provincial budgets and the defence budget), but gave him a stunning appeal among

Progressive Conservative voters in the Atlantic region, in Québec, in urban Ontario and even in some urban western ridings. Taking over the Liberal leadership in 2004, Martin stood poised to cannibalize large chunks of the "conservative spectrum." Manning had built a Western base for a more populist conservatism, one that dominated the federal elections of 1993, 1997, and 2000, but because of the first-past-the-post system, which discounted hundreds of thousands of votes for him and his successor, Stockwell Day, in Ontario and Québec, this movement was restricted to the West.

Canadian conservatives faced a survival risk in 2003–2004 as the Chrétien period rolled to an end and spectrum opponents within the conservative family faced their greatest postwar Liberal challenge: Martin's deficit-fighting popularity on the centre-right.

While Paul Martin's duty as finance minister was to confront the large deficit that the recession and the Tory inability to cut transfers during sensitive constitutional and Free Trade negotiations had left him, his decision to do so on the back of transfers to the provinces (slashed by thirty-three percent) and slashing defence created the opportunity for a united Conservative party to once again build balance after Liberal excess. Martin had created a fiscal disequilibrium, in which the provinces lacked the fiscal capacity to meet their own Section 92 health, education and welfare objectives. This imbalance would open the door for Stephen Harper.

Harper rebuilt the Tory balance after years of Tory-Reform-Alliance competition, not singlehandedly, but with intense focus and singular tenacity and will. He did so by linking the strains of prairie populism, by having a sense of modesty about the role of government, by moderating the tax burden on middle-income Canadians, by showing accountability, by giving the provinces the fiscal capacity to fulfill their Section 92 constitutional responsibilities, by renewing the defence system and by designing a more principled foreign policy.

His approach to "nation and enterprise" was policy-centred, respectful of voters' intelligence and inclusive. It saw him grow Tory seat totals in three successive elections (2004, 2006, 2008), during which he formed national governments after two. This was a remarkable feat for any leader of any political party—not in terms of how far he went, but due to how far back he started from and how much progress he made in such a short time.

It is important here to outline the steps forward as well as the setbacks along Harper's conservative trail. No leader can make all the right decisions all of the time. But few leaders have had the task of actually assembling a new political party from factions that were close to both calcification and mutual destruction.

In *The Long Road Back,* published in 2006, I detailed the many steps and stages that had caused the conservative family to divide into two political parties and the long road back to political competitiveness, led by people like Stephen Harper and Peter MacKay. I also talked about the contributions made to that process, sometimes unwittingly and sometimes purposefully, by people like Jean Charest, Preston Manning, Joe Clark, Bill Davis, Gerry St. Germain, Loyola Hearn, Scott Reid and others. I will not repeat that account here. Those who foment division and lead political insurgencies also often contribute, through sins of commission and omission, to what happens constructively afterwards. But I do believe that history and the media, and maybe even some partisans of the conservative cause, have begun to discount the importance of what Stephen Harper achieved when he reached out to Peter MacKay and brought about the rebirth of a unified and coherent Conservative Party as an alternative governing and policy choice for Canadian voters. It was a remarkable and profound turning point that had a positive effect on the entire political spectrum, including other political parties, the nation's economy and its foreign and defence policy. Whatever history may say about the prime minister's overall record of achievement and setback while in office, this accomplishment must be acknowledged as one of the signal acheivements of Canadian history.

I do not and did not ever regard this book as an ideological exercise—certainly not one about the sterile debate between right and left. That debate may well be what factions within the Republican Party in the U.S. continually embrace. Yet that is not in any way what the Canadian conservative dialectic consists of.

The Reform Party, not unlike H.H. Stevens's Reconstructionist Party of the 1930s that fractured R.B. Bennett's vote, was less about ideology than it was about its economic and populist roots. And western Canadian politics has profoundly different roots from those in Québec, Ontario and Atlantic Canada. Family trees unite genealogies that start elsewhere. In the West, the strong presence of American immigrants in the 1890s, the relative lack of serious Loyalist immigration in the 1790s and the particularly horrific realities of the "dustbowl" Depression produced a populism and a restiveness that informed the development of Liberal, Conservative and CCF (NDP) roots and sensibilities in that part of the country.

Other factors helped to work the soil in which Reform could flourish and prosper: the remarkable political skills of individuals such as John Diefenbaker (he of the first Canadian Bill of Rights), Preston Manning (whose Reform Party slogan was "The West Wants In") and Peter Lougheed (whose first piece of legislation was the Alberta Human Rights Act), and the epic struggle of the West against the confiscatory National Energy Program.

There had been some east-west crossover leadership figures like Diefenbaker and Bennett and those with national networks like Mulroney and Clark. But between the late 1980s and the earliest days of the next century two sets of competing roots began to set up rival and politically opposed cultures and campaign organizations. This was not just manna for the Liberals. It also threatened the conservative family with permanent federal irrelevance.

Essentially, the grassroots in the western political soil had grown to become a very different crop from that dominating the furrows of eastern Tory political fields.

This was the core challenge that Stephen Harper had to address as he returned to Alberta after one term in Parliament by Mr. Manning's side, having served as policy guru for the Reform Party. Preston Manning had been unable to broadly transplant the Reform-Alliance seedlings in eastern Canadian political soil under our winner-take-all riding system. Much of the broad experience with voters in Québec, urban and suburban Ontario, and Atlantic Canada rested with the Progressive Conservatives. Western populism, without competent eastern political capacity, would not be enough. Eastern PC capacity without populism had crested under Mr. Clark in the federal election of 2000 at twelve seats, one of which was in Québec (with the remarkable André Bachand), with the rest in Atlantic Canada. These two factions had no prospects for growth except, to the Liberals' glee, at each other's expense. And that the 2000 election should have been so disappointing, despite an early perception that Mr. Day, as a new and telegenic Alliance leader, had both appeal and momentum, only deepened the gloom on both sides. The famous "firewall" letter of January 2001—signed by Stephen Harper, then president of the National Citizens Coalition, and others—sent to Premier Ralph Klein, urging the government of Alberta to "build firewalls" around the province to prevent the Chrétien government from encroaching on legitimate provincial rights, was itself not so much ideological as it was an appeal to history.

The re-elected Chrétien government seemed quite comfortable under finance minister Paul Martin in overtaxing the economies of the Prairies so as to finance a myriad of federal "boutique" programs. So, the notion that Alberta Tories, Reformers and academics should want to reassert full Section 92 rights for the province in as robust a way as possible (no more robust, by the way, than Jean Lesage's Liberal "maître chez nous" for Québec, almost four decades earlier) should only have alarmed those who would prefer Canada to be a unitary as opposed to a federal state.

In his outreach to the Progressive Conservatives, Stephen Harper, whatever his other electoral or political ambition (and, in democracies, ambition is vital if we are to find the energy to move forward and make changes for the better), he was also reaching out to keep Canada from being a one-party state. One-party states often drift into corruption, as they are run by self-dealing elites. And they usually spawn the kind of exclusion that threatens the essential trust sustaining the larger community beyond government and the courtier class itself.

Now, to put two competing political genealogies together, one must find a way to accommodate both sets of roots and family trees. If you ignore one side, the peril of fragmentation is never more than a few short steps away. Stephen Harper and Peter MacKay (who had won the Tory leadership after Clark stepped down in 2003) understood that. During the long summer of 2003, what these two men built, with agreements their negotiators produced, underlined just how well they appreciated both the opportunities and the perils of coming together.

The core English-French partnership of the eastern consensus is as inviolate as the populism of their western relatives. The compassion and "nation and enterprise" approach of Macdonald-Borden-Meighen-Bennett history is as vital as the Diefenbaker-Manning-H.H. Stevens populism. Those who would simplify or caricature this balance of roots as a left-right debate understand little about conservative history and even less about Canada itself.

Chantal Hébert, in her thoughtful book *French Kiss: Stephen Harper's Blind Date with Quebec*, makes a compelling argument for Stephen Harper's surprising result in Québec during the 2006 election by pointing out two things: the sponsorship scandal had taken its toll on the Liberals in Québec, but more importantly,

Liberals were taking Québec for granted. Here is what she had to say about the latter: "there was no indication that Martin was burning to be proactive on Québec issues... Stephen Harper... had clearly given the issue more thought than Martin had and, oddly, his approach to federalism was often closer to that of the Liberal ministers from Québec than Martin's was." And later she adds that Stephen Harper "emerged as a new federalist voice in Québec at a time when it seemed that most Québecers were well past listening."

In fact, the open federalism *(fédéralisme d'ouverture)* that Stephen Harper spoke to at a Chamber of Commerce speech in Québec City in the 2006 campaign said to Québec what Sir John A., Lord Elgin and the Québec Act had said over the decades: we respect your differences, and our federal system must be able to do so as well; the "take it for granted" or "ignore it and it will go away" approach of the Chrétien Liberals is not ours. That signal was vital to the Conservatives' ten-seat breakthrough. And the absence of attention to this principle, in the Treasury Board's strategic review of cultural program cuts before 2008's election was, among other reasons, why that ten-seat progress stalled deeply in 2008.

To date, despite pressures from many sides, Stephen Harper has resisted the right-left caricature and, by and large, has operated as a paterfamilias at the head of a family table where diversity is a compelling and enduring strength. He has been broadly inclusive in terms of policies and priorities. Of course, successfully portraying one's efforts in this way is a very separate challenge. Stephen Harper faces, as have all other leaders before him, the need to reflect both parts of the Conservative legacy in the principles and policies he embraces. For Mr. Davis in Ontario, this balance could be seen in his support of the monarchy and the police and the Lord's Prayer in classrooms as he built French-language schools, started TV Ontario and purchased a minority interest in Suncor when the oil sands investment was repaid with profit to Ontario. Every Conservative faces this balancing task, and the instruments one chooses are important symbols of how the balance is being sustained. This is especially true when the party one leads is the result of two "legacy parties" attempting to shape and sustain a "new" party. Initiatives that seem ideologically self-indulgent, or that appeal to only one side of the balance, always carry high risk. That doesn't mean they should always be excluded from policy choices. But it is folly for them to dominate; the insertion of more toughness in the law-and-order agenda and the reduction of taxes are all part of this balancing challenge. One need not support them all or their degree of intensity to understand the imperative to which they relate. But the balance itself can never be deserted by any Conservative seeking to be politically competitive. Over any period of time, both parts of the conservative legacy need to be present in the overall policy mix.

And that challenge remains at the core of the ultimate success of the Harper period in office. His achievement to date, in effecting a unification of two warring factions, has been characterized by uncommonly gracious and inclusive gestures and judgements over the span of time vital to the process of unification. A modest setting aside of some of the more narrow ideological tendencies of the early Reform movement (hostility to aspects of Québec policy, elements of immigration policy) for more unifying ideals and purpose characterized his outreach to the Progressive Conservatives. A compelling respect for the role of a distinct Québécois society within Canada has shaped his approach to constitutional issues and policy. His compassionate apology to our First Nations over the residential-school sins of other governments, at other times, was one of his most shining moments. His international championing of democracy and of those Canadian values that have served Canada well throughout its history is also indicative of a sense of outreach, coherence and noble intent. These are the hallmarks of a consensus-broadening lift that has allowed him to increase seat totals in all of his elections. These are the instruments of any successful Tory rebirth. They are the kinds of instruments that always succeed over narrow or mean partisanship (which is very attractive in the Ottawa bubble, and is profoundly more "Liberal" than Tory). In Ottawa, the Tory is the perpetual outsider. But it is by choosing the instruments of outreach and generosity that Harper has succeeded. For any Tory, this is always the best way to proceed.

10

CANADA
IN THE WORLD
Balance and Principles

C anada and Canadian conservatives do not live on an isolated island, unaffected by the larger world. That a Tory "nation and enterprise" domestic policy perspective carries over into an approach to a principled foreign and defence policy based in idealism and realism should not surprise. Canada's challenge, as a middle power and as a country profoundly dependent on trade, has never been simple. There are alliances, like the constantly effective and underrated Commonwealth, which are essential to increasing our leverage and reach in a world of great economic and military powers, among which we are not the most powerful. It is vital that our broader national commitment embrace diplomacy, development, defence and democratization, as well as a unified view of how all of these must come together in a coherent and integrated way.

It is important to our understanding of Canada's international challenges and obligations to remember that some of our fellow Canadians would, quite frankly, rather not be bothered with them. They would, and I mean no disrespect or condescension in saying so, be quite happy if our political narrative at home were utterly dominated by elective surgery wait times, student loan and debt levels, financial market regulations, same-sex marriage or appropriate levels of child care or agricultural subsidy. While these endless domestic issues will always be part of a pluralist democracy's internal political debate, to allow our national politics be overtaken by them at the complete expense of Canada's international obligations and responsibilities would be self-indulgent. It would disconnect us not only from our values and our history as an ally and international partner, but diminish, to the point of self-denial, the extent to which our domestic policy choices are affected by the clarity or failure of our international posture as Canadians. It is one thing to stare at one's own navel, when we have yet another of our existential crises with respect to Québec, or when we persist in our endless neuroses with respect to the United States. Any country with our history and geographic location can be permitted such self-indulgences on occasion. Letting that myopia become a habit is deeply counterproductive.

There are strengths and weaknesses to having a strong sense of obligation beyond one's borders. Consensus at home on domestic and local issues is hard enough to build and sustain. Consensus at home about foreign wars, conflicts or even compelling international causes is a whole other level of political challenge—especially in a democracy where, from its very beginning, society developed in a multinational way. It was reflective of the compelling sixteenth-, seventeenth- and eighteenth-century empires whose competing outreaches founded the Americas and soon faced the "exceptionalist" self-image of the burgeoning American colonies and states.

To be fair, that complexity has not always been managed well by Conservatives. In fact, the different historical factions that Sir John A. Macdonald brought together—the ultramontane Québec *bleus*, the reform Irish partisans under Thomas D'arcy

McGee, traditional Tories and Conservatives from the Macdonald core—would all have had different views of the world, of our connection with the Empire, of the role of the armed forces and of our appropriate relationship with the United States. The complexity of these views was endless, even within one particular faction, and not easily managed among them. Similar complexities exist in Canada today and they are no less difficult to manage, reflect and respect.

We must be realistic and practical about what is authentic, what matters and why history is important to contemporary politics and public policy. And if history is vital, so is some balance and perspective. If that perspective is essentially conservative, then it is also profoundly conservative not to seek to impose one's own society's ideologies on those elsewhere. Canadian foreign policy needs always to embrace this modesty and to engage on this matter when others do not.

Vital interests, such as the national security of our people, our right to live free from fear of intimidation, our right to conduct our domestic debates and processes in an open and democratic society, our right to clean water and clean air, and our right to safety in our neighbourhoods and public places, are not sustained by accident. They are only there because we are prepared to engage our resources as a society to ensure that they are protected. If that is true about our vital interests at home, it must be equally true about our international goals, as Canadians in the larger world.

The inherently conservative position is one of dealing with international and global realities as they are and to be wary of those who prefer to build foreign policy by imposing what "ought to be." It is also intrinsically conservative to embrace the harsh and compelling reality of the imperfectability of humankind. Change, whether national or global, is not always better. Reason and logic do not always prevail or even dominate.

Most of Sir John A. Macdonald's global priorities beyond Canada were about artful negotiation with the British Colonial Office to secure Canada's national and confederal development (1863–70) and his stout rejection, once the Americans would not consider a trade agreement that was genuinely reciprocal, of the somewhat less reciprocal variety that the Grits had proposed. Not until Borden inherited the country (which Laurier had served so well) did a model of Tory policy towards the larger world emerge. And it was a model that would come to define Tory international policy for Canada—with a few notable exceptions—to this day.

On occasion, Toryism infects Liberal common wisdom, just as conservatism has been infected by more centrist aspects of competent liberalism. *Canada's First Century, 1867–1967,* Donald Creighton's masterful analysis of Laurier's departure from the Liberal character type and the incompetence of his predecessors, especially Mackenzie and Blake, leaders who were both eminently beatable by the Tories, speaks volumes about the potential capacity of Liberals, on occasion, to step out of the intellectually self-confining indulgence to welcome a more pan-national but regionally sensitive leadership style and mission.

What Laurier fashioned was a Canada still very much directed by Britain's overall foreign policy; the country saw its only global reality reflected in its more active role in the councils of the Empire itself. He dispatched troops to aid the imperial effort against the "oppressive" Boers in southern Africa. And while the Naval Service Bill of 1910, based on a motion proposed in the House of Commons the previous year by Conservative George E. Foster, points to a desire for national self-determination and was the first genuinely independent defence initiative (supported by Laurier and Tory leader Borden together), the truth is that Laurier demonstrated no interest whatsoever in any independent Canadian role or voice on matters of foreign policy or the state of the world beyond the Empire.

Borden, while in principle supportive of the joint Laurier-Borden resolution of 1909, had to bridge isolationist and imperialist traditions and biases in his own party. He did so by shaping, from opposition, a Tory naval policy that saw a uniquely Canadian naval force, constructed, maintained and staged in Canada, which would serve as a fleet arm in support of the Empire, should the Empire came under threat. Putting country first, he cooperated with Laurier on this, as he also did on the later creation, by joint resolution, of the independent Public Service Commission of Canada, taking a step above the traditional partisan game of patronage-based appointment at all levels of the government ranks.

After the election victory of 1911 and the 1914 assassination of Archduke Franz Ferdinand in Sarajevo, Borden ended up leading a wartime government with a remarkable four hundred thousand soldier commitment to the Allied side in World War 1. Unlike Laurier, who was happy with a benign, imperial connection, Borden struck out to ensure that Canadians would fight as one Canadian army abroad, that Canada would be counted as an independent player in the Imperial War Cabinet and, above all, because of the highest per capita sacrifice of any allied nation, that Canada would sit and speak on its own behalf at the Versailles negotiations and sign, along with the other dominions, the armistice treaty as an independent combatant. This was Tory nationalism and internationalism at its very best.

The Empire and all its historical linkages and resonance clearly changed in the post-World War 1 reality. But the jettisoning of old traditions and institutions is not the usual Canadian Tory way. When the British proposed, in December of 1919, that Canada and other dominions have delegates at the peace negotiations who would be consulted "when the questions directly affecting them are under consideration," as was put forward by British prime minister David Lloyd George to the Imperial War Cabinet, Canada flatly and bluntly refused. From as early as 1914, when a relatively amateur Canadian cabinet combined with a civil service that numbered barely in the hundreds to begin the awesome task of assembling the troop strength that would join the war effort, Robert Borden became the champion for greater Canadian voice and independence.

These roots of commitment and nationalism, as a basis for independent international engagement, would not and could not be set aside when peace was negotiated and Canada's role in the new postwar world was being determined. The risk of course was that the great historical powers, in concert with the already "exceptional" Americans, latecomers to the war, would conspire to dilute the independence or equality of Canada's status. But in presaging his actions prior to the Treaty of Versailles negotiations, Borden stated on January 4, 1916: "It can hardly be expected that we shall put 400,000 or 500,000 men in the field and willingly accept the position of having no more voice and receiving no more consideration than if we were toy automata."

The divisions over conscription, which were deep and pervasive between English and French Canada, would, as a legacy, also initiate a fresh "faultline" that would harden both the country and the Tories—and parts of the country against the Tories. (This term was later coined by *Globe and Mail* columnist Jeffrey Simpson in a 1993 book entitled *Faultlines: Struggling for a Canadian Vision.*) But despite this piece of difficult history, Canada's war effort and sacrifice engendered the courage essential to secure independent Canadian admission to the League of Nations and to the International Labour Organization, two products of the Versailles negotiations and peace accords.

The "independent" theme of this Tory patriotism would have long reach in the decades ahead: involvement in World War II, Korea, the Cuban Missile Crisis, the UN charter, Cyprus, the Golan Heights, Bosnia, the Congo and Afghanistan. And it would be a further refinement of Canadian conservatism, making our brand uniquely reflective of the historic, geographic and demographic forces that shaped Canada itself.

Conservatives also supported sending reinforcements during the Chanak Crisis, but after the election of 1922, Mackenzie King refused to call Parliament back to hear officially of Britain's possible need for reinforcements at Chanak, a need of which Churchill, who was Colonial Secretary at the time, had hinted. His action was not responsible leadership or coherent national government. It was shallow, tactic-driven, evasive and regional animosity-driven governance. And this same evasive approach, which contributed to unnecessary and excessive casualties in the air, at sea and on the land, through insufficient preparation, training, armaments and investment, would highlight a Liberal tradition only broken after the war by King's decent and accessible minister of justice (and subsequently external affairs) Louis St. Laurent, who actually understood the importance of deterrence and Canada's obligations and responsibilities. Liberals would return to Mackenzie King form under Trudeau and even more so under Chrétien. Paul Martin would try, to his credit, to begin military reinvestment (after slashing defence budgets earlier as finance minister) but he did not serve as prime minister long enough to see his initiatives through.

The war effort of 1939–45 and the eager role many Canadian Conservatives (and Liberals) took as citizen soldiers, airmen and sailors did not but solidify Tory views. Many Liberals, of course, did the same, as did prominent CCFers. And, as citizens, they developed on the battlefield, beneath and on the seas, and in the air their own views of Mackenzie King's "conscription if necessary but not necessarily conscription" negotiation of domestic tensions.

Throughout history, the Tory "Ready, Aye, Ready" approach (the motto of the Canadian navy) has been part and parcel of Canadian obligations and responsibilities globally. The bravery and massive sacrifice of Canadians—at Dieppe, up the spine of Italy, at Ortona and Monte Cassino, at Juno Beach and through the liberation of Holland, bringing the war to Germany as part of

Bomber Command as it had been rained down upon London, in Hong Kong and in keeping the sea lanes to Britain and Murmansk open—would earn Canada a voice in the post-1945 world.

On foreign policy, Canada's conservative tradition and its differentiation from the more extreme American neo-conservative foreign policy bias is seminal. It is also vital to understand the myths around the Pearsonian period and confront them directly in the form of a coherent Conservative foreign policy. A Canadian conservative view of peace is that it is a constructed, shaped and desirable reality—not a difficult, inert reality shaped by indifference or passivity.

As I recently wrote in the *International Journal,* in a tribute edition to John Holmes, for Tories peace is not only the result of diplomatic consensus, the engineering of treaties, or the intervention of "honest brokers" and well-intentioned or trusted intermediaries. Peace, to be the policy goal, must confer more general benefits to potential combatants than war, insurgency or terrorism. Sadly, there has been, with the best of intentions, a view held by some parts of the Canadian foreign policy arm (largely Liberal establishment) that international brokerage politics, with professional Canadian diplomats punching above Canada's weight as a middle power, is a unique instrument through which peace might be sustained and secured. The hard fact that Conservatives understand is that the golden period of Pearsonian diplomacy was made possible for Canadian diplomats because Canada had been part of an alliance that stopped the Axis powers, albeit with the devastating and unavoidable destruction of Japanese and German military and civilian targets, after a war initiated by fascists that claimed fifty million lives all around. And we had played more than our fair military role. As a result, we lost, on a per capita basis, a tremendous amount of blood in the process. This earned us a place at the tables where instruments of peace like the UN, NATO and the Universal Declaration of Human Rights was shaped.

Canadian diplomats of Mike Pearson's generation performed above and beyond in so many fora to bring great credit to Canada and meaningful benefit to the world. But those points of constructive leverage were available to Canada because they were earned by Canadian soldiers, airmen, sailors, riveters and home front participants before, during and after World War II and a few years later on the battlefields of Korea. They were earned opportunities because the courtly and decent Louis St. Laurent, Mr. Pearson's prime minister through the early 1950s, not only maintained a huge Canadian military presence in Germany with other allies, against the Soviet threat as understood then, but did so in a way that saw Canada become a major tripwire in confronting the Warsaw Pact nations through to the 1980s. And when an Egyptian blockade of the Suez Canal in October 1956 threatened to boil over into a world war, and Britain, France and Israel attacked Egypt in an effort to take control of the canal, Pearson was to solve the crisis by getting all sides to agree to the creation of a neutral United Nations force to maintain peace in the region. Justifiably, this earned him the Nobel Peace Prize in 1957. All of this occurred before the fall of the St. Laurent government and was driven as much by our pivotal role as a self-reliant and deployment-capable NATO partner, trusted by allies like France, the U.S. and the U.K. and understood by the Israelis to be both safe and trustworthy, due to our "Canadian desire for peace."

During the Suez Crisis, allies France, the U.S. and the U.K. were in sharp mutual disagreement. And Israel, whose birth had been aided by Canadians like General E.L.M. Burns, faced Gamal Abdel Nasser, the Egyptian leader who was both a keen Soviet client and, in the context of dictatorships of that era, a popular Arab leader throughout the Middle East. The planet faced a serious escalation of the thermonuclear threat. And Canada had the capacity to move, without any ally's assistance, five thousand soldiers, equipment and supportive air units—on our own ships, in our own navy, on our own aircraft carriers—to be in theatre quickly. Our military capacity was real and trustworthy, and we had a constructive, well-conditioned and well-trained force.

Our positioning within the alliance earned us a share of the voice. Israel, the USSR, the United States, the U.K. and France, not to mention Egypt, needed peace. In that context Mr. Pearson did extremely well; but without the military capacity the initiative would have been hollow. Tories understand this. Liberals and New Democrats still try to negotiate with this reality.

During the Suez Crisis, we were taken seriously. Yet when Canada tried a similar initiative at the UN before the Second Gulf War in 2003, despite the estimable diplomatic experience, standing and exceptional skills and reputation of Ambassador Paul Heinbecker—who had served as a senior cabinet secretary for foreign policy under Mulroney and as ambassador to Germany before his UN posting—few cared and less listened. Context, and what we had or had not earned as leverage, mattered in 1956 and it mattered in the lead-up to the Second Gulf War. Yet years of diminishing our military capacity, Jean Chrétien's essential disinterest in foreign policy except as a backdrop to "Team Canada" boosterism and federal-provincial sales promotion (not a bad thing, but disconnected from any vision or world view) had created zero leverage to back up Heinbecker's superb efforts and initiatives.

The Tory context for an active peace option is a balance of economic and social interests, shaped in part by military reality on the ground. Without that balance someone will always find war a more compelling option. That was surely the bias of the Iraqi junta headed by Saddam Hussein. In the post-9/11 U.S., considering intelligence failures that had in the recent past misinformed (and underinformed) American presidents about the dynamic context changes leading to the Yom Kippur War of 1973, the Hezbollah destruction of a U.S. marine barracks in Lebanon, the fall of the Shah of Iran, Pakistani and Indian nuclear weapon development, the attack of al Qaeda on the USS *Cole,* and the attacks on the Twin Towers in 1993 and 2001, erring on the side of caution and "looking the other way" was likely a less viable presidential option than many armchair quarterbacks have since concluded. The notion that America and the U.K. chose to assume the worst on the risk of weapons of mass destruction in Iraq would only surprise those who do not see keeping one's own people safe as the first and foremost priority, above and beyond any other strategic geopolitical goals, and central to any rational foreign policy. That intelligence may have been flawed, or that strong biases towards action existed among some advisors, does not, in and of itself, establish that the president of the United States or the prime minister of Great Britain knowingly acted in something other than their profound sense of the public interest.

Conservatives believe that one cannot engineer peace only through the vital instruments of tinkering, wordsmithing and treaty design. One must first have or support a plan to create the conditions for peace. Economic deprivation and zero economic prospects are not suitable preconditions for peace. When we look around the world at the hotspots that are very much on the agenda of the American president or our prime minister and their counterparts in Europe, Asia, Africa and the Americas, behind every insurgency, behind every border dispute, behind every buildup of violent or terrorist or criminal options is a broad overlay of relative poverty. Defence of the status quo, in places where many people are getting poorer, even if global free trade is reducing poverty worldwide, always fuels conflict.

There is a reason that depressions and wars run together in history. There is a reason that those with nothing to lose end up, in desperation, targeting those who do. There is a reason the poorest parts of the world see huge, disproportional investments in armaments.

Beyond diplomacy and intricate treaty or consensus design, there must be a conservative realpolitik that is based on real survival needs on the ground, between and within nations. These include safe borders, all the basic needs of Maslow's hierarchy, and the needs of any national community to preserve identity and culture. In simple terms, Israelis will not accept peace if the price is the extinction of their state; Gazans will not accept peace if it freezes them in poverty and stateless despair; Iran's neighbours will not accept peace if it makes nuclear intimidation from a chaotic Shia fundamentalist quasi-democracy inevitable; Iran will not accept peace if its right to peaceful economic development is held in trusteeship by others.

Classically the wealthier countries with reasonably democratic and economically prosperous societies have more choices, especially peaceful and diplomatic choices that set conflict aside for the sake of resolving disputes, dealing with commodity or labour shortages, or handling surpluses and distributional issues. Those nations mired in poverty and massive inequality are often already police-state or police-state "democracy light" regimes, where using force is normative most of the time. While warming trade and exchange options with China and Russia are good trends to be encouraged, both of these countries, which have nuclear arsenals and, in China's case, a rapidly and massively expanding military, do still fall in the "democracy light" police-state category. While diplomatic types, Old China Hands, friends of China and academics who study Russia all justifiably wish for a more dynamic and positive engagement between Canada and these two BRIC countries, naïveté in defence of happy outcomes is no virtue.

It is traditional for Tories to seek a mixed instrumental strategy that increases the positive incentives. It is one thing not to negotiate with terrorists on issues like hostages when it appears to reward inhuman activity. But not talking with groups that have embraced terrorism would have made the Northern Irish settlement, the establishment of the state of Israel, the Dayton Accords relating to the Balkans, the South African evolution towards democracy and many other regional victories impossible.

The most serious challenge facing Canada in the Pearsonian era was the rebalancing of the postwar world. This entailed dealing with the dynamics and risks of the Cold War and finding some point of Canadian leverage in a bipolar world. That leverage was about more than cocktail chatter in New Edinburgh, or sherry at Massey College. It was about building the standing and deployable capacity, humanitarian and military, needed to defend legitimate economic, social and security interests. In simple terms, there is not a foreign policy goal—from international security to humanitarian and development progress, to stability in the Middle East, to the protection of democracy, human rights and the rule of law, or even to the compelling notion of "the responsibility to protect," embraced by Liberal foreign minister Lloyd Axworthy— that can mean anything without the capacity to deploy. This fact is central to any conservative foreign policy agenda.

For Conservatives, there are in essence two pillars that support the cornerstones of civility and opportunity upon which Canada and the civilized (or civilizing) world depend for progress and stability. One is made from the granite of order and restraint that promises tyrants, invaders, adventurers, aggressors and intimidators, state or non-state, that they will face deep, uncompromising force in response to unprovoked aggression. For that pillar to be real, continued increase in defence spending is required by Canada and our allies. Enhanced intelligence and naval, special force and related joint expeditionary assets will determine whether the forces of darkness or light, nihilistic insanity or stability, will prevail.

The second pillar, that of social and economic opportunity that rewards democracies and those who eschew violence with increased social and economic justice, is just as important and requires just as much investment, if not more. In fact, one can (and Canada should) make the case that the more we invest in specific diplomatic and economic goals in pillar two, the less may be necessary for pillar one. But as we speak, we need more of pillar one because the world has underinvested in pillar two. The embrace of the central role of two freedoms, freedom from fear and freedom from want, supports a framework best discussed as "national security conservatism." National security conservatism sees increasing income security among the world's most poor as essential to personal, global and national security and a supporting pillar of a sane, international order. The idea that Canada can meet a "responsibility to protect" without the ability to deploy is a farce. Inefficient and unproductive aid only weakens pillar two (economic security), making more of pillar one (robust military and security capacity) necessary. It is, in championing the two freedoms, a distinctly Canadian conservative balance abroad not very different from the "nation and enterprise" approach at home.

The complexity of the real world requires that Conservative foreign policy makers engage more openly and creatively with partners like France, Japan, Germany and even Russia and China to collaborate more fully in the global buildup of both vital pillars. We are who we are: a diverse multinational democracy with a defining history in peace and war which also sets the values, allies and interests that shape our future. If we want that future to be shaped by others, there is always the low-risk, "pontificating from the sidelines" strategy for Canada made popular in the Trudeau era. That kind of future, formed only by others, constitutes, in the beginning and in the end, the greatest risk of all and should be unacceptable to Canadian conservatives. "Sitting idly by" is made real by failure to continue the expansion of our strategic deployability for humanitarian, stabilization or combat purposes, and failure to engage in foreign policy and initiatives on a level that makes a difference. It is within our power to decide that we will, from Afghanistan to the Ukraine, from the Golan Heights to Inuvik, from Harare to Beirut, have a say in that future and not sit idly by while others shape our future.

There is no premise upon which we can shape our foreign, development and defence policy for the coming decades other than that of geopolitical integrity. By geopolitical integrity I mean that the critical elements of our foreign, defence and humanitarian policies should come together in a coherent manner that is mutually reinforcing and consistent. And they must come together in a way that actually reflects what we say—and ensures that what we say actually reflects our value as Canadians.

In this context, I would like to emphasize one particularly Canadian value and that is the one of civility—a core premise that determines how differences of opinion and genuine dissent are framed and facilitated in our democratic society. It is a value that is central to a society where freedom and not fear shapes the social discourse.

The purpose of our geopolitical integrity is clear: acting diplomatically and militarily in concert with allies and international organizations to reduce the risk of major conflagration, to reduce or prevent human suffering, to repel aggressors and to repel ethnic cleansing. Such a purpose is a reflection of the civility and other values we have at home and the freedom from fear we want for others.

A foreign policy statement of substance and value that reflects Canadian leadership would stipulate those activities abroad that Canada will not tolerate, those values and vital interests we think are at stake and those prerogatives Canada is prepared to assert in defence of those values and vital interests. Threats to our national security, efforts at ethnic cleansing or genocide, state or non-state commitments to eradicate nations or cultures or other religious or cultural groups, and the threat of weapons of mass destruction and violence against civilian populations all need to be factored into a Canadian framework for foreign policy engagement. And while the military capacity to enable Canadian reach and impact is vital, also vital is having the ability to disarm post-conflict factions, to rebuild societies' infrastructures, to promote democracy and to enhance social and economic self-sufficiency.

The extent to which a country allows the gap to grow between what it says and believes and what it is actually prepared to do determines the degree of international influence that a country has. The dilution of influence reduces a country's leverage on issues of trade, economy, environment and the general world order. Conservative foreign policy, reflective of the appropriate balance of our history, requires an awareness of our values, an awareness of what we will commit in defence of those values and an awareness of our capacity to actually keep those commitments.

In assessing our geopolitical integrity it is imperative that we do not just look into our own hand-held mirror. We must understand how others see us as well. It is common wisdom that Canada is viewed well abroad for all the good that we do, in development, in peacekeeping, in police training and all the rest. In fact, individual Canadians and their specific efforts are very well regarded—but Canada as a whole? Before Afghanistan and the purchase of large aircraft, we were deeply strained when asked to deploy a thousand troops on any mission for either military or humanitarian purposes. That has changed. Our remarkable military performance in Afghanistan, the procurement of new airlift and armoured capacity, the use of unmanned and combat air assets, the performance of Canadian forces in the initial assaults on the Taliban, the protection of Kabul during the early days of democracy, and the holding of the line against the insurgency in Kandahar province are all developments that have changed the view of our capacity, performance and national will.

We need to rethink total Canadian investment and complement. We should have a regular force level of 150,000 people (now under 70,000), and we should have an effective active reserve of 50,000 (roughly double present reserves). We need these numbers not simply to address present capacity needs, but to make sure that a robust strategy of geopolitical integrity is attainable, the kind of integrity that any coherent and balanced conservative foreign and defence policy should perforce require. Balance and principle in our global stance calls for discipline and determination and a clear focus on who we are and the values we share. Avoiding principle, commitment and engagement or withdrawing before a job is done is not who we are and is not the Tory way.

11

THE BATTLE FOR A BALANCED FUTURE

Canadian, not American, Conservatism

A merican neo-conservatives, who, before Vietnam, began their activist intellectual lives as liberals, argued after Vietnam for more muscular pro-democracy, more American military and political engagement around the world. They remain, to this day, an active force, whose influence in the increasingly centrist Obama administration should not be under-estimated. Whatever the hubris of the newly elected Democrats in 2008 on national security or on Iraq, policy differences between the Obama and Bush administrations are not as large as they may appear. From the excesses of the radio talk show extremists to the debates about the future of the Republican Party, there is much to enjoy but little to learn. To be fair, American neo-conservatism is by no means monolithic. It has cultural strains, neo-liberal strains (as in right-wing Democratic Party players), strong economic and national security strains, free enterprise strains, nativist strains and isolationist strains. It is important to avoid oversimplification here or loose and careless labelling. The new Tea Party strain is but one fibre in an ever more multi-hued fabric.

The Tea Party reality, perfect for winning off-year elections—
which are usually about protest and sending a message—speaks
in a very American way to the fragmentation that the U.S. right
wing has generated since the Goldwater days of the 1960s. Part
evangelical and part libertarian in its inspiration (clearly with its
own set of contradictions), the Tea Party seems to essentially be
a vehicle shaped for and by anger, some real and some contrived.

At a time when Canadian conservatives have united from
across the spectrum into one highly competitive political party,
and American conservatives both inside and outside the Republican Party are going through a particularly fractious time (as
often happens after substantive election setbacks), the issue of
American conservatism and its potential to influence the Canadian conservative spectrum is very much with us. Articulate and
thoughtful American conservative theorists and commentators
like David Frum, recently of the American Enterprise Institute
and formerly of the Manhattan Institute in New York (and who
is originally and also a Canadian), and David Brooks of the *New
York Times*, respectively, speak of either a "new majority" or of
a "progressive conservative" Republican case that is not quite so
rigid on the environment or health care, the central reality is that
forces on the more narrow right still seem to be in the majority.
Frum, who is the true heir to the William F. Buckley intellectual,
conservative tradition in America, has attempted to urge more
realism on the Republicans. He has encouraged them to move
beyond their arch positions on health care and their aggressive
foreign policy, which is tied to overreaching and unsustainable
engagements. But his reasonable and pragmatic voice will need
to become louder before he can fully countervail, or even partially
balance, those who are holding to the more visceral, extreme neo-
conservative vision.

. The problem with American conservatism for Canadians is
related to its very different roots and origins. Essentially they

were more exclusionary. American conservatism began with the American Revolution, itself an essentially anti-conservative enterprise of the most profound kind. And, from the beginning, Revolutionary Conservatism was an amalgam of religious propriety around essentially Protestant denominations, as well as an exclusionary movement that left out the Loyalist Tory segment of its own population. This Loyalist Tory form of conservatism, which valued the Crown as an established symbol of order and respect for authority, history and the natural laws, was expunged by the revolutionary forces, making what was left both narrow in reach and shallow in depth. "Patriots" would brook only loyalty to them, not to larger ideas or historical foundations.

The Loyalist Tories were in no way anti-democratic, but they were profoundly anti-republican. They fled north in large numbers and became the bedrock of both English-Canadian society and Canadian conservatism. When American conservatism—an amalgam of hyper-patriotic, exceptionalist (aren't we special), Whiggish, reason-based, government-designed, melting-pot orthodoxy—took hold in the United States, it was Toryism, a far more inclusive and accommodationist version of conservatism, that took hold in Canada. The Canadian Tory version encompassed different faiths, denominations and identities as part of its inherited reality, and this was what became dominant.

Since the Vietnam War, the dilution of what remained of traditional, change-skeptic American conservatism by intellectually robust neo-con-neo-liberalism, the kind that welcomes greed, military adventurism, and a reduced state capacity, has produced an even greater gulf between the two North American conservative brands. And over the years this American neo-conservative thrust has laterally merged with the evangelical movement. It is truly the ultimate of ironies that it was American conservatives who spoke and legislated around the separation of church and state. And yet, American history has provided anything but such a separation. Canadian Tories, on the other hand, who legislated no such division, actually built a society that was, and is, far less prone to using the dominant faith or faiths to impose one religious belief upon another or upon society as a whole.

In the United States, the pursuit of the public interest has become something of an accidental outcome of all the private interests battling themselves to exhaustion. The implicit and self-centred liberalism of "life, liberty and the pursuit of happiness" has so infected American conservatism that it has become paralyzed by countervail. Conversely, Canadian Toryism remains more effective because it neither diminishes the importance of the public interest nor the responsible underpinnings of citizenship vital to any order capable of protecting freedom in any real-life sense. We believe that civility and having room to manoeuvre in economic and social terms matter.

One critical aspect of Canadian conservatism that American conservatism does not, and has never, embraced is the reality of subsidiarity, or the simple notion that local communities should have decisions made by the level of democratic government closest to them geographically. Canada's provinces and territories have fiscal and practical powers much further advanced than those allowed under the U.S. Constitution to individual American states. This is one example of how Tory respect for the politics and priorities of place shaped a different country and society: one where Saskatchewan could experiment with medicare, where Québec could experiment with its own day care or pension plan, where Nova Scotia could make its own decision to nationalize a private utility and where Manitoba could do exactly the opposite. And none faced sanction or were forbidden to do so by Ottawa.

Canadian conservatives do not generally seek modest and restrained government for ideological purposes. We seek restrained government because it is a better protector of local particularity, identity and freedom of action, and is less likely to permit excessive state intervention in areas it is unable to serve. Some American conservatives encourage dysfunctional government on domestic issues to ensure that private interests (health care, finance) can proceed unbothered by power exercised by elected authorities in the public interest. It is as if their anger and frustration at King George III, at the time of the revolution, continues today and is directed at all governments. History is not destiny, but how we respond to it does determine our future. History in Canada, while not necessarily predictive, has been *vitally* instructive.

America's debt and borrowing levels are at a critical high. As this book goes to press, China is the largest holder of U.S. currency in the world and the Chinese are speaking openly about alternate reference currencies. Except for former Massachusetts governor Mitt Romney, no Republican has come up with a meaningful alternative to the proposed Democratic plan to deal with the fact that millions of Americans live without health care. This speaks volumes to the lack of Republican domestic policy depth in the United States. These Republicans are disengaged from the traditional William F. Buckley and Teddy Roosevelt conservative strain that merged with the realpolitik of the Rockefeller/George H.W. Bush version of the Republican tradition. This latter view was more expansive, more reasonable and more fair and sensitive to a broader mix of American society.

At the turn of the twentieth century, Teddy Roosevelt confronted the great energy and corporate trusts and produced an anti-combines policy that gave small business and genuine competition a fighting chance. George H.W. Bush used his background as CIA chief and as ambassador to China to help shape a realistic world vision that saw limits to U.S. power and engagement and embraced, under the encouragement of G8 colleagues like Brian Mulroney, a meaningful collegiality with both allies and the United Nations in major undertakings (such as the liberation of Kuwait). Remarkably, after the successful U.S.-led coalition's destruction of Saddam Hussein's regime, the neo-conservatives advising his son, George W. Bush, seemed utterly blind to constraints facing the ability of the Pentagon and State Department bureaucracies to deliver peace on the ground in Iraq after regime change. This impaired vision, this unnatural and frankly un-conservative embrace of government overreach, underlines the core weakness of the present neo-conservative disengagement from reality relating to American foreign and defence (and even domestic) policy. A strong American military capacity is, without a doubt, vital for the world. An exceptionalist misunderstanding of the realities of global forces, be they military or civilian, combined with a clear tendency to under-prepare for the inevitable post-conflict adjustment imperils the success of American foreign and defence policy worldwide. This is why Canadian conservatism must take its own path and pursue its own unique development based on its own Canadian roots and history. Canada has very different domestic and international exigencies than the U.S. Being loyal to our allies (a true conservative value) is important, but it does not mean that we should repeat their mistakes.

Canadians have the right to choose not only their leaders and legislators, but also from among the various political options arrayed before them. The reason political parties need to be bottom-up organizations is so that they can ensure this right. A political party that is a power-management system, run by central elites who want to protect their own interests, not only loses touch with the electorate, but works in an unreal political context that is not viable in the long run. In the U.S. today, despite the mythology that anyone can be president, the deeply money-centred campaign realities and the serious absence of spending controls mean that only those who are awash in cash or close to those awash in cash can aspire to high office. The role of money has replaced the importance of policy. This is a perversion of democracy and a serious disabler of the potential for Americans to decide their own future. That imbalance also has a tendency to produce seriously flawed public policy, resulting from sins of omission and commission. One example that immediately comes to mind is the heavy lobbying done by private prison corporations for tougher sentencing laws and more funding for prison expansion. The highest-ever incarceration rate of Americans, a rate well above the rest of the civilized world, is the kind of reality that emerges from this kind of imbalance. The same is true of course of the long, and still ongoing, struggle for a health care insurance with any meaningful universal quality.

The way ahead is littered with detours, wrong turns, setbacks and very deep ditches if the approach taken in Canada is not driven by Canadian conservatism of the kind shaped, developed, nurtured and refined by Canada's unique history, geography and demographics. Ours is a compassionate Canadian conservatism that started when the French arrived in the sixteenth century. It was nurtured through the Ancien Régime, developed during the British regime, defended by French, English, Irish and Dutch loyalists and militia members, along with First Nations, in the battles that stopped the American invaders in their tracks during the War of 1812. It was moulded through evolution with the Crown, not against it. It is, in its Canadian modesty and pragmatism, very different from the divine right of kings and the exclusive embrace of the natural order that dominated European conservatism. Most importantly, it is the inverse of the "life, liberty and pursuit of happiness" exceptionalist neo-liberalism that fuels American neo-conservative excess. Canadian conservatism adopts responsibility as an equal value to freedom, not as an after-tax thought. Canadian conservatism puts nation and community first. It justifies personal and corporate wealth creation on the grounds that they are instruments that help expand the greater good—not instruments that are to be pursued exclusively and for their own sake.

Thrift, balance and proportion are Canadian conservative principles, and vital ones at that. The Wall Street excesses of recent times speak to the fact that prudence and fairness were obviously put well behind greed and unsustainable risk on the U.S.'s priority scale. Some actors in the American neo-conservative context value enterprise and profit, in the winner-take-all-sweepstakes, as concrete expressions of a masters-of-the-universe management of events. Canadian conservatives value the symbiosis of "nation and enterprise," where public policy choices and private sector investment coexist under a broad public interest umbrella. Profit is not the end purpose, in and of itself, and neither is wealth. But nor are they dirty words. Governments should never erect undue barriers to profit or competitive economic activity and investment. To do so would be to dilute the engine of economic expansion and social progress. But profit and wealth creation, simply for their own sakes, must not be allowed to leave a greater wake of destruction and suffering than what pre-existed them—socially, environmentally or economically. And the wedge politics of American conservatism, which seeks to use narrow-gauge, tough-guy issues like gay marriage or abortion (often through simultaneous referenda) to intensify divisions, while politically understandable, speak to the very opposite of the kind of society the Tory tradition in Canada tries to build and to which historic Toryism in Canada has been dedicated.

The Canadian Tory tradition has little room for the mean-spirited and immature. It is one that respects the other political parties as legitimate competitors with differing views in a broad parliamentary democracy—views that will, along with Conservative views, fall in and out of favour from time to time. This is what democracy is about. It is a path that should seek to attract achievers from business, science, arts and culture, farming, journalism, academe and community or volunteer leadership into Conservative Party politics at the grassroots level. And members should feel confident and comfortable in knowing that, if elected, they will have a personal impact on the policy and direction of Canada in a collegial cabinet system in which who is in charge does not diminish who can play a part. The recent Senate appointment of Pamela Wallin, former consul general to New York and distinguished broadcast and print journalist, with a large non-partisan following across Canada and especially in her native Saskatchewan, is a good example of the kind of recruitment that Canadian conservatism needs to promote and advance. Feminists trust her, business leaders have always sought her counsel and Canadians and Americans have trusted and do trust her judgement. Narrow ideological neo-conservative excess would keep people like Pamela Wallin from being recruited; no active, engaged Conservative Party could afford that kind of exclusionary bias.

So, a realistic Canadian conservative view must embrace the need to be brutally frank about the intrinsic problems inherent in American conservatism. The Canadian vs. American conservative comparison manifests itself in endearing, quaint and sometimes destructive ways. The proximity of our two societies, economically, socially and culturally means that the influence of American conservatism, with all of its good and all of its bad aspects, is always part of the Canadian weather map. The survival of the unique Canadian conservative version is not simply a "wouldn't it be nice" option. It is absolutely essential if the Canadian Conservative Party is to be a genuine participant in public policy debate of matters concerning our provinces and country. It was Mr. Diefenbaker's contemporary, the prime minister of the United Kingdom, Harold Macmillan, who argued that "a successful party of the right must continue to recruit its strength from the centre and even from the left centre. Once it begins to shrink into itself like a snail it will be doomed." In that view, he mirrored Disraeli's success before him and Sir John A. Macdonald's looking to Canadian history for guidance. Choose the narrow, ideological American option and you consign Canadian conservatism to oblivion.

Canadian conservatism is not about anger, as it appears so much of American conservatism has become. Traditional American liberals, who supported Senator Henry Jackson on the right of the Democratic Party, who had roots in Americans for Democratic Action and civil rights engagements, who became the apostles of neo-conservatism, were angry at the Democratic Party for not defending the values of democracy more forthrightly worldwide. And they were even angry at Richard Nixon for withdrawing from the Vietnam War, which was started by American liberals under John Kennedy and continued by Lyndon Johnson; they were angry at a public narrative in much of the press that saw value in détente with the Soviets, as embraced by Henry Kissinger, as well as potential in overtures to the Chinese. They broke from the civil, somewhat isolationist, but always intellectually engaged paleo-conservatism of William F. Buckley and adopted a type of robust re-engineering of Republicanism, moving away from the noblesse oblige of the Nelson Rockefeller crowd (he was Mr. Kissinger's first political patron), and sought instead to radicalize the Republicans after Henry "Scoop" Jackson's defeat within Democratic party ranks. Jackson was the very conservative Democratic senator from Washington State who could not overtake the traditional centrist Hubert Humphrey, Johnson's vice-president, who himself had to fend off the Bobby Kennedys, George McGoverns and Eugene McCarthys on the more pacifist left.

The Ronald Reagan period was a time of neo-conservative progress in the United States, while the genial American president, universally likeable and apparently decent and fair-minded, made headway. This was important in Canada because both the Reform Party in its inception and some Canadian Progressive Conservatives were intrigued by the mix of intellectual intensity, ideological clarity and campaign technology American Republicans developed during the Nixon and post-Nixon years. Narrowly cast direct-mail fundraising campaigns (which I helped design in Canada in the mid 1970s under the leadership of Bob Stanfield, when I reported to the PC national director, John Laschinger), push-polling that was more about shaping a view than measuring it and hard or tacit cooperation with evangelical and single issue lobbies (IRA, pro-life) all helped to shape a potent neo-conservative thrust vitally positioned to counter the many labour and related organizations that always worked the other side of the street. The birth of Fox News, launched in 1996, took the conservative arguments advanced in Buckley's *National Review* or the *American Spectator* to a new intensity and volume, minus some of the intellectual depth and civility. It is not hard to see how this would be very attractive. Why engage your political opponents around arguments, facts and policy preference when one can conspire to attack them personally, or have them attacked personally by officially unconnected fellow travellers, especially when there are media more than eager to live-blog the interaction without even a scintilla of editorial judgement or prudence. For parties in opposition or parties without any hope of winning an election, this trash-talk route in America is as good as any. And while fascination with the bump and grind of it all is, to any political junkie, understandably irresistible, one who seeks to adopt it or adapt it to Canadian Conservative politics does so at considerable peril. In Canada, there is real evidence that it does not fit in with our political culture.

The opposition scare campaigns against Stephen Harper during the last three elections (2004, 2006 and 2008) have failed to keep him and the Conservatives from gaining more seats. The famous skewed photograph of Jean Chrétien in the 1993 Campbell campaign backfired horribly, in large measure because Liberal organizers were able to play on grassroots Tory discomfort with the perceived approach. The wild overstatements and fears raised against Ontario's Mike Harris in 1995 did not prevent a Tory majority—twice! Attacking the coherence, logic or balance of someone's policies, or questioning their intent or capacity, is a legitimate part of the mix. But screeching arch epithets or unsustainable character allegations advances no cause and usually triggers a serious voter blowback. There is a difference between criticizing, however vigorously, opponents' policies or lack of same. Their logic, judgement, engagement and competence are always open to debate and attack. Their motivation and character will emerge in the cut and thrust of debate.

Canadian conservatism does not come from a tradition of excluding opponents' right to participate, or questioning their right to differ or offer another view. We gain in strength when we build a broader consensus. It is turning inward that causes us to lose ground.

The current contagion of American conservatism is already being gobbled up by the new excesses of the Tea Party. This appears to be a latter-day version of early liberal neo-conservative anger, minus the intellectual rigour and contemplative counter-analysis of established foreign and domestic American policy. It is more a populist anger. Despite protestations to the contrary, some of this may reflect the frustration of the size of the Obama victory in the Congress and Senate, and the deeply disturbing nature of the financial meltdown.

Whatever its motivations, it is a contagion Canadian conservatives and Conservatives cannot afford to indulge. To do so is to set aside the sustaining traditions, histories and moderate balances that has made Canadian Conservatives relevant and engaged competitors in provincial and federal government for the full range of our history. Canadian conservatism is about freedom and responsibility. American conservatism embraces only freedom, and in its most selfish extreme. Canadian conservatism believes in moderate but fair taxation. American conservatives believe in none. Canadian conservatism is based on a balance of nation and enterprise. American conservatism has no interest in that balance. Canadian conservatism helped build the Commonwealth of Nations, which is about the rule of law, democracy, parliamentary government and development aid across fifty-four countries, 2.4 billion people spanning every colour, race, continent, religion, language and culture in the world—an idea deeply inimical to the American neo-conservative world view. Canadian conservatives have never advocated starting a war or attacking anyone, but have always supported robust Canadian military response to protect the principles we share with allies or to protect our allies when they are attacked by others. American neo-conservatives have a long list of potential military targets. They, in their excess, are about setting aside the balance in public, national and international policy. Canadian conservatives are about the balance in all three. Setting that balance aside is the ultimate indulgence and the ultimate dereliction of duty to the country and its future. And that indulgence would not be, in any way, forgiven by the Canadian voter.

Conclusion

THE ROAD AHEAD

There are potential traps in the future for Canadian conservatives. Traps around undue centralization of both government and party; traps in letting civil service elites dilute vital commitments to a robust and deployable military and humanitarian capacity; traps in creating enemies of the media unnecessarily; traps around restricting who can or cannot serve in government, so that good people stay away; and traps in letting bureaucracies indulge in over-regulation. Unfortunately, these are traps of the kind that one can fall into far too easily. It is in the nature of large bureaucracies to first fend for themselves. This is as true of Ottawa as it is of the larger provinces. It is not about malevolence or disrespect for the public or the rights of Parliament; it is about using excessive regulations, unduly large budget bills, obfuscated public reporting and "strategic review" budget cuts to maximize the bureaucracy's options and discretion at the expense of the citizen, small business owner or farmer. Too much of this sort of thing has proceeded unchecked in recent years, and Conservatives and conservatives should always be deeply vigilant about these excesses.

The Liberal Party is resilient and always able to attract talent. Defeating Liberal cynicism is a good thing, but taking the Liberals for granted is always a mistake. They have not yet deserted the "default" position in Canadian politics, although their grip has been loosened by Stephen Harper's successes.

The various traps are made more inviting by the tension every Conservative government has always faced, between being open to a broad range of ideas and possessing strong discipline and central control. Either one of the options includes extremes that can greatly harm Canadian conservatism for decades. The party has never been about an "either one or the other" choice. It has been about finding the right balance between coherence and policy integrity at the one end and openness to grassroots ideas and pluralism at the other.

Successful national and provincial leaders like Macdonald, Borden, Lougheed, Flemming, Stanfield, Duplessis, Robarts, Davis and Roblin all found the right and workable balance necessary to have sustained periods of Conservative governments broadly trusted and liked, however much some choose to malign them today.

Stephen Harper has been remarkably successful to date at finding the right balance, helping to broaden it and, in doing so, building a new Conservative Party and a new Conservative government that most pundits thought utterly impossible at the beginning of the decade. But the search for the right balance that can best serve Canada and broaden conservative appeal, nationally and internationally, must be, for any party leader, never-ending.

Any time that any Conservative leader in any era determines that she or he has already found the right balance, and that the balance needs no lessons from history or the grassroots, the great "imbalance" of detachment and aloofness begins. That imbalance is a part of what has kept Conservatives out of office for decades at a time—much to the detriment of Canada's social, economic, productive and intellectual well-being. Looking for the new balance, and being open to the new strains of tomorrow's conservatism, is the beginning of wisdom. Ending that search or thinking that it is unnecessary is always the height of folly.

The central challenge for Conservatives in government is to be the advocates for those who are outside the charmed circle, either by region, income or social status. This is more important than being advocates for the bureaucracy, whose interests are intrinsically self-centred. When the bureaucracy advises against innovation, when it laments or obviates policy choices, when it circumscribes or crushes parliamentary accountability—as most bureaucracies do naturally, whoever is in office—it is crucial that engaged Conservatives do not become the bureaucracy's agent. There are a myriad of examples that ring alarm bells: bureaucrats who use wildly excessive administrative authority in new laws to limit personal freedom or right of appeal; bureaucrats who invite governments to pass laws that defy the Charter of Rights and Freedoms while advising ministers and parliamentary committees that they do not (only to be summarily struck down by the courts); bureaucrats who seek to claw back vital defence resources at precisely the time they are needed most; bureaucrats who derail, delay or dilute reasonable accountability to Parliament; and bureaucrats who oppose tax cuts, greater revenue sharing or transfer stability with the provinces because it diminishes their prerogatives and program-design options.

These are present and ongoing realities in Ottawa and they need to be resisted. What must also be resisted is the siren call to excessive partisanship. From Lord Elgin to John Macdonald, from Cartier to Borden, from R.B. Bennett to Mulroney, there were times when the public interest was not only more important than partisan interest but inimical to it.

Afghanistan is that kind of issue. Social security and safety net modernization is that kind of issue. Health care streamlining and efficiency and pension reform are two such issues. Support for defence and security investment is very much that kind of issue.

Stepping beyond partisanship does not mean deserting one's own principles or base. Quite the contrary. It means that one actually searches for ways in which to address the concerns of other stakeholders in the democratic process. It is not always possible to go beyond partisanship, but on pressing issues of national purpose it is always wrong not to try. Mulroney did so on Free Trade and the Constitution; Davis did so on the Charter of Rights and Repatriation. On issues where a genuine, broadly consensual way ahead is crucial, extending one's hand to the opposition is very difficult—but this is precisely what Tory government forces in the House and Senate should attempt. If done fairly and rebuffed, there is no harm done. If never attempted, then the system of government, its parliamentary institutions and underlying principles are brought very much into disfavour. And this never reflects well on those in government. It is not naïve to extend one's hand. It is not weak to seek collaboration. The fact that Liberals rarely have, should not discourage Tories from trying.

The kinds of challenges that Conservatives will face in the years ahead will no doubt reflect the complexity of a rapidly changing world. Economic power is shifting to the West in Canada and to Asia in the larger world. America is facing a crisis of domestic and international confidence. Nihilistic forces of violence and brutality are alive in state and non-state organizations worldwide. Core economic challenges are more complex, as are the regulatory balances necessary to sustain both solvency and opportunity. Risk management is a new assertive priority in national and international affairs.

Now is the time for steady, adaptive, principle-based leadership. And this is what Canadian conservative history and tradition can teach today's conservatives. Understanding the balances of that tradition and the exigencies of its core principles and tenets has never mattered more.

Speaking at the annual Sir John A. Macdonald celebration in January of 2007 at the Albany Club in Toronto to an enthusiastic and diverse crowd, Prime Minister Harper reminded all present, in one of the best speeches ever given by any prime minister, that a component of the Liberal conceit was the belief that Canada actually began with the 1982 Charter of Rights and Freedoms. This amusing poke at the Trudeaucentric view that Liberals of a certain age hold of all things Canadian evoked an instantaneous response from the audience. Tories of all shades and stripes— from the right, to the left—whom Harper had so deftly combined into one political coalition by reaching out to Peter MacKay, all agreed, whatever their other points of disagreement, on the core calumny of Liberal conceit: that beyond one act of constitutional revision in 1982, there would be no peaceable country of laws, rights and collective will in Canada at all. The prime minister cited the many nation-building measures of Macdonald, Borden, Bennett, Diefenbaker and others to pierce this offensive and ahistorical Liberal delusion.

Whatever the momentary media passion in the land about the ego-tickling stimuli of Twitter, texting or YouTube, the hard truth is that history matters. It matters to the future because it is the reason for the choices we face today.

Conservative history in Canada is one of victories and defeats, policy successes and setbacks. What has survived is what has stood the test of time: Macdonald's railway, his defence of the Northwest from American-inspired insurgents; Borden's stand at Versailles; Meighen's support of universal suffrage; R.B. Bennett's social reforms; Diefenbaker's Bill of Rights; and Mulroney's anti-apartheid and pro–Free Trade idealism and his pragmatic GST legislation. These brave stances and substantial investments were all politically unrewarding for the incumbent prime minister and the Conservative Party at the time, but right for Canada in the long run. They were part of a larger vision of economic and political expansion and social fairness. They were intrinsically conservative and Conservative. And while it is true that grand, eloquent, visionary engagements can be overdone and can dilute credibility, what parties propose and governments do is part and parcel of a preference for the kind of Canada and world we are all trying to build. Vision is not intrinsically subversive. Making the link to the broader goal is essential. And sharing with Canadians what that Canada and world should look like in terms of the outcomes we seek is not folly. In fact, if done properly, it can create difficulties for those who oppose these measures only for tactical purposes.

The uniqueness of Canadian conservatism is its ability to not, in its fealty to Canadian values, history, geography and demography, be held captive by conservatism elsewhere. The conservative social principles that served in parts of Europe over the centuries could not, for a moment, hope to survive unchanged in the geography of a country that was larger than any ten European countries combined. Canada's geography and demography called for intendants, governors, seigneurs, local military personnel, commanders, agreements with First Nations and fortifications distributed over vast territories. And, above all, it called for pragmatic, not dogmatic, compromise, achieved creatively. That, by definition, required the shared government and decentralization that became the very essence of Canada.

European conservatism has its origins in the preservation of aristocracy and all its privileges, in the continuation of a strongly theocratic state and the divine right of kings, and in the perpetuation of feudal structures inimical to the progress and dignity of those not "well-born." This system evolved over centuries to embrace a strong association between property and freedom and a preference for tradition. Beyond the preservation of this kind of social order, where land ownership, usually through inheritance, meant essentially everything, there was not much of a role for government, especially if it disturbed how the upper classes went about their business in any way. It was a system that saw leadership in government, military, academe and enterprise tied very closely to one's standing in society, which depended entirely on one's ownership of land or association through kinship or marriage with those who did own land.

There were remnants of all this in early Canada. But these remnants were quickly superseded by the exigencies of a frontier: the need to have local order and community coherence, the need to provide support for the geographical enterprise, the need to reconcile English and French, and the need to face the challenge of potential American absorption.

No English-speaking or French-speaking country has on its longest border a similar cultural phenomenon. Economically— and in many other ways—our neighbour to the south is a huge blessing. But no blessing comes without a cost. And for Canada, from 1776 onward, maintaining our values, our sovereignty, our social and economic priorities and our identity has been a central part of every government's remit. That remit is as important to French language and cultural preservation as it is in our approach to health care or parliamentary and confederal government. It is not only about identity but about the day-to-day benefits of having a unique Canadian approach to government, politics, social policy and global affairs. "Unique" here does not speak to purpose. It is a necessity if Canada is to survive.

The conservative view of sovereignty in Canadian history has always reflected not only de jure legal status, but also de facto engagement in the preservation of the balance between freedom and responsibility, and individual and community, in a sovereign society that manages its own affairs.

Domestically, that has always meant a striving for equality of opportunity for all, with a minimum of excessive government bureaucracy, regulation or intervention. In Ontario in the 1970s, what this meant for Bill Davis and his finance minister Darcy McKeough was addressing the poverty of senior citizens. Not with a new welfare program that would dilute personal sovereignty and dignity, but with a universal tax-based guaranteed annual income supplement that topped up all tax filers who were above a certain age and beneath a basic income floor. It involved no new bureaucracy or "how to live your life" rules from the Ontario Tory government. It was a simple top up, via the tax system. Poverty among seniors, who were predominantly women, dropped from almost one third of the target population to three percent. Not perfect, but very effective and cost efficient.

As we near the 2013–14 negotiating period for federal social transfers, the government has a rare opportunity to take this same approach to tackling poverty, which has not been reduced to a level of less than ten percent of our general population for decades. Provinces could wind down welfare, and the federal government could create income-based refundable tax credits. Federal transfers aimed at provincial welfare could be redirected elsewhere, as could provincial welfare dollars, into places like early education or more advanced elder and palliative care. Whatever the method, it's possible that sovereignty for the individual and sovereignty for communities could be enhanced. As the negative pathologies that are created by poverty—putting the poor in expensive prisons (more than any other income group); into the health care system and into the ranks of the illiterate and the unemployed—are diminished, the resulting savings would allow governments at all levels to manage programs and costs more rationally. That conservative respect for the individual freedom of citizens, the sovereign capacity of governments and the burden on the taxpayer is the kind of balanced approach traditional program-happy and social-engineering liberals and social democrats are unlikely to ever embrace. And the vision of a society of genuine equality of opportunity, as opposed to the more socialist bias towards a society of equality of outcomes, is very compelling.

Conservatives understand that sovereignty is not a goal but, in fact, an instrument towards a goal. The end goal, of course, is a better life for more people and a strong democratic state within which people can advance and prosper with a strong sense of self-worth and opportunity and without fear of intimidation, foreign threat, civil disorder or unreasonable constraint of reasonable freedoms and rights. In Canada, that means a conservatism that is at home with prairie and agricultural populism and the stability of the Crown. It means a conservatism that embraces individual enterprise and initiative and that seeks its moderation on the levels of both taxes and the reach and scope of government itself. It means a conservatism that embraces tolerance and inclusion because our national strength as a small population, large geography country makes all hands on deck not an option but an undeniable requirement. It also means that we learn from the mistakes of others to avoid repeating them ourselves.

Arch and narrow conservatism, badly articulated and defended, made Labour leader Tony Blair very successful. Narrow ideology, rigid neo-conservative excess has the potential to severely limit any hope for a Republican rebirth in American politics, mid-term elections notwithstanding. Successful European conservatives like Sarkozy in France and Merkel in Germany, despite their transient problems, seem more and more Canadian in their moderation and Red Tory-like social consciences. David Cameron in the United Kingdom reflects it in many ways as well, with his one country, and one world, "big society" conservatism. "We are all in this together" should bother no conservative anywhere who admires Canada's history of balance.

Balance is not a goal in and of itself for Canadian conservatives and Conservatives. It is a vital means to a critical outcome, and its importance lies in its potential to help Conservatives attain their goals, at home and abroad. At home: a balance between provincial and federal roles helps Conservatives to avoid oppressive federal centralization; a balance between what governments raise and spend at one end and what private and not-for-profit sectors are free to achieve at the other helps Conservatives to sustain tax fairness; a balance between rural and urban priorities helps Conservatives to respect the exigencies and rights of both; and a balance between the key freedoms—from fear and want—helps Conservatives to secure a better life for more people. Abroad: a balance between spending on national security and spending on the eradication of global poverty further helps Conservatives to secure a better life for more people who can experience freedom from fear and from want and become stronger as a result.

The right balance needs always to be sought and defended at home and abroad because it is the absence of balance that creates the most serious of domestic and geopolitical threats to Canadian ideals, values, prospects and security.

And the challenge now is to define a broad and compelling agenda that is about more than managing through the economic difficulties caused by the American credit and housing bubble collapse. The agenda must also take Canada to the next level of economic expansion and social progress, where equality of opportunity matters.

Let me suggest a set of priorities about the Canadian dream that attempts to translate Sir John A.'s mission to our time and place: to build a Canada where the accident of one's birth, disadvantaged or otherwise, does not limit one's ability to succeed and contribute; to build a Canada where there is a greater commitment to excellence and better access to education and health care; to build a Canada where equality of opportunity and free enterprise sustain and strengthen each other; to build a Canada where the federal-provincial relationship reflects the needs and aspirations of our people and not just the vested interests of our political establishment; to build a Canada where the military can advance, at home and abroad, with logistic, combat and high-tech expeditionary capacity, with the right human, fiscal and material resources, and with the values of freedom, tolerance, democracy, non-aggression, national sovereignty and respect for fundamental human rights; to build a Canada where the government neither overstates its role nor understates its responsibilities, reflecting the historical reality that we are not a society of ideologies but a community of ideals, and a pragmatic and fair-minded one at that; and, finally, to build a Canada where economic performance and social progress are linked through a clear understanding that you cannot have one without the other. Societies that are prepared to decouple one aspect from the other or that have lacked the passion to unite them in the first place are no better or worse than we are. They are just different. Uniting the two, however, without wild swings to the left or the right, is the Canadian way and at the very core of our economic and political culture.

In the same way as Macdonald would have been dismissed by some moralists and social conservatives on the far right today as a Red Tory with a drinking problem, or as Churchill would clearly have been dismissed by Mrs. Thatcher, were he a cabinet contemporary, as a hopeless "wet" with delusions of grandeur and social justice, so too would some of the passionate purposes above be dismissed as less than practical, in view of contemporary and competitive pressures.

The Canadian idea itself has always been less than practical and intrinsically inefficient. So what? Many things that really matter, like love, research, civility and compassion, are also intrinsically inefficient. With our Canadian mix of using private and public resources, of sustaining not only our founding cultures, but those that have enriched us from abroad, we have dared to leave Henry Ford's American melting pot vision with the other pots and pans and have built something more reverential of diversity. That diversity is a compelling human resource, one which contributes to economic strength and vitality.

The sort of one-nation (in the sense of breaking down class divisions) Toryism that reflected the common age of Disraeli and Macdonald and the one-nation Toryism that reflected Sir John A.'s negotiated federalism, with a respect for both diversity and nationality, seem less than robust these days, within all of the political parties at the federal level. Tactical obsession will do that to the best of intentions. Someday, hopefully sooner rather than later, that may change.

We need to have the courage to use statecraft in a more heroic way if we are to truly shape a prosperous and humane future.

It has always struck me that among the many strengths we share as Canadians—decency, compassion, moderation, tolerance—we also have a particular weakness, a weakness that combines wishful thinking, nostalgia and confusion. I would like to call this weakness the Canadian Disease. This problem often manifests itself in a deeply felt devotion to various instruments of public policy. A devotion so deep it confuses instruments with the goals they are used to achieve.

Health care is a classic example. The Canada Health Act, at the base of our universal access health care system, is not a set of goals in and of itself, but a set of instruments that Canadians have put into place for a purpose—namely, that each individual Canadian has the best available medical, diagnostic and hospital services in the country without regard to his or her individual ability to pay. The ultimate goal is better health and longer disease-free and impairment-free lives, along with reduced financial worry. The instruments involved here, some of which are nearly fifty years old, have been elevated by some to holy grail status. This is a classic example of the Canadian Disease contagion. That virus paralyzes both political debate and creative policy development. This produces a form of "path dependency," where governments and politicians and even lobby groups go back and forth in the same policy path or rut, because it takes far less energy to do so than might be required to hop out of the rut and start a new path. John Diefenbaker did not succumb to path dependency when he crafted the Canadian Bill of Rights that passed Parliament in 1960. Nor did Brian Mulroney succumb to it when he negotiated the Free Trade Agreement, implemented the GST or helped to lead the charge on Commonwealth sanctions that led to the defeat of apartheid. Succumbing to that path dependency was not what Joe Clark did when Canada led the way to settle Southeast Asian boat people in Canada and elsewhere. And Stephen Harper was not intimidated by political risk when he reached out to Peter MacKay in order to break a corrosive conservative family guerrilla war. Nor did he back away from the challenge when he offered a fulsome, heartfelt apology to aboriginal Canadians for residential school excesses and cruelties imposed by previous governments on previous generations. Why is it that these moments of vision, humanity and courage stand out well beyond the day-to-day tactical skirmishes that so occupy parliamentary parties and their media overseers? Largely because they matter. The conservative and Conservative way ahead should be about principles and engagements that matter. The imprisonment of path dependency and the Canadian Disease is no basis for moving ahead. In fact, it is the ultimate knuckling under to the bureaucratic bias towards deep and distressing inertia, both at home and abroad.

The inertia virus has, of course, gone crazy on the issue of sovereignty. And I would say candidly, that if there was ever a case of a conceptual pandemic of serious proportions, one that is debilitating to a society as a whole and prejudicial to its prospects, this issue clearly fits that bill.

Sovereignty is a vital national instrument. It is not a goal. We use it to shape domestic policy within our own borders; we share and divide sovereignty in the creation and negotiation of federal and confederal constitutions; we protect it through the patrol of our airspace, land mass, sea lanes and coastal waters; and we use it to make agreements with other sovereign nations that duly and democratically elected Canadian governments deem to be in our national interest. Sovereignty is not hoarded, nor is it locked away. It is there to be used to advance the legitimate social and economic interests of Canadians on a host of fronts.

But the Canadian Disease virus has produced a very strange behavioural pattern in which, beyond the trade specialists and proponents of a dynamic outreach across normative bilateral perspectives, the traditional creativity we are known for as a country in our international statecraft dimensions is very much constrained. So the same Canada that helped write the UN charter, that created the concept of international peacekeeping, that helped create the Commonwealth, that had a key role in the creation of the Universal Declaration of Human Rights, moves today with an almost paralytic lethargy on the most important challenge and opportunity that it faces: namely, how to better govern and engage a world whose prosperity and stability is now deeply at peril. As a large trading partner dependent on trade income and markets for our own quality of life and for our own freedom from fear and want, this question of engagement is very much in our interest.

We are members of the world's largest volunteer association of nations, the Commonwealth, which shares no ideology of the right or left, but rather a sense of the value of democracy, freedom, human rights and development that spans rich and poor, east and west, Christians, Muslims, Hindus, Sikhs, Confucianists and those of every other faith in the world, every race, colour and creed.

The Commonwealth is the ultimate conservative-balance organization; it respects the local particularity of religion, culture and practice, and the countries within it are united by common law traditions, common parliamentary traditions and one English language. We can and should be much more engaged in strengthening its reach, and extending its democratic and aid capacities. It has the nimbleness the UN has long lost and the cultural sensitivity Europe is unable to muster regarding Turkey, an able and important ally. The Commonwealth has room for both Pakistan and India, despite their mutual anxieties, and has had the courage to confront tensions such as those in Rhodesia and South Africa, two countries that used racist oppression as a base for public policy. The Commonwealth needs to do more and embrace a more robust stance on its core values. And Canada should, in collaboration with other Commonwealth members, seek to broaden its global and humane reach through the organization. A similar embrace of the more long-term (and, as of yet, not comparable) potential of La Francophonie is also worth a look.

As I argued when I was president of the Institute for Research on Public Policy, just before coming to the Senate, a critical global priority for Canada should be the creation of a North American Community in which our sovereignty and influence is enhanced.

The opportunity to create a community that enshrines democratic principles, enhances economic growth and opportunity, deepens trade and regulatory cooperation, increases social justice and economic development, and forms a basis for a hemispheric Community of the Americas should excite and inspire. The progress made in Québec City at the 2001 Summit of the Americas, where trade integration was coupled with important democratic and social priorities, should, in any healthy society, inspire immense creativity and enthusiasm. And yet we would have to admit that beyond the civil servants, trade lawyers, scholars and business practitioners engaged in this work as part of their honourable professional service to us all, the Canada we know is reticent, angst-ridden and extremely evasive in terms of any strong national popular commitment.

Now, there are obvious reasons why politicians are reticent, even though there are even better public reasons why they should show more courage. Laurier was defeated on a proposal for "reciprocity" far more modest than the FTA for which Mulroney, showing immense courage, eventually won a mandate in 1988. Mackenzie King almost signed an agreement with the Americans after World War II, and then demurred. (Demurral was the operative word for much of his successful career in public life.) The Chrétien government was, when in opposition in the 1980s and 1990s, clearly opposed to the FTA and NAFTA until a policy conference in the early 1990s in Aylmer, Québec, where they wisely decided as a party to bury the hatchet on Free Trade and move on. Brian Mulroney's courage, along with that of Michael Wilson, on the Goods and Services Tax probably did much to cut Tory poll standings and make electoral defeat almost an assured outcome. So courage has its genuine political costs.

I am very much persuaded by Mancur Olson's argument put forward in *Power and Prosperity* that when it comes to the importance of institutions to facilitating trade, "without the right institutional encouragement, a country will be restricted to trades that are self-enforcing." And I make the case that the enlightened institution-building that created NATO, NORAD, the Commonwealth, the FTA, and NAFTA must not be allowed to grind to a halt because a contagion of self-doubt and insecurity is about to land. In fact, this is precisely the time to make the case to the country for a vibrant North American Community.

If sovereignty is an instrument to be used to expand freedom and opportunity, then surely the use by us of our own sovereignty to build a North American Community must also be seen as an attempt to create a larger society that reflects our values and priorities. This should be a Conservative and conservative priority. What are the goals such a community would serve?

1. Enhanced market size and trading opportunities for Canadian companies, employees and investors with less non-tariff and exclusionary barriers of various forms.
2. A continent-wide commitment to economic and social development, where models like our own equalization program or the European Union's Cohesion Fund could be adapted to serve economic and social development throughout the North American Community.
3. Cooperative environmental, social and military activities that magnify our individual capacities and have the

potential to deal with opportunities, threats and challenges that are larger than any one of the three founding nations: Canada, the United States and Mexico.

4. The creation of a North American Assembly, not unlike the early European Parliament, which could begin to give legitimate expression to the concerns we share with our allies and partners to the south, and which could provide the opportunity for legitimate democratic linkage across national borders.

A North American Community is not about the victory of the right or the left in this country, the United States or Mexico. With just a touch of statecraft and leadership, it could be about the coming together of our Canadian commitments to both economic performance and social justice with a far-sighted vision that sees Americans and Mexicans as among the very best allies in the world. Who in the world would we rather have as allies and fellow travellers in pursuing the twin challenges of economic performance and social justice?

What September 11 brought home to us all is that neither the Atlantic Ocean nor the Pacific insulates us from man's fabled "inhumanity to man." But September 11 also taught us that *in extremis* we get down quickly to the fundamentals of security, humanity and the key instrument of recovery. Open and secure borders are better than those that are closed in fear or slow-moving; planning ahead is better than panic and insecurity; common ground and joint institutions, built in mutual interest and practical reality, are far better than retreating into the narrow sovereignty of fear and misunderstanding.

Surely the rule that has defined our foreign policy priorities since World War 11—namely, that we secure our national interests best as an open, small-market, middle-power economy through an aggressive multilateralism—has never mattered more than it does today. A North American Community with institutions shaped in part by Canadians, by our ingenuity and creativity, by our sense of respect for cultural and linguistic diversity, by our desire for both economic and social progress, would be a serious and important goal.

The narrow-minded focus on sovereignty as a purely self-fulfilling goal, as opposed to an instrument with which to advance and share our national purpose and interests, is the refuge of those who fear the broader context of visionary thinking. That fear is completely out of keeping with the wider Canadian tradition that has been in place since the inception of Confederation in 1867. Macdonald's reach, Laurier's heart, Borden's muscle, Meighen's bridge, Diefenbaker's vision, Mulroney's courage and Harper's intensity do not argue for a Canada without reach or aspiration.

Jean Chrétien showed significant courage and leadership in terms of the Québec City Summit of the Americas and the declaration that emerged there. On Free Trade and in opposition to apartheid, Brian Mulroney stood in the tradition of nation builders like Macdonald and anti-racism leaders such as Diefenbaker. Paul Martin's role as chair of the G20 was also reflective of his very Canadian preference for economic performance and social justice. While it is a truism in politics that the urgent always takes precedence over the important, leaving the development of a North American community to the sands of time would give a whole new meaning to "abdication of duty."

The time is ripe for a Canadian White Paper on a North American Community that includes a suggested process for the way ahead, and for the environmental and security aspects of the relationship. The time is ripe for a White Paper that discusses what a North American Assembly would look like, how its members could be elected within the three founding countries, and what initial advisory, consultative and auditing role it might play, as the European Parliament did in its early days. The time is ripe for a White Paper that embraces a community that includes our Caribbean neighbours and friends and moves beyond some of the debilitating ideological disputes that, even today, hold this hemisphere back from its full potential.

An economic market with four hundred million participants linked by culture and language to the English, French and Hispanic worlds across the globe, with enhanced infrastructure, defence, respect for diversity, far-reaching social opportunity and mutual commitments and obligations, fuelled by reasonably unencumbered trade flows and impressive economies of scale, would certainly be a compelling step ahead for a better world.

To let the contagion of the Canadian Disease, or some unjustified insecurity keep us from this or keep our political leaders on both sides of the floor from embracing these opportunities would be to lose all sense of priority and perspective. The challenges and issues we need to face at home need not be set aside by this common effort towards a North American Community. They would be placed in a more realistic and prospect-intense context, which would, I predict, assist in their resolution, as would the enhanced national wealth created through broader economic integration.

We have reached the point where our national interests— economic, social, security and the rest—are now best served by a North American Community engaged in the economic broadening and institutional cohesion that generates focus and opportunity. There will be a huge effort on the part of the forces of reaction, the old proponents of "a little Canada" and the merchants of insecurity and polarization to systematically strip away our will to move ahead. Canadian conservatives across this country must ensure that we do all that our democratic system allows to not let those forces prevail. We must take the case beyond universities, law offices and specialized bureaucracies and trade associations and to our fellow Canadians, with respect and determination. And we should not wait until the next crisis or negotiation. We should begin the inoculation process against the Canadian Disease now by advancing the prospects, issues, challenges and opportunities of a North American Community on a go-forward basis. And we should circulate that White Paper in English, French and Spanish to legislators and business and labour leaders throughout our three countries. We must look beyond bilateral integration to the genuine promise of a North American Community. We owe it to our children, ourselves and our grandchildren to do so.

It would be the logical next step, building on Prime Minister Harper's focus on our own hemispheric neighbourhood in foreign and trade policy. And it would indicate exactly what the right balance between sovereignty and local authority on the one hand, and outreach and cooperation on the other, could achieve for today's and tomorrow's Canadians. The process can be started easily enough with a White Paper and broad national discussion; an America that might have been resistant before may well be more open today. Drugs, climate change, disease control, trade and poverty challenges know no borders. The exercise of sovereignty in the national interest truly requires a search for international solutions within one's own neighbourhood. It is a vision today as large as others that have driven our past. It need not be an over-the-top exaggerated promise. It can be a steady determination to open markets, strengthen liberty and development, and make Canada healthier and safer by attacking the poverty, protectionism and small-mindedness that are the real threats we face from the "near abroad."

In the beginning and in the end, Canadian conservatism is about balance. Balance that mediates between left and right, between the past and the future, and builds bridges over which progress can be made and new ideas can be sent. In peace and war, with our allies and partners, Canadian balance, competence, decency and fairness have become hallmarks. This is true of our men and women in uniform, it is true of our diplomats and it is true of successful Canadian governments. Excessive partisanship, on a consistent basis, is not a helpful contributor to that balance. Reaching out, frequently beyond partisan lines, is how to both broaden that balance to include others and build the large consensus Canada needs on the most challenging issues of our time.

Acknowledgements

I owe a debt to many who were of direct and indirect assistance and support throughout the three years of effort involved in this undertaking. The idea of a reasonably historical treatment of Canada's conservative roots really emerged from the work of many journalists who, on an ongoing basis, use "conservative" and "Conservative" in their respective Canadian, American, European or religious sense interchangeably. The frequency of this is such that it struck me as high time for a book like this; a rooted look at how Canadian conservatism differed would be a helpful addition to the narrative, wherever any reader might be on the political spectrum.

Publisher Scott McIntyre was a constant source of advice, patience and encouragement. Editor Susan Folkins used diligence, granularity and precision to help the manuscript to a more readable and less unduly pedantic form, an effort on her part for which I am greatly appreciative.

Pam Wallin's kindness in agreeing to do the foreword is deeply appreciated, not only because of her own vast skill and experience as a journalist, broadcaster, diplomat and author, but because of the unique perspective she now brings to her role as a Canadian Senator. Her ability to serve her reading and viewing publics and her country for decades as a non-partisan journalist and diplomat affords her a unique capacity to offer readers a fresh perspective on the arguments advanced in this effort. Her Wadena, Saskatchewan, roots ensure that her views are always grounded in the core frankness, independence and no-nonsense clarity for which she is broadly known and respected.

My family, Donna and Jacqueline, are always encouraging, and great sources of honest advice and unrelenting good and gentle sarcasm, which can illuminate an idea in so many ways. My daughter Jacqueline uses humour and a cogent analytical capacity to link disparate political and social pieces in ways that regularly give me fresh insights. Brothers Brian and Seymour, both in very different walks of life, have added the kind of honest and thoughtful takes on the broader world beyond politics that are deeply valuable to honing one's own world view. My executive assistant at both the Institute for Research on Public Policy and in the Senate, Cathy Ciavaglia, deserves credit for helping to ensure that those evenings, weekends and brief vacations, when this text was written, were actually preserved so that the time to write existed.

I owe a special debt to Rosemarie Brisson, whom I have known and respected since 1997 (when she was a key campaign volunteer for Helen Cooper, the PC candidate in Kingston), and who helped in a unique way. As my policy advisor in Ottawa, she applied her background as a civil servant, accomplished Kingston actor and theatre volunteer to ask tough, key questions throughout the writing process and always provided salient and deeply helpful advice. Her kindness, on weekends, evenings and holidays, in deciphering my handwriting (yes, fountain pen on yellow-lined foolscap—guilty as charged!) and clarifying issues and ideas through questions, debate and editorial advice was a crucial emotional and intellectual enabler for this book. A remarkable speech writer herself, her instincts and passion for public policy were and remain of incalculable value. Brain cells are supposed to degrade as one ages. Her engagement and penetrating focus may have, on occasion, reversed the trend.

I remember Adrienne Clarkson, when she was Governor General, reminding a room full of folks at an Order of Canada ceremony in 2003 that all of us in life stand on the shoulders of those who believed in us and those who would be astonished at any success at all. In my case, Conservatives, conservatives and Progressive Conservatives have facilitated an ongoing intellectual journey, of which this modest effort is a part. Formative forces including Bill Davis, Darcy McKeough, Roy McMurtry, John Diefenbaker, Richard Hatfield, Bob Stanfield, Brian Mulroney, Sterling Lyon, Nate Nurgitz, Barbara McDougall, Peter Lougheed, Peter MacKay, Norman Atkins, Dalton Camp and Stephen Harper all generated fresh insights, unwittingly and otherwise, about people and the interplay of ideas. And close friends and political co-combatants over the years including Harry Near, Bill Fox, Lee Richardson, Bill Liaskas, Graham Fox, Linda Frum, Katie Hermant, Kellie Leitch, Michael Meighen, Lowell Murray, Ian Green, Gerry St. Germain, Graham Scott and Tom Kierans all helped me, through countless discussions, to shape the conclusions and questions addressed in this book.

Outside Tory circles, Liberals and non-partisans like Tom Axworthy, Michael Kirby, Bob Rae, Sean Conway, Michael Robinson, Keith Banting, Janice Stein, Don Macnamara, Patrick Reid and Arthur Milnes have all been a rich part of discussions about Canadian political ideas, and idea sources themselves. All of the above are, of course, blameless in the mistakes, conclusions and excesses to be found here. These are mine alone.

September 2010
Kingston, Ontario

PERMISSIONS ACKNOWLEDGEMENTS

I would like to thank HarperCollins Canada for permitting the use of one or two of the ideas that appeared originally in my books *No Surrender* and *The Long Road Back*, first published by them in 1996 and 2006 respectively. I am very much indebted to the *International Journal,* published by the Canadian International Council, for their gracious permission to use sections of a recent essay, entitled "Grappling with Peace," that I authored for their Spring 2010 edition. Also, I acknowledge the Institute for Research on Public Policy, who kindly granted permission for me to use pieces of an essay, "Geopolitical Integrity for Canada," which I wrote in December of 2004 as part of an edited volume of the IRPP's National Security and Interoperability research series, entitled *Geopolitical Integrity.*

Bibliographical Note

A work of opinion and analysis, however reflective of my own biases and conclusions, also benefits from the intellectual thought of others. I have many debts to the work of other writers.

Donald Creighton's works on Sir John A. Macdonald *The Young Politician* and *The Old Chieftain* (Toronto, Macmillan,1952 and 1955) were of compelling value. Also very helpful were Sir Joseph Pope's *The Day of Sir John Macdonald* (Glasgow, Brook and Company, Toronto, 1915), Donald Swainson's *Sir John A. Macdonald: The Man and the Politician* (Quarry Press, Kingston, 1971) and the more recent and magisterial *The Man Who Made Us* by Richard Gwyn (Random House Canada, Toronto, 2007).

Chronologically, as *The Right Balance* progresses, there are other deeply helpful sources. Marcel Trudel's *Introduction to New France* (Holt, Rinehart and Winston, Toronto, 1968) was of immense value, as was being a student in the history department at the University of Ottawa when Professor Trudel was there. Mason Wade's iconic *The French Canadians, 1760–1945*

(Macmillan, Toronto, 1956) speaks with a level of diligence and magisterial clarity about the stages in French Canada's political, social and economic development, and was most helpful.

Professor Richard White's work *The Middle Ground: Indians, Empires and Republics in the Great Lakes Region 1650–1815* (Cambridge University Press, New York, 1991) was deeply helpful in helping me understand the inter-community linkages, both cultural and linguistic, between First Nations and the first French inhabitants. Arthur Lower's foundational *Colony to Nation* (Longmans Green and Company, 1946) has always been my preferred road map to Canada's early history, from the early arrival of the Europeans to the 1931 Statute of Westminster.

William Wood's *The Winning of Canada* (Glasgow, Brook and Company, Toronto, 1914) helped immensely with the Empire and colonial office linkages to British strategy on the ground in the mid- to late-eighteenth century.

In assessing the Loyalist dynamic, both within the American colonies and within Canada, Daniel Dulany's *Considerations on the Propriety of Imposing Taxes in the British Colonies* (1765) was of immense value, as was W. Stewart Wallace's *The United Empire Loyalists* (Glasgow, Brook and Company, 1914). Janice Potter-MacKinnon's *While the Women Only Wept: Loyalist Refugee Women in Eastern Ontario* (McGill-Queen's University Press, Montreal, 1993) was an invaluable source of information on Loyalist life, travails and culture, both during and after the colonial revolt against the Crown. No understanding of Canadian social and conservative roots would be complete without this remarkable historical study.

G.P. de T. Glazebrook's *A History of Canadian Political Thought* (McClelland & Stewart, Toronto, 1966) provided wonderful background on how our politics developed and evolved from New France to the pre-centennial era. Edmund Burke's famous *Reflections on the Revolution in France* (1790) not only revealed how core political thinking varied on the French Revolution, in the U.S., the U.K. and Canada, but when compared to Burke's earlier stout defence of the colonies and opposition to war, in the lead-up to 1775–76, it was a clear, if nuanced, indication of how this thoughtful British Whig moved to a more Toryist view of the world.

Dr. Janet Ajzenstat's outstanding analysis of Lord Durham, *The Political Thought of Lord Durham* (McGill-Queen's University Press, Montreal, 1988), helped immensely in my understanding of the difference between anti-Québec racism and universal liberalism, and also how this important difference is still not acknowledged by many French Canadian historians and their English Canadian counterparts.

Gerald Craig's *Upper Canada: The Formative Years, 1784–1841* (McClelland & Stewart, Toronto, 1963) provided depth and texture to my understanding of early survival points in Canada, through the War of 1812, to the Act of Union and the rebel-Tory pressures around responsible government.

S.F. Wise and R.C. Brown's *Canada Views the United States: Nineteenth Century Political Attitudes* (Macmillan, Toronto, 1967), David Mills's *The Concept of Loyalty in Upper Canada* (McGill-Queen's University Press, 1987) and Janice Potter-MacKinnon's *The Liberty We Seek: Loyalist Ideology in Colonial New York and Massachusetts* (Harvard University Press, Cambridge, 1983) all enriched the granularity of my understanding. S.F. Wise's "Upper Canada and the Conservative Tradition" (in Edith G. Firth, ed., *Profiles of a Province*, Ontario Historical Society, Toronto, 1967) provided additional background on the framework of Canadian conservative philosophical roots.

Richard Clippingdale's "J.S. Willison and Canadian Nationalism, 1886–1902" (Canadian Historical Association, Historical Papers, Ottawa, 1969) and his subsequent works *Laurier, His Life and World* (McGraw-Hill Ryerson, Toronto, 1979) and *Robert Stanfield's Canada* (McGill-Queen's University Press,

Montreal, 2008) were of significance in helping to address the philosophical contribution and relevance of these outstanding Canadian historical figures. O.D. Skelton's work on Laurier, *The Day of Sir Wilfrid Laurier* (Glasgow, Brook and Company, Toronto, 1916) was also especially useful in terms of its being a history written close to the actual event, in this case a political defeat; it is replete with impressions of Liberal loyalists.

Two books on Robert Borden assisted immensely in my assessment of Borden's initiation of modern-era Canadian nationalism: John English's *Borden: His Life and World* (McGraw-Hill Ryerson, Toronto, 1977) and Robert Brown's *Robert Laird Borden: A Biography* (Macmillan, Toronto, 1975).

Roger Graham's *Arthur Meighen: A Biography, Volume 2* (Clarke, Irwin, Toronto, 1963) and his *The King-Byng Affair, 1926* (Copp Clark, Toronto, 1967), along with John Boyco's recent biography *Bennett: The Rebel Who Challenged and Changed a Nation* (Key Porter, Toronto, 2010) and Arthur Milnes and Christopher McCreery's *The Authentic Voice of Canada* (McGill-Queen's University Press, Montreal, 2009), provided remarkable insight and featured literal "voice of" sources with respect to Bennett and the political transition that followed his rise to power.

James Struthers's *No Fault of Their Own: Unemployment and the Canadian Welfare State, 1914–1941* (University of Toronto Press, Toronto, 1983) contributed to my general knowledge of the labour economy before and between the Wars. Jack Granatstein's *The Politics of Survival, the Conservative Party of Canada 1939–1945* (University of Toronto Press, Toronto, 1967), probably the very best account of any era in Conservative Party history, was also an invaluable source of information on the roots of modern Canadian conservatism.

Nelson Wiseman's "The Pattern of Prairie Politics" (*Readings in Canadian History: Post-Confederation*, Sixth Edition, (in R. Douglas Francis and Donald B. Smith, eds., Nelson Thompson, Toronto, 2002), combined with Tom Flanagan's *Waiting for the Wave: The Reform Party and Preston Manning* (Stoddart, Toronto, 1995), assisted in broadening my understanding of political mindsets in the West.

William Christian and Sheila Grant's *The George Grant Reader* (University of Toronto Press, Toronto, 1998) afforded me a broader understanding of the breadth and depth of George Grant's work beyond his own *Lament for a Nation: The Defeat of Canadian Nationalism* (McGill-Queen's University Press, Montreal, 1965) which I essentially memorized word for word at fifteen years of age.

Andrew Gollner and Daniel Salée edited *Canada Under Mulroney: An End-of-Term Report* (Véhicule Press, Montréal, 1988) which, through its reading on national reconciliation, economic renewal, social justice and streamlining administrative machinery, helped refresh my recollection of strengths and weaknesses of the Mulroney administration before I joined it as hired help in 1991.

Bill Fox's *Spin Wars: Politics and New Media* (Key Porter, Toronto, 1999) is the best book written to date on the new media exigencies for modern political practitioners.

Many texts have helped my understanding of the neo-conservative movement over the years. Michael Novak's *The Spirit of Democratic Capitalism* (Madison Books, Lanham, 1982) and David Frum's more recent *Comeback: Conservatism That Can Win Again* (Broadway, New York, 2008) were wonderful refreshers on the purposes and challenges of modern American conservatism. Justin Vaïsse's *Neoconservatism: Biography of a Movement* (Belknap Press of Harvard University Press, Cambridge, 2010) was of genuine value and a remarkable, dispassionate analysis of a movement and its many strains.

All of the above-mentioned writers, historians and philosophers have created a wonderful series of frameworks, analyses and understandings that I have benefitted from greatly. They are, of course, to be held blameless if any of the conclusions I have drawn are inaccurate. For these, I take full responsibility.

Index

Aberhart, "Bible Bill," 132–33
Acadia, 32
accommodation, 23, 32, 34, 37–38,
    77, 82, 97, 112
Act of Union, 65, 66, 85
Afghanistan, 10, 88, 192, 209
Agricultural Rehabilitation
    and Development Act
    (ARDA), 140
Ajzenstat, Janet, 63–64
Alberta, 132–33, 162, 166
Alberta Human Rights Act of 1972,
    54, 171
Algonquian cultural zone, 33
alliances, 114, 177, 186
ambition, political, 44–45
American: in conflict with Canada,
    48–49; conservatism, 4–5, 91–92,
    195–96, 200–206; democracy, 15,
    16–17, 46, 197–201; dream, 17;
    government structure, 52;
    immigration, 133; industrialism,
    105; neo-conservatives, 90,
    194, 201; political parties, 7.
    See also United States
American Constitution, 15
American Empire Loyalists, 18
American Indians, 53

American Loyalists, 42, 46
American Revolution, 18, 36, 37–38,
    47, 196
Ancien Régime, 5, 24, 26, 27, 35,
    81, 200
Anglican Church, 75
Anglo bias, 71
Anglo-Montrealers, 68
anglophone minorities, 78
annexation, 68, 75
"Annexation Manifesto," 75
anti-democracy, 44
anti-establishment, 133
anti–French Canadian bias, 75
Anti-Inflation Board, 150
armed conflict, 48–49
armoured capacity, 192
arrogance, 11–13
Articles of Confederation
    (1865–67), 40
assimilation, 71
Atkey, Ron, 144
Atlantic Accord of 2005, 163
attorneys, 45
Australia, 8
Axis powers, 128–29, 184
Axworthy, Lloyd, 189
Axworthy, Tom, 145